MICHAEL A. ATTALIDES

# CYPRUS

MICHAEL A. ATTALIDES

# CYPRUS

*Nationalism and international politics*

Q PRESS EDINBURGH 1979

© Michael A. Attalides 1979

Published by Q Press Ltd
58 Queen Street
Edinburgh EH2 3NS

Typeset in 10/11 C.A.T. Baskerville
and printed by Billing & Sons Limited
Guildford, London and Worcester

Designed by Ruari McLean

ISBN 0 905470 08 7

# CONTENTS

# ACKNOWLEDGEMENTS

This book was made possible through the generous financial support of the Berghof Stiftung für Konfliktsforschung GmbH. I am also grateful to the Otto Suhr Institut of the Free University of Berlin which, by inviting me to conduct a seminar on the problem of Cyprus during the academic year 1974-5, gave me access to its library, time to relect and the opportunity .to discuss with interested scholars. The German, Cypriot, Greek and Turkish scholars who participated in the seminar played an important role in the crystallization of my ideas.

The following people read parts of or the whole manuscript and commented on it: Costas Carras, Nils Kadritzke, Peter Loizos and Tassos Papadopoulos. They are responsible for improving the style and accuracy of the book, but not for the judgements contained in it, or for any errors of omission or commission.

# INTRODUCTION

Most literate people in the world know that the problem of Cyprus is "a problem of Greeks and Turks". In other words it is a problem of opposing nationalisms. Journalists have often treated the problem as one deriving from a traditional hatred between Greek and Turk. Social scientists have often treated it as a problem of psychological or social adaptation of two culturally distinct groups to each other. Nationalism however is a more complex phenomenon than that. The appearance of nationalist movements clearly depends on internal changes in societies, but in many cases nationalist movements attempt to modify state boundaries or areas of sovereignty.

Nationalism is a kind of social movement which can spring up purely from internal transformations in a society. But frequently it interacts with the interests and pursuits of other states. This provides endless scope for complication in human affairs. The intensity and non-rationality of nationalist feelings do not adapt easily to international accords, balances of power and understandings. They are also vulnerable to manipulation or aggravation.

Though nationalism can be an extremely important force in internal and international politics, it is not clear that one explains very much by attributing a certain course of events to "nationalism". In fact the danger of explaining complex courses of events in these terms is evident if one examines some of the possible varieties of "nationalism". It encompasses many varieties of group identification and types of political action. Some nationalist movements advocate changes in state boundaries and some do not. If a nationalist movement does not advocate such changes, it may be the official ideology of an established state. By contrast it may be a movement to subvert the existing state structure. Anti-colonial movements for example are subversive in this way without necessarily advocating any change in the boundaries of the political unit. If the movement advocates new state boundaries, this may mean either separation from the existing state or the unification of a number of smaller states.

These differences of course would have significant effects on the course that nationalist movements take and on their effect on international relations. But there are other important variations in nationalist movements. Their occurrences may have as a necessary precondition certain universally recurrent social changes,[1] and their ideologies generally assert unity and lack of division within the society.[2] But it would be hard to insist that, unlike other ideologies or patterns of thought, nationalist movements do not mobilize different sections of a society or different classes at different points in time, with varying degrees of intensity. If this is so, it would also be likely that sectional or class interests were relevant to the kind of elective affinity that developed between the adherents of a nationalist movement on the one hand, and its aims and the content of its ideology on the other. Nationalist movements assert such varying bases of unity as language, religion, or class. So they have very different implications for the social arrangements or rearrangements which they advocate. This being so, they are likely to be influenced by class or segmental interests. The fact that nationalist movements identify a great variety of enemies is also related to this point. Social groups which differ between them on whether they define colonialism, communism, or a neighbouring group which speaks a different language as the main opponent, must have other significant differences in their social composition and pursuits.

These sketchy comments on nationalist movements suggest that in their development and in their outcome they are only comprehensible as products of the society in which they develop, the kinds of adherents that they attract and the kinds of aims which they pursue. The interests and power of their opponents, including other states, must also be very important influences on their development. In fact the point has been made that these influences are often more important than any characteristics of the movement itself.[3] A movement which develops within a colonial domain involves the additional consideration that the colonial power influences the internal social structure of the colonial society as well as the international power relations of the movement.

Following this line of thought, it has been found useful to think of "nationalism" in Cyprus, and the course of the "Cyprus conflict" by using three ideal-types of nationalist movement. The first type could be called "European nationalism" because the intellectual origins and content of nationalist movements in nineteenth-century Europe were described so elegantly by Kedourie.[4] Naming it "European nationalism" implies that this is only one variety of the phenomenon.

European nationalism is the type of political and intellectual movement which developed in many European countries in the nineteenth century. The movements were based on the assumption that groups of people with a common language, independently of existing sovereignties and jurisdictions, formed "a Nation". "Freedom" for such people consisted in forming a State of their own.

The process of the formation of the Greek nation-state is distinguished by being perhaps the most protracted in Europe. It lasted for almost a century and a half from 1821 until just after the

Second World War. The Turkish nation, and Turkish nationalism, on the other hand, formed itself during a relatively brief period of the twentieth century. It was defined, by Mustafa Kemal, as complete on its formation.[5] The two nations were formed by a tortuous process of disentanglement of borders, mixed populations and symbolic sites.[6] Some of the people involved were not just 'mixed' in the sense of geographical residence. In some cases they had mixed cultural characteristics. Turkish-speaking Christians and Greek-speaking Muslims were not uncommon.[7] The "Cyprus problem" can in some senses be clearly placed within this process, and this has been done by both Greek and Turkish nationalists and by other observers.[8] But it is central to the interpretation of nationalism that whether this is a valid view or not has become an issue both in internal Cypriot and in international politics.

The second ideal type of nationalism is "anti-colonial nationalism".[9] In contrast to the first ideal type, it has frequently de-emphasized the significance of linguistic or other cultural divisions. It frequently defined "colonialism" or its post-colonial variant "imperialism" as the common enemy.[10] Also, unlike European nationalism, it pays attention to economic and social issues and the economic divisions in societies, though frequently it argues that they should be set aside temporarily. It has been argued[11] that this kind of nationalism is sometimes indistinguishable from communism. This model was very influential among both Greek and Turkish Cypriots, particularly after the Second World War, but conspicuously failed to become the dominant one.

The third ideal type of nationalism can be defined in terms of two sub-types. Unlike the first and second ideal type they do not aim to create new state boundaries, or to transfer sovereignties, but rather to reallocate power and resources within a state. It is possible of course for these types of nationalist movement to develop into or merge with the previously outlined types. The first, for lack of a more accurate term, could be referred to as "sectarianism". The term refers to jockeying for power and resources between religious, linguistic or other culturally defined groups, in order to distinguish such competition from that which is based on occupational or class groups. A particularly formative phase of the Cyprus conflict can be traced to this kind of competition between Greek and Turkish Cypriots immediately before and after independence. It eliminated crosscutting trade union and cooperative ties and spilled over into nineteenth-century nationalism. This was reinforced by some extraordinary conditions which had been attached to the new state's independence.

The second sub-type may be termed "regionalism". It is the tendency of the elite of a particular region of a state to engage in a "struggle for domain" with the state authorities, if it has distinct, territorially defined economic or political interests. This form is introduced because in some senses it is a relevant way of describing the relations between the Government of Cyprus and the Government of Greece, particularly during the period of dictatorial rule in Greece. It must be emphasized immediately though, that the sense in which Cyprus was a "region" of Greece was limited. It was primarily related to some degree of control over the means of violence in Cyprus by the Greek Government.

The interests and powers of other states are important in assessing the consequences of nationalist movements. In the case of Cyprus, this naturally implies Greece and Turkey. They have at various times been defined by Cypriot nationalists themselves as having a special relationship to Cyprus. In fact they form part of the field of nationalism which is being interpreted. But beyond these two countries, other large powers had a considerable and relevant influence on the Cyprus conflict. They exercised this influence in the course of pursuing their global interests. These powers, Britain and later the United States and the Soviet Union, are to be referred to as "imperial powers". The use of the term makes it obvious that one's thinking has been influenced by ideas that imply that there are world powers which seek to dominate weaker states to varying degrees, and that they do so in order to satisfy what are defined by the imperial powers' leaders as the interests of their own citizens. But it is best to make it clear at the outset that there is no intention to discuss whether the rulers of societies with free-market or planned economies are more or less prone to act in this way. There is even less intention to enter the controversy about whether such behaviour is an outcome of ways in which the economies of such states function. It is sufficient for present purposes to think in terms of strategic interests and their conflicting aims. Most of this book is concerned with how these aims intersected at various times with indigenous political processes, and the nationalist field which included Greece and Turkey. A formal causal analysis, or even an attribution of relative weight is almost impossible. One of the reasons for this is the complexity of the fact that, while Greece and Turkey are centres of opposed fields of nationalism, they are also both members of NATO, which is a more or less cohesive system of international alliances headed by one of the imperial powers, the United States.

It is possible, however, to point to some relevant factors in the development of the situation which led to the invasion. This, it is hoped, will widen a little the comfortable London journalist's point of view that "The harassment of the Turkish minority by the Greek majority in the 1960's ... was the basic cause of last year's explosion."[13] Such a simple attribution of causality is unsophisticated about the way in which groups of people come to define each other as enemies, and too smug to be held by people whose own society has shaped events to a great extent. This is particularly significant for an ever-present problem. An attribution of causality has hidden assumptions about possible "solutions", which come as secondary consequences of naive attributions of "responsibility".

Chapter I places the Cyprus problem in its international context. It reviews the development of the interests of the imperial powers in relation to Cyprus, and shows how they have intersected since the beginning of British rule with indigenous political movements. Chapter II traces the development of Greek "European nationalism" in Cyprus, and explains the reasons for its intensification and eruption into violence in the nineteen fifties. Its specific characteristics as a nationalist movement are explained by the social characteristics of its leaders and its internal opponents. Chapter III looks at the reasons for the late development of Turkish "European nationalism" on Cyprus. The Fourth Chapter is about the increasing autonomy of Cyprus from Greece, and the development of "regionalist" differences between the Greek Cypriots and Greece, particularly after 1963. Chapter V examines the problems of power sharing between the Greek and Turkish Cypriots and the difficulties in coming to an agreed constitutional settlement after 1968. Chapter VI examines the difficulties of the Greek Cypriot political forces in facing an ideological renunciation of Hellenic nationalism. Chapters VII and VIII look at the coup by the Greek military dictatorship in July 1974 and the succeeding invasion by Turkish forces and the implications of the continuing occupation of a large part of the island by Turkey.

Benjamin 1874    Communist - Relations with Russia

land
language
politics
religion

# CHAPTER I

## Small island and imperial powers

When the Ottoman Turks invaded Cyprus in the sixteenth century they destroyed the Venetian feudal structure which ruled the mass of the Greek-speaking, Orthodox Christian population in Cyprus. The process of incorporating Cyprus into the Ottoman Empire gave Cyprus some basic socio-political features which survived in same form into the twentieth century. Muslim peasants were settled on the lands of the dispossessed Venetian aristocracy.[1] The land was initially held by military and administrative officials of the Ottoman Empire, but with time largely passed into small-holding peasant ownership. In this way, villages and village-quarters of Turkish-speaking Muslim peasants came to be interspersed over the whole of the island with the Greek ones. This dispersal remained as a firm and apparently immutable geopolitical fact until the population uprootings of 1964 and 1974-5.

The Muslims who settled in Cyprus were, within the religious subdivisions through which the Ottoman Empire was ruled, part of the dominant *millet*. Since Muslims in general, and Turkish Muslims particularly, were the dominant *millet* of the Ottoman Empire, they developed a European nationalism later than the other peoples of the Empire. In Cyprus they had no distinct representative institutions because of their notional membership in the ruling group and it was only from this group that recruits were drawn for the state institutions. By contrast, among the Christian *millets* of the Ottoman Empire, nationalist movements were fuelled partly by awareness of their subordinate position in the Empire. Greece became a state in 1828, with national aspirations to expand its then very limited borders at the expense of the Ottoman State. In Cyprus itself the Christian *millet* was ruled through the Church whose most senior representative, the Archbishop, was also the Ethnarch. The Greek community of Cyprus was found by the British administration to have a well developed system of political representation through the Church and a degree of nationalist consciousness within their leading groups. By contrast the Turkish Cypriots had neither independent political organization, nor a mainland Turkish nationalist movement to attune themselves to. So that in this sense, as well as due to the fact that they were a minority, there were few barriers to their leaders' identification with and acceptance of the colonial organization which the British established.

1

# CYPRUS

The fact that Cyprus had been a significant source of tax-revenue for the Porte and the fact that the imperial Ottoman Government was indebted to British stock-holders resulted in a situation where the revenues of the Cypriot exchequer continued to flow out of the island to British stock-holders after the British occupation. This appeared to the Cypriots to be blatant economic exploitation. Though the two ethnic groups were sometimes in agreement on this issue, for the Greek Cypriots it was one of the main issues fanning nationalist agitation.

These conditions served as the base point for the development of relations between Greek and Turkish Cypriots. A schematic view of these relations over the past century shows how Greek and Turkish nationalism developed asynchronously. The relation of the two ethnic groups to the colonial power was asymmetrical. Some of the roots of the Cyprus problem lie in this fact. But a key to its increasing aggravation lies in a periodic non-congruent interaction between the kinds of nationalism which developed on the island and the interests of the imperial powers.

Up to and for a while after the Second World War, Turkish nationalism in Cyprus was relatively quiescent, while Greek nationalists demanded Union with Greece. The colonial power, Britain, resisted the demand, which was cast in terms of the right to self-determination by the majority of the population. This resistance contributed considerably to the escalation of Turkish Cypriot nationalism and Turkish mainland involvement. The Cypriot State set up as a compromise in 1959 was weakened through a series of sectarian conflicts which spilled over into a resurgence of Greek and Turkish nationalism.

In the conditions in which it surged up again in the early 1960's, however, Greek nationalism in Cyprus was likely to exhaust itself. The Greek Cypriots gained control of the Cypriot State and adopted a non-aligned policy with the economic and diplomatic support of the Soviet Union and some of the Arab countries in order to achieve fully unfettered independence which might have led to incorporation with the Greek State. Since Greece was a member of NATO this was unlikely to be successful strategy. Together with internal social transformations, it resulted in regionalist conflict between Greece and the Greek Cypriots and the development among Greek Cypriots of consciousness of a group identity distinct from Greece.

The United States fairly consistently opposed this process. It generally supported lines of development leading to a subsuming of the Cypriot State to Greece and Turkey and so, at least indirectly, encouraged Greek and Turkish nationalism.

The Soviet Union emphasized the exclusive responsibility of "imperialism" for the centrifugal tendencies in the Cypriot State. In a

2

subtle way this also reinforced Greek Cypriot nationalism, because it enabled Cypriots tending to the left to see the Cyprus problem almost exclusively in terms of the threat to Cyprus from Greece or Turkey or the United States, while largely overlooking the necessity to reincorporate the Turkish Cypriots into the Cypriot State.

"England" according to Sir Ronald Storrs, an ex-governor of Cyprus who wrote his autobiography when officials of imperial powers could still be frank, "occupied Cyprus for strategic and imperial purposes, and not as rescuing or pretending to rescue Cypriots from Turkish misrule."[2] The occupation of the island had been debated in the British press in the 1840's.[3] In 1878 the opportunity to acquire what appeared to be an important base for controlling access to the Suez Canal arose. In exchange for undertaking to prevent the dismemberment of the Ottoman Empire by Russia, Britain acquired Cyprus "to be occupied and administered".[4] Disraeli had not foreseen that within four years Britain would acquire a far more useful base for the purpose, Egypt.

Cyprus, already a British possession of no economic significance, also lost some of its strategic significance to the British Empire. These facts, combined with the fact that it was a European colony, largely inhabited by Greek-speaking people, made possible the development within Cyprus of a fairly liberal internal policy. This in turn allowed the Greek Cypriots to educate and organize themselves for a long and pervasive struggle to remove British colonial rule. Greek nationalism was intensified by the inherent contradiction between liberal educational and other legislation and ultimately authoritarian rule by a colonial power. The historical irony of the period until the Second World War was that neither the Greek Cypriots nor mainland Greece succeeded in bringing enough pressure on the British Empire to release Cyprus at a time when it appeared not to be crucial to it.

The reasons are complex and would not have been worth entering into here were it not for the fact that they are connected with the issues of the "Eastern Question", whose current resurgence in Cold War form is partially responsible for the recent fate of Cyprus. To a large extent the answer is that Greek governments did not militantly pursue the incorporation of Cyprus simply because they considered that it would at some stage be in British interests to hand the island to Greece.

Britain's acquisition of Cyprus was not only connected with the specific purpose of controlling Suez. It was also connected with the more general policy of dominating the Mediterranean in order to prevent Russian access through the Straits and in order to protect the route to India and later to the oil producing areas. This is the general context in which Britain protected the Ottoman State and acquired Cyprus in repayment. Early in the twentieth century this scheme

3

changed.[5] British-Russian *entente* drove Ottoman Turkey to reliance on Germany, and to alliance with the Central Powers on the outbreak of the First World War. One minor consequence of this was the annexation of Cyprus by Britain in 1914, and its conditional offer to Greece in 1915.[6] The offer depended on Greece joining the Allies and was rejected by the Greek Government which at the time tended to neutrality. In fact, Greece later joined the war on the side of the Allies, while Turkey contributed to the collapse of Russia by closing the Straits.

At the end of the war, the Ottoman State had itself dissolved and the Kemalist Republic had established good relations with the Soviet Union. Britain supported Greek expansion into Asia Minor, which was however militarily unsuccessful. While Turkey had, as it did until the mid 1930's, good relations with the Soviet Union, it was natural for Greece to assume that its own claims on Cyprus were unlikely to be overriden in favour of Turkey. But the claim was postponed for too long.[7] Immediately before and after the Second World War, the increasing power of the Soviet Union induced Turkey, once more in fear of "Russian" (Soviet) expansion to move to closer relations with Britain and Germany again and in 1952 to alliance with the United States in NATO. It also became through the NATO alliance an ally of Greece. So, ironically, it became possible in terms of world power politics to compete with the latter over Cyprus. Detente accompanied by conflict with Greece over Cyprus has, since 1964, apparently once more thrown open the question of Turkey between "Russia" and the "West".

The intensity of the *enosis* movement, the Greek-Cypriot movement for incorporation with the Greek State, increased during the twentieth century and reached a peak after the Second World War. The reasons for this were some of the internal social transformations in Cyprus which were partially unintended consequences of colonial policy and competition between Greek Cypriot political forces for dominance. These forces took little account of the international constellation of Great Power interests. Britain and France were still determined to safeguard some of their interests in controlling the oil sources of the Middle East. Strategically they had suffered increasing setbacks after the Second World War, which made Cyprus increasingly important. The Arab liberation movements had resulted in some governments coming to power which were opposed to European or U.S. control of the Middle East. They had also made the position of others, which were pro-western, insecure. The positions of the United States on the one hand, and of Britain and France on the other, were not identical on Middle Eastern policy.[8] The United States probably suspected that in the pursuit of their narrow imperialist interests, Britain and France would damage the overall cause of the "Free World" in combating the "world communist conspiracy". In these terms it was possible for the United States to be understanding of those anti-colonial movements against Britain or France which did not appear to lead to radical social changes or orientation towards the Soviet Union. In 1950 a Greek Cypriot nationalist delegation was received in Washington and it presented to the State Department copies of a plebiscite demanding *enosis*. In their address to the Secretary of State for Foreign Affairs, Dean Acheson, the delegation included a paragraph apparently calculated to appeal to the difference between U.S. and British Middle Eastern and generally colonial policy. It was pointed out that the maintenance of colonial rule in Cyprus created fertile ground for the spread of communism.[9] The Greek Ambassador to the United Nations, A. Kyrou, writing on Greek foreign policy in 1955 goes further. British colonial policy, he points out, in some respects actually favoured the communists in Cyprus.[10] Both Greece and Cyprus (in the person of Archbishop Makarios who visited the United States in 1952) addressed themselves to the United States for support in ending the colonial status of Cyprus.

The perception of the leaders of the Greek Cypriot nationalist movement were not inaccurate in one respect. The United States had started establishing its presence in the Eastern Mediterranean by taking over the support of the royalist, conservative forces in the Greek Civil War from Britain. This fact was instrumental in allowing the Greek Government to pursue the Cyprus problem. They could not have conducted a diplomatic campaign for the acquisition of a British Colony, while Greece itself was dependent on the same colonial power for military and economic assistance. And there is no reason to suppose that the United States would not on the whole support the idea of Cyprus, a Greek island in the anomalous position of being a British colony, joining Greece. The latter had become a member of NATO in 1951 after the Right had been firmly established in power and the Left thoroughly crushed. This would have been true had not Turkey acquired an increasing interest in Cyprus and had not Turkey become an increasingly important factor in U.S. containment policy.

An incidental consequence of the liberal elements of British rule in Cyprus was the tolerance of self-administered education by the two ethnic groups. But a less than liberal series of tricks in the balance of representation of the two groups in the Legislative Council of the colony was also part of British policy. The effects of divisiveness in the Legislative Council, the consequences of separate educational systems, the Greek nationalist movement, all provided favourable preconditions for inter-ethnic conflict. There was a ready base for such conflict present. It was utilized as a last resort of British policy in the attempt to maintain colonial rule in Cyprus in the 1950's. Mainland Turkish claims would then be encouraged with an appearance of justification.

5

Britain was forced to withdraw from Palestine in 1948. In 1954, one year before the armed Greek Cypriot campaign for *enosis* started, they were also forced to sign a treaty with Egypt involving the evacuation of the Suez Canal. By the same treaty however they were to return there in the case of an attack on Egypt, one of the Arab League Countries or Turkey.[11] Where were they to return from? Cyprus at last justified Disraeli's reasons for acquiring it. The British Middle East Headquarters was moved to the island as the Greek Cypriots were secretly organizing for armed rebellion and as the Greek Government took the Cyprus issue to the United Nations. United States policy at this time was that Greece and Britain should avoid public conflict in the U.N. and settle the issue by bilateral negotiations.[12] Though the U.N. at this time was dominated by the Western Powers, an appeal by Greece would still have presented an indication of cracks in the alliance to the rest of the world. Sir Anthony Eden was not, however, about to put the interests of the "Free World" before those of Britain; only the Suez expedition in 1956 showed that Britain was no longer powerful enough to take an independent stand. In 1955 he was explicit on the reasons for Britain's refusal to hand Cyprus to Greece:

> ... I have never felt, and I do not believe now, that Cyprus is an Anglo-Greek question and can ever be treated as such. It is equally unrealistic to lecture Turkey as to the view she ought to take about an island no farther from her coast than is the Isle of Man from us. ... Our duty if called on, ... is to safeguard the strategic needs of our country and of our ally (Turkey). Neither the NATO obligations ... nor the Baghdad Pact, nor any agreement in the Middle Eastern Area or the Persian Gulf, or anything else, none of these can be speedily and effectively carried out today unless we have the assured and unfettered use of bases and use of facilities in Cyprus ... Her Majesty's Government must be concerned as every other Government is concerned, to protect the vital interests of its own citizens. The welfare and indeed the lives of our people depends on Cyprus as a protective guard and staging post to take care of those interests, above all oil. This is not imperialism. It should be the plain duty of any Government, and we intend to discharge it.[13]

It is worth outlining how British policy set out to secure these interests. As early as 1953, according to a serious report,[17] the Foreign Office had been urging Ankara to take more interest in Cyprus, a matter on which Turkey had until then indicated little interest in public. The official British view, however, as expressed during the United Nations General Assembly debate of the first Greek appeal for self-determination for Cyprus in 1954, was purely legal. By the Treaty of Lausanne of 1923, British Sovereignty in Cyprus was internationally recognized, and Sovereignty is inviolable. Cyprus is an internal British matter.[15] This, however, cut little ice in a world where "self-determination" and "anti-colonialism" were virtually universally accepted ideologies. Informally, other, and for the moment equally unsuccessful approaches were being tried. A member of the British delegation asked the head of the Egyptian delegation to vote against the inclusion of the Greek appeal in the agenda, so that he, a representative of a Muslim country would not suffer from bad conscience for contributing to the incorporation of a substantial number of Muslims in Cyprus into an Orthodox State. The Egyptian was reported to have included in his reply the statement that "... you British have learnt nothing and forgotten nothing".[16] The delegate of another of the influential Arab States, Syria, replied to the British argument that Cyprus was necessary for the defence of the Arab countries by pointing out that, "Till today the crucial problems of the Arab countries have been with the West."[17] In spite of such reactions, and in spite of presumed American pressures to negotiate with Greece, the British Secretary of State for the Colonies was confident and unfortunately prophetic when in July 1954 he told the British House of Commons that,

> ... it has always been understood and agreed that there were certain
> territories in the Commonwealth which because of their particular
> circumstances could never expect to be fully independent ...[18]

But the time when such crude statements of imperial interests could be publicly maintained was past. More subtle means were necessary once international political issues were publicly debated. And there was no better ideal to appeal to than the protection of the rights of a minority, particularly if the minority in question was Turkish. This accorded with broader, not only British but also American considerations in Eastern Mediterranean policy.[19] The "Solomon like proposal to cut the island in two was a tactical step designed to neutralize the Greek appeal for self-determination."[20] It seems to have first been taken officially at the end of 1956, when the British colonial secretary proposed in the House of Commons that if the Greek Cypriots persisted in demanding *enosis,* the Turkish Cypriots should be entitled to separate self-determination and that if they chose to join Turkey, the island should be divided. The same line was taken in subsequent United Nations discussions of the problem.

Of course the British did not invent Turkish claims on Cyprus. They merely gave them international respectability. Turkey had indicated interest in Cyprus publicly on previous occasions. In 1951, the Turkish Foreign Minister had observed that he saw no reason for a change in the status of Cyprus. If it happened that there was, the change should take place with the participation of Turkey and with due regard to Turkish rights. But in general he thought that the activation of the Cyprus problem would be harmful to the unity of the Free World.[21] When the Cyprus problem was "internationalized" by the Greek Government's appeal to the United Nations for self-determination for Cyprus in 1954, the Turkish Government, both in private communication to the Greek Government and in the United Nations, favoured the maintenance of British rule in Cyprus. They opposed the union of Cyprus with Greece and argued that if there were discussions on the constitutional status of the island, Turkey should participate in order to safeguard its interests.[22] These interests were defined in the United Nations debate in 1954 as being due to "racial, historical and contractual reasons", and then more precisely delimited as opposition to self-determination for Cyprus on the grounds that the continuation of the colonial status of Cyprus "is important for the defence of southern Turkey and of the Northern Mediterranean in general".[23] At the London conference, called after the beginning of the Greek Cypriot armed campaign in 1955, Britain invited Turkey to attend as the third interested party. One purpose of the conference appeared to be the official introduction of Turkey into the Cyprus problem.[24] And before it began Sir Anthony Eden sent a telegram to the Turkish Government urging it to express its opposition to *enosis*.[25] The Turks stated that the greatest change they could accept from the current state of Cyprus was some degree of internal self-government on the condition that the Greeks renounced the principle of self-determination.[26]

The idea introduced by the British at the end of 1956 was rather different, and, "it apparently took some time for the argument to take hold in Turkish minds. But when it did, the Turkish Government adopted it wholesale."[27] Before this, Turkey merely supported the British position in favour of the *status quo,* that is the continuation of colonial rule in Cyprus, with an added disincentive against decolonization in the claim that if Britain were to ever abandon Cyprus, it should, under the provisions of the Treaty of Lausanne, revert to Turkey. Once the British led with the argument for "double self-determination", the Turks could take a much more active part. By the spring of 1957, the Turkish Prime Minister, Adnan Menderes, was arguing that the uttermost sacrifice which Turkey could make on Cyprus was to accept partitioning Cyprus.[28]

By 1958, the British representative in the United Nations was able to confirm that Cyprus was not a colonial dispute between itself and the Greek Cypriot majority and in fact not even an internal British problem, but rather

> *(...* a complex international problem) to which no simple slogan such as
> self-determination provided a solution *)*

and that

> A considerable number of Turkish Cypriots live in the island, people
> who look to Turkey as their fatherland. The island is of great strategic
> importance to Turkey, covering its southern ports and has a long
> association with Turkey in the past.[29]

As a manoeuvre by Britain to maintain Cyprus, the official
involvement of Turkey proved a failure. It had an important
unintended consequence in making the application of the principle of
self-determination to Cyprus impossible, because it would have
resulted in union with Greece. The Turkish Prime Minister had
stated his country's readiness to go to war as early as May 1956 in
order to prevent this.[30]

The U.S., as the senior ally of all the, by then, involved parties, felt
impelled to try and resolve the situation, which had developed by early
in 1957. A brief review of U.S. interests in the Eastern Mediterranean
to this point indicate the direction of resolution that the United States
would be interested in. As was previously pointed out, the United
States was suspicious of Anglo-French imperialism. On the other
hand, France, and particularly Britain were the most important allies
of the United States and had common interests when it came to more
general strategic issues. On the Cyprus problem, it appears that views
initially diverged considerably. One of the reasons might have been hit
on by Labour Party M.P.s. In spite of what Sir Anthony Eden
maintained, they insisted that the British bases in Cyprus were not
used for NATO purposes, but exclusively for British ones. Richard
Crossman said that he had discussed the issue of the bases with
British generals in Cyprus, and

> ... they know nothing of NATO in Cyprus. And they know nothing
> purposely, as the intention is for the island to remain British.[31]

The Greek Government had, in the case of *enosis* promised NATO
bases not only in Cyprus, but additional ones in Greece. In 1953, the
Greek Prime Minister had said to the British Ambassador that in the
case of *enosis.*

> ... one would be able to say not just that Cyprus had been annexed by
> Greece, but that Greece in its entirety had been annexed by Britain.[32]

But Greece was in NATO, and dependent on U.S. military and

economic assistance. A Greek Cyprus would serve NATO, not specifically British imperial interests. Britain still maintained an independent foreign policy. The invasion of Egypt was still three years ahead.

It is not therefore surprising that Greek policy-makers might think that the United States would favour *enosis*. The suspicion has been expressed that the U.S. aided the Greek Cypriot anti-British organization, EOKA, since it was in favour of *enosis* and was anti-communist.[33] The United States may have for a while considered supporting the Greek position. The Greek Ambassador to the United Nations at this time was certainly under this impression,[34] though it has since been argued that the United States had made it perfectly clear that no matter what it favoured as a solution, it would do all it could to block an open discussion of the issue at the United Nations.[35] Greek impressions might have been reinforced by various reports and events.

A usually excellently informed American journalist had written in 1949 that the U.S. Government had been drawing the attention of the British Government to the increasing strength of communism in Cyprus. The U.S. had "virtually parallel strategic interest" to Britain in the use of Cyprus as "a bastion between the exit from the Dardanelles and the entrance to Suez". The British Colonial Office had up to this stage regarded the *enosis* movement as more of a threat to its aims than the growth of communism in Cyprus. But the Foreign Office and the Defence Ministry were now taking the situation in hand. The report was on the occasion of municipal elections in Cyprus. And the intriguing fact reported was that

> Possibly as a result of last minute efforts by the British Government of Cyprus to reduce the strength of local communism, yesterday's municipal elections in the Crown Colony swung in favour of the right-wing candidates.[36]

The line of divergence between Britain and the U.S. seems clear. Britain would like a balance between communist and right wing (pro-*enosis*) forces in Cyprus. The old divide and rule idea holds in many contexts. The U.S. has nothing to loose by an overwhelmingly strong *enosis* movement at this stage, since even if successful in its aims, it would result in Cyprus becoming part of American-protected Greece. For the British this would be a loss since they would not then control the island for their specific imperial uses.

In May 1955 a Mr Irving Brown of the AFL-CIO in his capacity as representative of the ICFTU turned up to give a press conference in Athens after a visit to Cyprus. At this conference he attributed responsibility for the growth of communist influence in Cyprus and for inter-communal tension to British colonial policy.[37] In fact, given the general strategic situation in the Middle East, it is unlikely U.S. policy-makers were thinking of *enosis* as a solution to the Cyprus problem, or that if this were entertained, it was no more than one of a series of possibilities.

In 1953 Dulles had shocked the British by taking an active part in the conception and organization of a barrier composed of anti-communist Muslim nations between the Soviet Union and the Middle East. This was shocking to the British since this area was till then considered to be in the British sphere of influence. These nations were Turkey, Iran and Pakistan. By 1955 the Baghdad Pact was signed.[38] Turkey, with common borders with both the Soviet Union and the most obstreperously anti-western Arab nation, Syria, was particularly valuable in this scheme. With the Democratic party in power under Menderes it seemed particularly reliable. In any event, the long-term position of Turkey on the "Eastern Question" now seemed to lie with the Western power dominating the Mediterranean. The U.S. was increasingly stepping into British shoes in this role. Soviet demands in 1945 for territorial concessions from Turkey, and a revision of the agreements for the control of the Black Sea Straits must have worried Turkish policy makers.[39] But though Britain, mainly interested in the Middle East oil resources, could devote her whole attention to Turkey as an ally against Greek claims for Cyprus, the United States had to give more consideration at this stage to the Greek position. This was for two reasons. Already the Balkan Pact, created in 1954 as an alliance between Greece, Turkey and Yugoslavia against the Soviet oriented Balkan countries, was in the process of dissolution largely because of the Cyprus problem. Also, some solution needed to be found to make Cyprus available to NATO rather than British uses.

At the NATO Foreign Ministers conference in May 1957, Dulles presented his plan for Cyprus. Cyprus would become part of NATO and would be ruled by three commissioners, one Scandinavian, one Portuguese, and one from a Mediterranean country. Internally it would have some degree of self-government. An American official delegate visited Athens and Ankara later in the summer to persuade these governments to renounce their claims in the interests of the Alliance.[40]

Each of the involved parties had reason to accept a solution along these lines during the next year and a half. Though the ruling Conservative party policy in Britain appeared to be pushing for partition, the Labour party had announced that if it came to power it would give the right of self-determination to Cyprus. Since this would have resulted in a vote for *enosis*, it contributed to greater readiness by Turkey to achieve an alternative solution. For Greece and the Greek Cypriots, independence was an alternative to partition. The level of intercommunal violence in Cyprus and the announcement of the Macmillan plan in 1958 for condominium in Cyprus between Britain, Greece and Turkey were signs of what was coming. In fact the fear existed among the Greek Cypriots and the Greek Government that the British would withdraw to their bases and let Turkey invade and partition Cyprus.[41] As for the British, the strategic use of Cyprus was being vitiated by the effort needed to keep it. By the end of 1958, it needed to keep 30,000 troops in Cyprus in order to keep the Cypriots down.[42] It was virtually a choice between Cyprus as a base, and bases in Cyprus. The British military decided that bases in Cyprus were sufficient. Besides Britain was being seriously pressed by the United States and its NATO allies to renounce its sovereignty in favour of an independent Cyprus as a step to bringing the Greek and Turkish allies together again.[43] Between November of 1958 and February 1959, the Greek and Turkish Foreign Ministers agreed on a solution based on the independence of Cyprus.[44] The Zurich-London agreements were also formally endorsed by Cypriot representatives.

The essential characteristic of these agreements are that they transformed a colonial dispute into a far more complex colonial dispute:

> Britain found itself unable to complete the job of decolonization. For both strategic and political reasons, it left Cyprus with severe limitations on its sovereignty. Not only did Britain itself retain certain sovereign areas on the island, but it also left the new government with a constitution which has since proved unworkable, but which it cannot change except with the consent of the three "protecting powers", each of whom, like Britain, has rights of intervention. In this situation President Makarios has some justification when he claims that the events on Cyprus since Christmas 1963 are part of the continuing struggle for independence. In effect, the London and Zurich agreements, by which Britain sought to ensure a minimum of stability on Cyprus after its own departure ... have ended by extending the scope of a colonial conflict from one government to three.[45]

There was some idea in the air that Cyprus would, after independence, join NATO. This possibility is referred to in letters sent to General Grivas by both Makarios and the Greek consul in Cyprus at that time.[46] But in any event, the presence of three "guarantor powers" with entrenched rights of intervention in Cyprus collectively or singly "had the advantage of making it evident to the whole world that this was a state in which the immediate interests of the Atlantic Alliance were involved".[47] The editor of the conservative Athens newspaper *Akropolis* sent the following report from Zurich while the discussions were continuing:

12

## Small island and imperial powers

The reinforcement of the security of Greece and Turkey dominates the talks of the Prime Ministers of the two countries, which began yesterday. The communist threat and Russian pressure creates for Greece and Turkey common immediate dangers ... It is obvious that the guarantees that Turkey seeks must be seen not only as strengthening the defences of that country, but also from the aspect that they are in a certain way guarantees of Greek security and of the independence of the new state which might face an internal threat from communist infiltration.[48]

At that time it seemed that there was little to impede the main goals of the United States in the new republic which were that:

First, the Republic of Cyprus should develop political stability and join together with Great Britain, Greece and Turkey to form a solid bulwark against communism. Second, Cyprus should stress economic development, free democratic institutions and a pro-West orientation. Third, the U.S. should enjoy unrestricted use of its existing communications facilities on the island. Fourth, the British Sovereign Base Areas should remain inviolate and available to any Western Nation for any purpose.[49]

U.S. communication facilities were in Cyprus before independence and included radio listening and broadcasting stations, jointly controlled with the British.[50] In 1974 however it was revealed that Cyprus was a base for over the horizon radar installations for the detection of ICBM launches in the Soviet Union.[51] British bases after independence occupied just under 3% of the area of Cyprus, which was excluded from the territory of the Republic, remaining a Sovereign British possession. (This is a fact that has lent considerable ambiguity in later years to calls for "the withdrawal of foreign troops from Cyprus".) Cyprus was still important for Britain's "East of Suez" policy, but the main interest on the part of Britain was in the security of the Persian Gulf for British interests.[52] The bases apparently however increasingly lost their specifically British imperial purpose to become, by 1963, bases for the British strategic reserve, "to act as a reserve strategic power for CENTO, and in a sense for NATO itself. They provided the British V-Bomber force, and the Canberra light bombers with a base from which to vary their angle of attack on the Soviet Union."[53] They were also important for strategic reconnaisance, presumably over the Mediterranean, the Middle East, and perhaps the Soviet Union.[54] The Treaty of Establishment of the Republic provides that should the bases cease to be in the possession of Britain they cannot be transferred to another power, but would become part of the territory of the Republic. Of course this was unlikely to limit their use by other NATO powers in case of nuclear

13

war.[55] But it was by no means clear that without the goodwill of the Cyprus Government the bases could have been used in more limited wars, for example in the Middle East. To ensure such goodwill some twenty million dollars in aid were given by the U.S. to Cyprus from independence to June 1963.[56]

Cyprus itself became "the first country in the world to be denied majority rule by its own constitution".[57] The mechanics of administration imposed in a fixed way on the new republic guaranteed both a continuation of "european nationalism" and sectarian conflict between Greek and Turkish Cypriots. Each reinforced the other. There is no evidence that any Cypriots other than the communist party of Cyprus, AKEL, at this time objected to the strategic positioning of Cyprus through the London and Zurich agreements. But Greek Cypriots of all political alignments had cause to resent the agreements because they had denied them *enosis* for the sake of the links between a minority of the population and a strategically important power, Turkey. They also resented the fact that this minority had been given more rights in the administration of the island than is probably known anywhere outside of white-dominated Africa. The Turkish Cypriots were placed in the unfortunate position of being guardians of the whole paraphernalia of the Zurich-London agreements, as well as of having to bear Greek Cypriot resentment for their aiding the British in ruling Cyprus. The Greek Cypriots were placed in a position where both the further pursuit of Hellenic nationalism and the pursuit of post-colonial nationalism would meet with firm outside blocking. But at the time they could not be expected to understand this.

Makarios had already, early on in his leadership of the campaign against the British, realized that small and weak countries can gain leverage by placing themselves in a line of dispute between opposed imperial powers. As early as 1953 he had declared his intention to seek aid "from East and West" in the struggle against the British. As archbishop and leader of the Greek Cypriot anti-colonial fight he had attended the non-aligned nations' conference in Bandung in 1955. As Head of State after independence his scope for "non-alignment" became much greater. If Cyprus was to rid itself of the limitations on its independence imposed at Zurich and London, it would obviously be with the support of those countries, the non-aligned ones and the communist ones, who felt threatened by the British bases and the NATO guarantors of Cyprus. The central paradox of Cypriot foreign policy, that is the pursuit of *enosis*, incorporation with Greece which is a NATO country, with support from the non-aligned and communist countries did not have to be examined too closely. The first step, achievement of unfettered independence, would work to the benefit of the Greek-Cypriot majority, whether the second step were *enosis* or

14

not. There is also the question of whether any prudent and far-sighted leader would have any choice but to try and take his country away from an alliance in which Turkey carried such weight. Within the alliance, any renewed instability in Cyprus would again work in Turkey's favour. And such signs were evident when Turkish boats were intercepted carrying arms to Cyprus even before the formal declaration of independence.[58] Obversely though, for the Turkish Cypriots, "unfettered independence" carried with it the unwelcome possibility of *enosis*.

This aspect of Cypriot foreign policy impinged on U.S. interests on a number of points. Instead of forming an anti-communist barrier with Greece and Turkey, Cyprus gave the local communists a respectable political role, including seats in the House of Representatives. Within the first two years of independence the Cyprus Government had signed a series of trade agreements with the Soviet Union, which caused a "wave of concern in the State Department".[59] As early as the Summer of 1961, the *New York Times*[60] rang the bell of "communist danger" in Cyprus. The president of Cyprus attended the conference of the non-aligned nations in Belgrade in 1961, and was to attend the one held in Cairo in 1964. He also developed close relations not only with Tito but also with Nasser, a man not likely to use any influence he gained with the Cypriot president in favour of the protection of the British bases in Cyprus. On many occasions before 1963, Makarios stated that he would "react in many ways if the Bases were used against the Arabs".[61] In 1963, at the Afro-Asian People's Solidarity Organization Executive Committee meeting in Nicosia, Makarios reaffirmed his intention to reject all military alliances.[62] All these actions placed Cyprus in some respects outside a camp of which others, the Turkish Cypriot leaders, the Governments of Turkey, Greece and the United States were firm members.[63]

As these developments had taken place, it was natural for the Cyprus Government to try and use its new international orientation during the next Cyprus crisis. At the end of 1963 an attempt by the leaders of the Greek Cypriot majority to revise the constitution resulted in intercommunal fighting and threats of Turkish invasion. The Cyprus Government rejected mediation or peace-keeping by NATO and appealed for assistance to Greece, the Soviet Union and Egypt, as well as to the United Nations. This set in train a sequence of events that was to transpose the Cyprus conflict to a bigger league than the one it had belonged to up to this point. The 1954-60 manoeuvres over Cyprus had taken place in a world where the two great opposed alliances were still solid blocs and where the Cyprus problem was a minor corner of the chess board in a rigidly global game. Neither Greece nor Turkey would seriously consider altering their alliances for the sake of Cyprus. By 1963 detente had begun with the Test Ban Treaty. This made small Western nations less anxious to shelter under American wings. They could make a show of troublesome independence, without leaving the Alliance. Since 1956 the Soviet Union had increasingly abandoned the Zhdanov-Stalin doctrine of "two blocs". It now believed that conflicts between capitalist countries were more likely than a world confrontation between the capitalist and the communist blocs. This made it possible for the Soviet Union to use such conflicts for the purpose of "anti-imperialism".[64]

In this world situation after 1963, because of the treaty structure with which it had been surrounded, Cyprus threatened the very cohesion of NATO. The rights of intervention which had been established to ensure that Cyprus remained Western could work so long as Greece and Turkey were mindful of joint intervention. When they were about to intervene in support of their respective ethnic groups, the treaties became instruments for inducing war within the Alliance. There was a structural paradox in the international situation. The Soviet Union, while supporting Cyprus against NATO interventions, could also choose to support the point of view of one or the other of the competing NATO allies. This introduced a much more significant dimension into the conflict. Cyprus, though it was the pawn that had caused all the trouble, became after 1965 disposable if a major gambit were in sight. Where the major issue was the cohesion of the NATO alliance, Cyprus as a non-aligned country became the centre of contradictory policies on the part of the United States and the Soviet Union. On some occasions the United States strengthened the independence of Cyprus if this was necessary to prevent a Greek-Turkish conflict. On some occasions the Soviet Union over-looked threats to the independence and non-alignment of Cyprus if there was a possibility of detaching one of the allies from the Alliance. This does not mean that subsidiary games were not played which had as a centre the strategic and political significance of the island itself.

Initially, the 1963-4 conflict was seen by the United States as an opportunity to re-establish the internal balance of forces in Cyprus in favour of greater western orientation,[65] and to forestall the Cyprus Government's appeal to Moscow for military aid against the possibility of an invasion by Turkey.[66]

A "NATO plan"—which was in fact an Anglo-American plan which the Greek and Turkish Governments were induced to accept—was formulated[67] which would have involved a ten thousand-man NATO peace-keeping force landing in Cyprus. The degree of suspicion that the Cyprus Government entertained for NATO peace keeping is indicated by the fact that the then President of the Cyprus House of Representatives, Mr Clerides, stated that this would amount to an occupation of Cyprus by NATO.[68] It was believed in Cyprus

16

that the NATO commander in chief, Lemnitzer, had sent telegrams to the Greek and Turkish Governments urging them to land troops on the island, so that a NATO mixed force would follow them in order to interpose itself between them and confront the Cyprus Government with an accomplished partition of Cyprus.[69] The Cyprus Government steadily opposed any NATO initiatives for the solution of the Cyprus problem, and with the support of the Soviet Union insisted on the issue being dealt with by the United Nations.[70]

The Soviet Union[71] took an increasingly active part in the dispute, starting with a statement at the end of January 1964 condemning the London Conference at which Greece and Turkey were persuaded to accept a NATO peace-keeping force. (Turkey is unlikely to have needed much persuasion, given the likely consequences of such a peace-keeping force). By August 1964 the Soviet Union had announced that it was ready to help Cyprus in the event of an invasion and in September a Cypriot delegation to Moscow was promised heavy arms. Naturally the Soviet Union did not regard this aid as being in the cause of *enosis*. It indicated a preference for the self-determination of Cyprus which it was aiding to orient itself to "unfettered independence" and demilitarization rather than *enosis*.[72] During the year, Egypt had provided some assistance in military equipment to Cyprus.

Though on the whole Greece and Turkey were agreed on the common interest which they had in preventing this trend in Cyprus, they had distinct disagreements on how it should be done or who should do it. By June the Greek Foreign Minister had covertly transported five thousand Greek troops to Cyprus.[73] General Grivas was to arrive during the next month with the encouragement of "western diplomatic circles",[74] to command them and to help check pro-communist feeling in Cyprus. Makarios vainly complained to the Greek ambassador that the number of troops were "far above" what had been agreed with the Greek Prime Minister.[75] Turkey meanwhile was threatening to solve the problem by landing its own troops. During 1964 there were four Turkish invasion scares.[76] The realization of the threat was likely to result in war between the two allies.

Even short of war, Greece and Turkey were indicating trends of action that were undesirable to the United States. In the case of Turkey these trends would continue long after 1964. After a strong letter from President Johnson, arguing against an invasion of Cyprus, to Inonu, the Prime Minister of Turkey, the latter said in an interview that "If our allies do not change their attitude, the Western Alliance will break up ... a new kind of world will then come into being on a new pattern, and in this new world Turkey will find itself a place."[77] The Greek Prime Minister, George Papandreou, in spite of strong American pressures, was refusing to enter into direct

17

negotiations with Turkey. In spite of some disagreement with Makarios, he was by and large supporting Makarios' position that the problem should be dealt with through the United Nations.

From the point of view of the United States, the problem of Cyprus presented itself as a dual one. On the one hand, trends in an independent Cyprus might result in the strategic interests of NATO in Cyprus being threatened. This could happen either through an indigenous political change, or through determined non-alignment. On the other, if either Greece or Turkey intervened dynamically, or even if the dispute continued, NATO cohesion would be threatened.[78] The first problem could be solved by terminating the independence of Cyprus, and the second by making the form of its termination the subject of agreement and territorial adjustment by Greece and Turkey. Since Greece for the moment had an apparently strong hand in Cyprus, through the presence of Greek troops, and since Greek nationalism could still be powerfully appealed to in Cyprus, the plan could be presented in such a way as to be acceptable to the majority of the population in the island. It could be presented as *enosis*, though it would in effect be partition. Views of Western diplomats that a solution along these lines would be optimal had been aired since the beginning of the crisis.[79] It had to be presented though, not as partition (to which virtually all Greek Cypriots would have preferred continuing independence, even under the Zurich-London agreements), but as *enosis*, which was in fact impossible due to the position of Turkey, military and political.

The discussion of this plan was conducted as a sideshow of a U.N. mediation effort between Greece and Turkey in Geneva in July. The U.S. point of view was presented by Dean Acheson. The basic idea behind the plan was that, to obviate the objections of the Cypriots to territorial concessions to Turkey and to a Turkish military base on Cyprus, these concessions would only be made after an unconditional declaration of *enosis*. Turkey would be reassured by a secret protocol, before the unilateral declaration of *enosis* by Greece.[80] Various versions of the plan have been published.[81] It appears to have evolved in minor ways during negotiations, but the basic elements are always: the cession to Turkey either in perpetuity or on long lease of a large base in the Karpasia area of Cyprus; three cantons with some form of local autonomy to be established for the Turkish Cypriots; and the cession of the Greek Aegean island of Kastellorizon to Turkey. The reason for the plan being a secret one is obvious if one considers the fact that Karpasia is not an uninhabited wilderness. It contains a large Turkish Cypriot population and a much larger Greek Cypriot one, who would presumably have to be removed to make space for a military base. There was also the suspicion that the establishment of Turkish cantons would in the long run have involved a rearrangement of the settlement pattern of Cyprus, not dissimilar to the one which took place during 1974. In any event, the establishment of a Turkish base would have given Turkey the military means for achieving such a rearrangement.

The Acheson plan provided in a sense for a "just" solution of the Cyprus problem, from the point of view of the leading power of the NATO alliance. Cyprus would be eliminated as a small non-aligned state in the Mediterranean. It would henceforth be taken care of by the relatively reliable allies, Greece and Turkey. The Greek Government would have something that it could call *enosis*. The Turkish Government would have a base in Cyprus, assuring it that the island would never be used militarily against its southern ports. It would also have a cantonal arrangement for the Turkish Cypriots providing the territorial basis for a possible later annexation of a part of the island. The fact that the plan could not be put into practice led to the heyday of Cyprus as an independent state.

One reason for the inapplicability of the plan was that Greece and Turkey found it hard to agree on exactly what constituted a fair division. There is no report that Greece and Turkey actually agreed at any stage. The first version of the plan, which provided for a sovereign Turkish base on Cyprus was accepted by Turkey as a basis of discussion, but rejected by Greece. The second version, which provided for a Turkish base to be leased to Turkey for twenty or twenty-five years was accepted by Greece as a basis of discussion, but rejected by the Turkish Government.[82] But the Government of Cyprus not only rejected both versions, it also rejected the argument that discussions between Greece and Turkey under the aegis of the United States was the correct way to solve the problem. Mr Clerides, the then president of the Cypriot House of Representatives expressed the problem as follows:

If union with Greece is to take place first and then Greece is to negotiate with Turkey what the rights of the Turkish community in Cyprus are going to be and whether there will be a Turkish or NATO base in Cyprus, then this is an unacceptable proposition.

This would amount to

An attempt to force the solution of the Cyprus problem from within the Western Alliance and to deprive Cyprus of the support of countries outside that alliance.[83]

Though the discussions in Geneva between Greece and Turkey led by Mr Acheson did not come to a conclusion, it is evident that the two governments were willing to continue negotiating. The Turkish Foreign Minister, Mr Erkin had said that "some interesting ideas had been produced during the Geneva talks".[84] And the Greek Prime Minister, George Papandreou, in his reply to a letter from Acheson, where the latter emphasizes the dangers of Cyprus falling under communist influence unless the plan were implemented, writes that:

> I agree absolutely with your view that this threat creates a common interest between Turkey and Greece which is greater by far than the exact lines which we draw on a map.[85]

Acheson himself said of the Geneva negotiations that "they had come very close to an agreement, but that President Makarios threw monkey wrenches into the machinery".[86]

The "monkey wrenches" came in three main shapes. The insistence that Cyprus was a sovereign state which would solve any internal problems on its own initiative was one; calling on the assistance of countries interested in the maintenance of Cypriot independence was another; and appealing to public opinion in Greece over the heads of the Greek Government was a third. The last one took the form of arguing that Cypriots would only accept pure *enosis*,[87] and not any of the adulterated varieties which it, by implication, accused the Greek Governments of considering the acceptance of. This point is more extensively discussed in Chapter IV.

The most successful stage of Cypriot foreign policy culminated in December 1965. After the presentation of the Acheson plan, a Greek Cypriot delegation visited Moscow in September 1964 where political consultations took place and Soviet arms were promised. In October, at the conference of non-aligned nations in Cairo, President Makarios went further than he had ever gone before and pledged himself to work for the abolition of the British bases in Cyprus.[88] In March 1965 the report of a mediator who had been appointed by the United Nations appeared, which substantially legitimated the Cyprus Government's claims in rejecting either the limitation or the elimination of Cypriot sovereignty. In October 1965 the Cyprus Government presented a set of proposals to the United Nations on minority rights for the Turkish Cypriots. While providing for wide and U.N. supervised guarantees for the Turkish Cypriots, the proposals would have eliminated their special position as guaranteed by the Zurich-London agreements. Finally, in December 1965 the U.N. General Assembly passed a resolution recognizing the unfettered independence of Cyprus. This direction of change appeared to have been strengthened rather than weakened when, in 1967, following further intercommunal incidents in Cyprus and a Turkish ultimatum and invasion threat, the Greek Junta, which was then in power, agreed to withdraw all the Greek troops which were stationed in Cyprus since 1964. What had been foreseen as a U.S. policy failure as early as November 1964 seemed to have taken place by 1967. Cyprus was getting out of hand, and,

> United States policy makers appear headed for another setback in the Eastern Mediterranean. The best informed diplomats here agree that Cyprus is likely to hang on indefinitely to its status as a self-governing state. That means the island will probably not become a part of Greece and will not be brought back into the Western Alliance ... will be neutralist, non-aligned and will play between the Eastern and Western Worlds.[89]

This could well have been so, had Turkish Governments not reopened the "Eastern Question" and had a dictatorship not established itself in Greece.

# CHAPTER II

## *The enosis movement: European nationalism as anti-colonialism*

European Nationalism and anti-colonialism are both fertile grounds for intellectual production. "Nationalists" writing about Cyprus have generally seen the history of Cyprus as a cultural movement starting around 2000 B.C. and continuing until the present and tending to unite Cyprus with other Greek cultural areas.[1] This view largely ignores the way in which group identity is expressed, the roots in everyday life of these expressions and, most significantly, the political constraints on such expressions. By contrast, liberal social scientists may under-emphasize the non-rational expressions of group national identity, or even the existence of cultural differences.[2] The real problem is to trace the fate of a movement which, from an ideology arguing the freeing of Cyprus from foreign rule, developed into an instrument of foreign domination while evoking in its adherents a fairly constant emotional reaction.

In spite of the fact that Cyprus was subject to a modern colonialism from 1878 until 1959, the reaction to this kind of rule was not "modern". The dominant anti-colonial movement was exclusively Greek Cypriot, and was led by a conservative Church hierarchy. At its peak it was a European nationalist movement based on the culture and language of one of the ethnic groups on the island. Of course, the Greek Cypriots had always formed more than three-quarters of the population of the island and had been, even during the Ottoman Empire, the dominant group economically, though a subject one politically. To understand the characteristics of this movement, the course of its development and the nature of its aims, one must look at its relation to British colonial policy on the island during the formative stages of the development of the movement.

There were perhaps certain distinctive liberal characteristics of British colonial policy in Cyprus, which were due to a distinctive relationship of rulers and ruled. The main use for Cyprus was strategic: the island had little economic significance for either metropolitan traders or settlers from the metropolis. Also, there must have been certain problems with the normal colonial ideology of a "civilizing mission". The majority of the population had the characteristics of a culture long regarded as superior by the British educational system and spoke a language obviously descended from classical Greek. As Storrs,[3] writing of his experiences as Governor of Cyprus before the war, points out "no sensible person will deny that the Cypriot is Greek-speaking, Greek-thinking, Greek-feeling Greek ...". In fact the colonial history of Cyprus is dotted with recognitions by British colonial and other government officials of the Greekness of Cyprus. The 1915 offer of Cyprus to Greece has been mentioned. It was preceded in 1907 by Winston Churchill's much repeated statement during an official visit to Cyprus on the natural and praiseworthy character of the Greek Cypriots' Hellenic sentiments.[4] In 1919 both Ramsay MacDonald and Lloyd George made statements implying that ultimately Cyprus would become part of Greece.[5] During the Second World War, the British Government's recruiting slogan in Cyprus was "Fight for Freedom and Greece".[6] The expressions of the liberal British press were much more explicit. "To explain to the Greek Cypriots that they are not Greek is to explain to the inhabitants of Yorkshire that they are not English" wrote the *Manchester Guardian* in 1954.[7] Cypriots were given conditions within the island enabling them to express such sentiments themselves.

These facts had to be reconciled with the reality of colonial policy. Political control must ultimately rest with the metropolis. The Imperial exchequer must not be placed under any charge from a colony. And the governed are, after all, the governed. The basic contradiction worked its way into virtually every aspect of the colonial political system and crystallized around several issues.

The British Government had undertaken to make good to the Ottoman Empire that part of its tax revenue which had been lost due to the transfer of Cyprus to British administration. Since the Ottoman government was indebted to British stock-holders and had defaulted on repayment, Cypriots found that for the first half-century of British rule they were paying substantial proportions of their low incomes to British stock-holders.[8] Even more to the point perhaps was how this must have looked from the perspective of the Cypriot legislators in the "toy parliament" of Cyprus. The principle of "no taxation without representation" was a gift to the Cypriots from British liberalism. But to approve the necessary budget for the island was to approve the payments to the British stock-holders.

Four years after the British occupation of Cyprus, a Legislative Council was established. Initially it had a membership of 18. Three members were Muslim and 9 were "non-Muslim" elected members. There were also 6 appointed members who were Civil Servants and the Governor had a casting vote.[9] The arithmetic indicates an early perception on the part of the British administrators of the potential alignments. After persistent Greek Cypriot agitation on the unfairness of representation in this way, the Legislative Council was expanded in

1925 to a membership of 24, of which 3 were Muslims. The Greek membership of the Legislative Council was increased from 9 to 12, but the Official members were at the same time increased to 9.[10]

Acknowledgement of the cultural equality and "European" nature of Cyprus was combined with exclusion from the higher posts of the Civil Service for Cypriots, discrimination in pay between Cypriot and expatriate civil servants of the same rank, and social exclusion.[11] Other facets of colonial rule were similarly contradictory. There were reforms which deeply affected Cypriot society, and which had effects on important parts of it, particularly the Church, which lost its representative function in relation to the secular power. Yet the Mufti as the Muslim religious leader retained ceremonial precedence over the Archbishop,[12] at least until 1930. The fact of nominal Ottoman sovereignty was given as one reason impeding the transfer of the island to Greece.

These problems were sufficient to cause dissatisfaction among the merchant and professional class of Cyprus. At the beginning of the twentieth century though, the demand for union with Greece does not seem to have been expressed with unanimous vehemence among this class. In fact there was some degree of political conflict centred around this issue, splitting the merchant and professional class, and through them the rest of the island, into "moderates"and the "uncompromising nationalists".[13] Also, while these problems served to incite dissatisfaction, they do not explain the channels which the dissatisfaction took, that is Hellenic nationalism. The reasons for the expression of dissatisfaction in this form have partly to do with British colonial policy, and partly with the relations of the Greek State to Orthodox, Greek-speaking communities outside its domain.

When the colonial political life of Cyprus was not dominated by the issue of the "Tribute" payments, it was dominated by the issue of "representation". A Legislative Assembly which went through all the motions of parliamentarianism existed. But the vote was always "fixed" in favour of the Government. At crucial times, when Greek and Turkish Cypriots might combine and defeat the vote of the official members, the decision was reversed by an "Order in Council" in London.[14] After extensive riots in 1931, the Legislative Council was abolished.

For Greek Cypriots there was an alternative avenue of political representation, unbound by colonial limitations, the Autocephalous Church of Cyprus. The official representative functions which it had enjoyed under Ottoman rule were limited by the British; and aid from the secular authority in collecting the contributions of the faithful, had been terminated. But some of its basic "ethnarchic functions", particularly its involvement with education, remained for almost 50 years of British rule and were confirmed by Privy Council and

Cypriot legal decisions.[15] This was enough to make the Church an important political institution and a political plum for competing factions. The nationalist issue could, from the viewpoint of the Church, both help in re-establishing the predominant position of the Church among the population and also suitably expressed the Church's disloyalty to the colonial power which had removed or limited various of its secular powers.[16]

The "disloyalty" of the merchant and professional class was an added reason inducing the British administration to introduce reforms which broke the hold of this class on the peasantry. The measures included the suppression of money-lending and the introduction of Credit Cooperatives. In the battle between the colonial government on the one hand, and the merchants and professionals on the other for the allegiance of the peasantry, the colonial government used measures of economic reform. The bourgeoisie had other reasons to extend the nationalist ideology, but the possibility of mobilizing peasants against the Government must have been an important one.[17] Besides the Church, the main means of the extension of Hellenic nationalism to the mass of the population was the educational system. The educational system however had, even before the beginnings of British rule in Cyprus, formed a link between the Greek-Cypriot bourgeoisie and the Greek State.

After the formation of the Greek State in 1828, it was natural for successive Greek Governments to assume that an island on which about three quarters (at that time) of the population were Greek would sometime be incorporated in the Greek State. There was no question that at least the elite of the island were aware of being Greek. In 1821 the Church hierarchy and prominent Christians all over Cyprus were executed on the grounds of preparing to join in the mainland Greek revolt against Ottoman Rule. "In only a few days ... the archbishop, the bishops, the high-ranking Greek priests, the merchants, the notables of the cities and villages, finally all rich or influential people have been slaughtered. ..."[18] Even the most servile or *rayah*-like Christian Subject of the Ottoman Empire must have been persuaded, by being treated as a revolutionary, that he had some connection with what was going on on the mainland. The severity of Turkish measures ensured that until the occupation by the British in 1878, there were no overt Greek nationalist actions.[19] Whatever education existed though for the Christian population during the Ottoman period was Greek. Quite early on there were signs not only of its being Greek culturally, but also of pursuing the ideals of Greek nationalism.

As early as the middle of the eighteenth century[20] a "school of Greek Letters and Music" had been set up by the Archbishop in Nicosia, and an Athenian teacher taught in it. By 1830, after the establishment of the Greek State, there were schools in the main towns, Nicosia and Larnaca, and some of the bigger villages which included Greek history in their syllabus. In 1860 the prominent citizens of Famagusta arranged regular meetings in the house of the school teacher and read (or perhaps had read to them), the mainland Greek newspapers. The newspapers were sent to them by the Greek consul in Cyprus. One need not go into the details of the history of Greek education in Cyprus to show that it developed to become a branch of the mainland Greek educational system. This was of course facilitated by the advent of liberal British administration. With the advent of the British, there was no reason to conceal the fact that one important function of education was to develop in the young a sense of identification with the Greek State. The history of a secondary school in Famagusta illustrates the point. In 1899 the drawing lesson involved drawing heroes of the Greek War of Independence. There was also a lesson about the *Philiki Etairia,* the secret society which organized the war. In the same year criticisms appeared in newspapers of parents who did not send their children to Greek Schools, reminding parents of the danger of the "Levantinization" of Cyprus. In 1908 the School Board wrote to the Greek Ministry of Education asking it to find a university graduate "of good character and holding to the pan-national ideal" to reform the school. In 1910 a service is reported on the occasion of the birthday of the king of Greece. In 1923 the school was recognized by the Ministry of Education of Greece as equivalent to mainland Greek secondary schools. Such secondary schools provided teachers for primary schools, which increased in number after the British occupation.

The number of "Greek-Christian" schools in Cyprus increased from 94 in 1881 to 238 in 1901.[21] In each community the priest presided over the educational organization, and each community elected a school board which appointed teachers. This was as it had been since Ottoman times. During Ottoman times the financial resources for education had largely come from the Church and the monasteries and so were limited. The expansion of primary education was made possible by the fact that with British rule school boards were empowered to impose taxation, and later grants from the government become available. Otherwise, the system of administration remained much the same until 1933, with the Church supervising the education system overall. Muslim education is discussed in another chapter. But it is worth pointing out here, by contrast, that at this time there was no national Turkish State, only an Empire in which Turkish-speaking Muslims were the dominant group. The Greek State's educational system was part of a state organization to inculcate in the young the need to expand the limited borders of the Nation.[22] Ottoman education might well have de-emphasized national characteristics which were disruptive of the Empire. In fact Muslim education in Cyprus at this time appears to have been largely religious:

> The subjects taught are the reading and the chanting of the Koran and the repetition of the religious code "ilmihal", reading and writing of the Turkish language, some Ottoman and general history and geography ... and, for the highest classes in some schools, a little Arabic and Persian.[23]

The results of Greek education became increasingly evident to British colonial administrators. It appears that there had always been more government intervention in primary than in secondary education, probably because this level was more dependent on governmental economic assistance. After 1923, the appointment of school teachers was largely taken out of the hands of local community councils and therefore out of the hands of Greek Cypriot politicians and the Church. In 1933 legislative measures put primary education completely under the control of the British Government.[24] In primary schools one could hear "God Save the King" being sung in Greek translation. No doubt this was done with tongue-in-cheek if possible, given the nature of the rest of the educational system. The attempt to bring secondary education under governmental control was unsuccessful, but it is interesting to look at the issues involved. They included the final struggle between secular and religious representation in political affairs for the right wing Greek Cypriots.

The riots of 1931 were followed by widespread repression on the part of the colonial authorities. Among other measures, the elected Legislative Council was abolished. It was replaced by an appointed Consultative Council. Both a nationalist Greek Cypriot intellectual,[25] and Storrs[26] in his biography, mention that in the mid-nineteen twenties there began to appear in British Government circles the idea, that if only the Greek Cypriots would not feel that they were Greek, they would be much more governable. Storrs actually thought that the idea of developing a Cypriot nationality was impracticable. Presenting the Greek Cypriots with a Cypriot flag would do nothing to stop the nationalist agitation. The Greek Cypriots were not merely negatively inclined to the British, they positively wanted incorporation with Greece. For the Cypriot nationalists thinking along Cypriot national lines was anathema. It was a British trick. A myth of Cypriot nationality would be invented in order to perpetuate British rule in Cyprus. The only form of conceivable liberty, Union with Greece, would be denied in perpetuity. After the riots of 1931, the symbols of the Greek nation, the flag and the Greek national anthem, were banned in Cyprus. (Until the beginning of the Second World War, when the British Government used these symbols to recruit Cypriots

27

to the British armed forces.) But finally, the British tried to deal with the Church and the educational system. Some of the Bishops were exiled. The Archbishop was not actually exiled, but when he died in 1934, there was an attempt to establish means of governmental control over his successor. In this the government apparently had the support of some sections of the Greek Cypriot influential class; the same ones it appears who had agreed to serve in the Advisory Council.[27] The issue of whether the government could or could not control the filling of the Archbishop's seat crystallized over the recognition of the *locum tenens* right to serve in the functions of the Archbishop in relation to the School Board. The "moderates" maintained that the issue should be raised only after the appointment of a new, government approved Archbishop. The nationalists of course supported the *locum tenens*.

From 1933 onwards, the British Government in Cyprus appeared to have made a persistent attempt to alter the Cypriot educational system in two ways. One was to make sure that if it was controlled by the Church, the Church would be politically controlled by the Government and not by the nationalists. The other was to force changes in the curriculum by withholding economic aid to schools which persisted in teaching the Hellenic-oriented curriculum. Both struggles ended in failure for the Government. Despite some division among the Greek Cypriot elite, all the British Government succeeded in doing was to keep the Archbishop's seat vacant until after the War. Meanwhile it appears that the *locum tenens* continued to have legitimacy for most Greek Cypriots as a national and religious leader. In 1937, however, a law forbade the official involvement of any religious personality in educational administration.[28]

One can look at the changes in the curriculum which were aimed at through the history of the Famagusta Gymnasium again.[29] In 1933 aid from the Government's education department was cut. In 1936 the board of prominent citizens which ran the school agreed to the curriculum reform which the Government insisted on as a condition for the resumption of aid. History and Geography, the Government demanded, would be taught in English. The traditional Greek schools, the Gymnasiums, would be limited to one on the whole island. The encyclopaedic nature of the curriculum would be changed in favour of the positive sciences, commercial subjects and languages. All courses should be oriented to British University entrance examinations. Greek history should not be taught as a special subject and more emphasis should be given to the teaching of the history of Cyprus. Teachers who accepted these changes would find it easy to get Government scholarships to go to England to study, in order to help in the reorganization of the school system on returning. "On the whole", however, "the reforms seem not to have been applied in practice as Greek Government recognition was not withdrawn."[30]

## The enosis movement

There is no detailed historical account of the reaction among intellectuals to the attempt to impose these changes. There are indications, in the chorus of accusations, which have until recently blamed the British Government for attempting to de-hellenize Cyprus. And it is likely that these attempts to infringe on the Church and on the educational system might partly explain the degree of nationalist fervour which subsequently gripped the intellectuals and the Church, and eventually left no dissenting voice among the bourgeoisie either. In contrast to other colonies the British had met opposition not on the part of anglicized subjects but rather on the part of people of strongly defined Greek culture. In any event this was probably one of the earliest of the movements against colonial rule. The British reacted to the movement, not only by opposing any change in the sovereignty of the island, but by also trying to change the culture through the educational system. At least they tried to change those aspects of the culture which the contemporary nationalist intellectuals heavily emphasized. But this was much worse than a mere refusal to change the sovereignty of the island. It was a threat to the personal identity of the increasing number of educated Greek Cypriots and to the status of the intellectual and religious leaders.

Apart from the outbreak of 1931, the *enosis* movement was peaceful until 1955. It does not seem to be the case that the 1931 riots were the outcome of a plan to instigate violence,[31] but was rather a combination of nationalist verbal agitation and spontaneous peasant riots. On the whole, nationalist aims were pursued through peaceful channels. They often involved petitions to the Crown. Frequent delegations went to London to see members of the Government and present the demands of the Cypriot political leaders. Filibustering in the Legislative Council appears to have been frequent while it continued to function. And on occasion, elections were boycotted.[32] The decision to resort to arms appears to have been taken by the conservative Greek Cypriot nationalist leadership after the Second World War, during a period of intense class conflict and considerable gains by the Left in support among the swelling urban population. It seems likely that this fact lent an additional characteristic to the Greek nationalist movement.

There is a pronounced difference between the nature of the demands made by the opponents of colonial rule in its early and later stages. It seems that there was a tendency in the early days of British rule to make demands related to issues of constitutional structure, economic measures and social reform, as well as the ultimate nationalist demand for Union with Greece. In 1888 a Cypriot embassy consisting of the Archbishop and the three most prominent politicians of Cyprus went to London to present a petition to the British Government, much as similar embassies had travelled to

29

Constantinople earlier. The contents indicate that consideration of the island's economic and constitutional problems was at the forefront. It was claimed that the average level of taxation had considerably increased since the British Occupation. (The British had abolished a number of taxes, but collected the ones that remained on the books efficiently with a consequent increase in the yield of taxation.) The petition inevitably demands the abolition of the Tribute and its replacement by a once and for all payment. The money would be raised by a loan made in the name of the island. The decisions of the Legislative Council should always be binding on the island's Government, and only subject to the Queen's veto. There should be two Cypriot members in the Governor's Executive Council which was solely composed of British officials. Measures should be taken to advance secondary education. An agricultural department should be established, and also an agricultural bank. Tobacco planting should be free and not subject to the Government monopoly's decisions. And a law should be promulgated regulating the relations of Church and State.[33] It does not seem that any demand was made for a change in the sovereignty of the island. The relatively low level of nationalist fervour at this time is also indicated by the fact that Katalanos, a mainland school teacher and nationalist, writes that at the turn of the century the anniversary of the Greek War of Independence was hardly celebrated at all in Nicosia and with little liveliness in the other two main towns, Limassol and Larnaca.[34]

The "national issue" became increasingly prominent, but still a tame version of what it was to become. In 1902 one of the Greek Representatives, on behalf of the rest, obtained an audience with the British High Commissioner in order to discuss the economic situation of the island. The High Commissioner claimed that if the Legislative Council set aside the "political question", that is *enosis,* then foreign capital would flood Cyprus, which it was now afraid of doing due to the nationalist agitation. The Greek Member replied that the Cypriots had no differences with the Government on the "political issue" because,

> the Cypriot people will seek with determination by legal and law-abiding means their national restitution, which they expect to obtain through the great-heartedness of the British nation.[35]

He did insist, however, that the Representatives had disagreements with the Government's economic policy.

In 1922 a memorial from the Archbishop to the Secretary of State for the Colonies asked for Cypriots to be granted full self-government and that Greek and Turkish Cypriots should participate in the Executive Council and in the Administration in proportion to their numbers.[36] Requests for constitutional change, after 1931, concentrated on the re-establishment of some kind of self-government. But the request of anything but *enosis* was rarer. However as late as 1939 a "Committee for Cyprus Autonomy" formed in London, produced a document which was approved by 200 persons and organizations in Cyprus and presented it to the Governor of the island. The document suggested a new constitution.

Yet, when after the war the Government offered, for the first time in the history of Cyprus, economic aid from the metropolis, a ten-year development plan and a constitution for self-government, the offer was rejected outright by the conservative Cypriots under the leadership of the Church. (An Archbishop had once more been elected without government regulation in 1946.) The Left, after considerable dithering, also rejected cooperation with the Government in the cause of reform, but that is a subject of another chapter. What is significant here is the change in the demands of the leadership of the nationalist movement.

Further research might establish how the Cypriot bourgeoisie responded to the challenge of the Government's reform measures in relation to the peasantry, and the threat of the increasingly strong communist movement, by dropping all demands for reforms, which they had so frequently previously demanded. They adopted instead the slogan of "*enosis* and only *enosis*". One would have to look at the transition in demands and political slogans in much more detail to be sure of this. But if the bourgeoisie's economic position was being threatened by British colonial reforms favouring the peasantry, and both the bourgeoisie and the Church were being threatened by revolution from an increasingly strong Left, they would be unlikely themselves to demand constitutional and economic reforms as they had done at the beginning of the British occupation. Not only was the idea of reforms dropped, but their consideration became a sign of betrayal. The Archbishop coined the slogan "Away with constitutions and ballot boxes. *Enosis* and only *enosis*." Since both its opponents used social reform as a threat, the bourgeoisie moved to the most contradictory position possible. Total rejection of any reform and incorporation into the Greek State would remove both of the threats. The Church was a natural vehicle of a messianic and anti-communist movement. After all, its successive stripping by the colonial government of its fiscal, political and educational functions made sure that it had nothing to loose but its chains.

The complete separation of demands for social reform and "national liberation" is in fact an extraordinary characteristic for an anti-colonial movement.[37] The internal history of the movement gave this separation an ideological impetus. But of course the fact was that the movement in any event had demanded the incorporation of Cyprus

31

with an existing and established state, Greece. And this alone meant that less prominence would be given to issues such as the political and social arrangements in the island after the removal of colonial rule. These facts combined with certain other characteristics of Greek nationalism in its Cypriot variant. They formed the political belief system of generations of educated Greek Cypriots. Since it was a set of beliefs that was inculcated in the whole generation that attended Greek Cypriot schools after the Second World War, it could not be discarded like a casually held political opinion when political conditions changed.

The *enosis* movement is not "European" nationalism merely in the sense that it has similar characteristics with movements that developed in Europe in the nineteenth century. The most influential intellectual formulator of Greek Nationalism, Adamantios Korais, was directly influenced by the ideas of romantic nationalist philosophers such as Herder.[38] Language was the essence of nationality, so a "purified" version of Greek was invented by Korais and adopted by the Government and the educational system. The ancient heroic virtues of the Greeks and the direct link of the modern Greek to ancient Greek culture and virtues are other themes of Greek nationalism which are given the status of dogma.

In Cyprus, where the cultural identity of the Greek Cypriots had been by turns glorified and repressed by the colonial rulers, these characteristics of Greek nationalism reached the proportions of a revelation. We have here an ideology which was originally highly idealistic. It was embodied in a bourgeois political movement which was challenged by movements of social reform. The cultural identity on which it was based was made the target of educational change. And the leadership of the whole movement was embodied in a religious institution. No wonder that the whole movement acquired highly non-rational characteristics, which emphasized distant descent, racial continuity and purity, and religious fervour.

These themes are well illustrated in the work of a prominent Greek Cypriot nationalist intellectual. One of the most prominent Cypriot historians writes about the motivation to engage in his work:

> I came across the work by Perrot and Chipiez *Histoire de l'art dans l'Antiquité* and I saw with puzzlement, that the eminent archaeologists maintained at many points that the Cypriots were Phoenicians. This made a great impression on me and since that time I was determined to prove that their assertion was mistaken.[39]

When Archbishop Cyril III declared in 1934 a literary competition with the subject, "The First Inhabitants of Cyprus", he took part, and was awarded first prize by a committee appointed by the Athens Academy. Some of his main conclusions are:

> ... the first inhabitants of Cyprus came from Asia Minor and in the thirteenth century B.C. the population of the island was finally formed, becoming purely Greek, and in fact composed of the same elements of which the population of mainland Greece and the other islands is composed.

The work ends with the Persian conquest of Cyprus. He does not consider it necessary to go into the historical period.

> I have avoided the examination of this period in the text, as the facts are known and are not essential for the purposes of this book. We have been extensively concerned with the prehistoric period, because it is there that one must go if he wants to classify a people to a certain race.[40]

This concern with racial purity and racial descent in the determination of nationality is apparently logically contradictory to the concern over the possibility of de-hellenization, but is in fact highly consistent emotionally. It is quite clear to all involved in a nationalist situation that the main vehicle of nationalism is the school system. The emphasis on racial purity is an intellectually weak but emotionally strong argument in favour of inculcating national consciousness. It makes the national claim just, since it is in any event biologically given.

In actual political usage, the characteristics of Hellenic nationalism in Cyprus discussed above gave it an extreme religious fervour. In 1950 a plebiscite was organized by the Church, which resulted in a virtually universal vote in favour of *enosis*. A speech delivered on the morning of the plebiscite, contained the following:

> When the bleeding and chained Greek race lay thrashing under the feet of the Asian conqueror, and found themselves abandoned by their natural leaders, their intellectuals and politicians, they turned in supplication towards the remaining clergy, who were themselves wearing rags instead of holy robes, ... and asked them not to allow the candle of Christ to go out, not to allow the light, the Greek light to eclipse totally.
>
> And then, the clerics of the Holy Church of Christ ... took from its blood-stained hands its ideals and secreted them deeply in their hearts. And from that moment, the life-saving labour of the Greek-Orthodox Church towards the Greek Nation begins. Then the "Secret School" begins, under the light of the moon, to create the miracle. There under the never-dying light which lit the icon of the Holy Virgin and the crucifix, the Priest-Teacher whispers in the ear of the enslaved Greek

33

child, that there were times when Greece, his Motherland, was Queen
of Nations, even though now her forehead bled from a crown of thorns.
  And the Priest of the enslaved Greek village exclaimed while carrying
the Crucifix "We bow before your sufferings O Christ, show to us also
Your glorious Resurrection", then, there appeared before his soul and
before the souls of his flock, not only the Cross of Golgotha, but also
Hellenism crucified, before whose sufferings he wept, And when
afterwards, he transmitted to the faithful the light of Resurrection, the
Resurrection of the Race was also symbolized in his patriotic heart. So,
was ritualized in the soul of the nation the inseparable Bond of
Motherland and Religion, which led to the National Risorgimento.[41]

To a secular European reader the passage may appear grotesque.
The speaker was however doing no more than indicating the pervasive
awareness of the role of the Church organization in maintaining and
extending some form of distinctive identity during the Ottoman period
of Greek history and the special place of education in this process. He
was speaking at a time when the British administration was once
more (after a period of wartime liberalism) attempting to suppress the
symbols of Greek nationality in Cyprus. By combining religious and
national symbolism, in the contexts of some of the most deeply
ingrained institutions of everyday life, the nationalist speaker could
appeal to the deepest levels of feelings of threatened cultural identity
and mobilize them to particular political acts. In this particular case to
vote for Union with Greece.

Cultural and national identity are inseparably merged in this kind
of nationalist rhetoric. Political ideology becomes one with personal
identity. The space for change and political manoeuvre is eliminated.
It is a good incentive for fighting against apparently hopeless odds, but
is dynamite in the light of any subsequent need for flexibility.

It is in this atmosphere that a decision was taken during the early
1950's to organize armed attacks on the British in Cyprus. The aim
was to force the concession of *enosis*. This was a stage of great
escalation, and not only because of the use of violence. Greece at last
took up the issue of Cyprus on the international level and in 1954
made the first appeal to the United Nations on behalf of Cyprus. It
sought the application of the principle of self-determination. Greece
was now under American rather than British tutelage.[42] Taking up
the issue of the Cypriots may also have been timely in view of the need
to reunify the country after an intermittent civil war of almost six
years. The leader of the *enosis* movement in Cyprus, Archbishop
Makarios, soon perceived the link between the fact that Cypriots,
though motivated by a cultural nationalism, were fighting against
government by a colonial power. Due to this they had common links
with the group of nations and aspiring nations which met for the first
time in Bandung in 1955, even though Cyprus at this stage was far

from itself aspiring to be a nation. Even the gaining of support by the Soviet Union appeared a legitimate aim. In June of 1953, Archbishop Makarios, speaking in Phaneromeni Church in Nicosia, took an oath not to give up the struggle for Union with Greece. And he added: "We will extend the right and the left hand to accept any help from East or West."[43]

A conservative nationalist movement thus began the fatal course of fighting communism at home while seeking its support internationally and aligning itself with the non-aligned countries in order to achieve incorporation with a state which was a member of NATO. Greece was no ordinary member of NATO. It was the first country which had had to be saved from communist insurgency with U.S. aid. It was natural that its conservative leaders would regard this alliance as virtually sacrosanct.

# CHAPTER III

## The Turkish Cypriots: from religious minority to a state within the state

For the first three quarters of a century of British Rule in Cyprus the Turkish Cypriots did not show strong nationalist tendencies. This relative quiescence made it possible for Greek Cypriot nationalism to develop with little attention to the presence of the Turkish Cypriots on the island. At various times some sections of the bourgeoisie, and also at times the communist party, paid some considerable attention to the political significance of the Turkish Cypriots, which is discussed in Chapter VI. But given the relative lack of nationalist consciousness and the lack of a nationalist movement among the Turkish Cypriots, these Greek Cypriot groups never considered it worth making a major political issue out of their presence. The problem never seemed serious enough to risk confrontation with the developing Greek nationalist fervour. When Turkish Cypriot nationalism erupted violently in the 1950's, it was hard for Greek Cypriots to accept that it was a real and important political phenomenon which had to be taken into account in their own political calculations.

The long quiescence of the Turkish Cypriots seems to have been a product of various factors. They all contributed to identification with Islam and the British Government rather than the Turkish State. (It must be remembered that the Turkish national State came into existence in 1923, whereas the Greek State had come into existence almost a century earlier, in 1828.) This is only a general statement. But certainly by comparison to Greek nationalism on Cyprus, Turkish nationalism appeared to be a mild phenomenon for a long period. This is due both to the late development of mainland Turkish nationalism, and to the particular characteristics of the Islamic, Turkish-speaking population of Cyprus.

Of all the linguistic and religious groups which formed the Ottoman Empire, the Turks were the last to develop a distinct nationalism. This was not unnatural since they were the masters of the Empire.[1] It was only by a process of differentiation and defection of other groups from Ottoman and Islamic forms of loyalty that specifically Turkish nationalism developed. Until the mid-nineteenth century, the rulers of the Ottoman Empire found it hard to conceive of an alternative to Islamic loyalty in the Empire. When in the late 1850's, a special commission discussed the question of recruiting

Christian subjects of the Empire to the army, Gevdet Pasha, in giving evidence, put his finger on the essential elements of Ottoman loyalty. This loyalty he pointed out is Islamic-religious. If there were Christian soldiers in an Ottoman army,

> ... in time of need how could the Colonel of a mixed battalion stir the zeal of his soldiers? In Europe, indeed, patriotism has taken the place of religious devotion, but this happened at the end of their feudal period; their children hear the word fatherland (*vatan*) while they are still small, and so years later the call of patriotism has become effective with their soldiers. But among us, if we say the word "fatherland" all that will come to the minds of the soldiers is their village squares. If we were to adopt the word "fatherland" now, and if, in the course of time, it were to establish itself in men's minds and acquire the power that it has in Europe, even then it would not be as potent as religious zeal, nor could it take its place. Even that would take a long time, and in the meantime our armies would be left without spirit.[2]

The malleable and pragmatic view of group loyalties, and the means by which they can be inculcated, presented by a practical man of affairs is an interesting counter-balance to the idea that nationalism is a spontaneous phenomenon occurring universally under certain conditions. But of course nor is malleability without limits. For the very reason that the ideological core of the Empire was Islamic loyalty, attempts to build an "Ottoman nationalism" failed. This was attempted by Ottoman constitutionalists and liberals in the Committees of Union and Progress and by the Young Turk Government which came to power in 1908. The dynastic and religious form of loyalty was to be undermined not by a constitutional loyalty encompassing the various linguistic and religious groups, but by the gradual defection of linguistic and religious groups from any loyalty to the Empire at all. The Young Turks were initially Ottomanists, but were pushed increasingly towards Turkism by the defection even of Muslim subjects of the Empire from loyalty to it.

As a literary and intellectual movement, Turkism was first expressed around 1900.[3] It was at first expansionist and in its political expression visualized the incorporation of Turks who were outside the Ottoman Empire. In fact in 1917-18 it led to military adventures in Trans-Caucasia and Central Asia. It was Ataturk's realization that the internal consolidation of a secular modern state involved the renunciation of "Turanism" or the pan-Turk ideal that resulted in the establishment of a Turkish nationalism based on the Anatolian homeland as the official policy of the Turkish Government. (In a broad historical perspective, the massacre of the Armenians of Asia Minor in 1915 eliminated competition from another group for the establishment of a territorial homeland in Anatolia. The last act was the expulsion of the Greeks in 1922.) "Tụrkiye", meaning a secular Turkish state in Anatolia was first used officially in 1921.[4] But in certain senses, the state had preceded the nationalism. And in 1930 Ataturk founded the Turkish Historical Society to inculcate the theory of modern Turkish nationalism based on the Anatolian homeland.[5]

Just as Greek nationalism in Cyprus developed as part of a wider Hellenic nationalist movement, so Turkish Cypriot nationalism had no preconditions for development before the 1920's, when a Turkish mainland nationalism developed. But in fact conditions in Cyprus delayed this development further.

Muslims in the Ottoman Empire were notionally part of the ruling group of the Empire. The precise meaning of this in the historical development of relations between Turkish-speaking Muslims and Greek-speaking Christians in Cyprus is complex and would take one far out of the scope of this book. It would involve a detailed examination of the social structure of Cyprus during three-and-a-half centuries of Ottoman administration. But some comments can be made about the relations of Christians and Muslims in the State and in the economic structure of Ottoman Cyprus. It seems that the two lines of "stratification" were not aligned with each other. In the economic sphere it seems that the dominant group in the middle of the nineteenth century was Christian. There is also evidence that there was, on occasion, class solidarity between Christian and Muslim peasants. But the State structure which was based on religious differentiation gave a clear superiority to Muslims.

Christians were not legally eligible for military service in the Ottoman Empire before 1855, and in practice after that time as well. Christians were subject to sumptuary laws, for example in dress.[6] They were legally compelled to show deference to Muslims.[7] And although the Christians were not allowed to possess arms, but Muslims were.[8] Until the Tanzimat reforms, Christians were not allowed to have bells or bell towers in their Churches, and in practice they were not allowed such things after the reforms also.[9] But the most explicit indication of the notional membership of Muslims in the ruling group, besides the facts already mentioned of the exclusive right to military service and to bear arms, is in the administration of the State. The system which the British found in Cyprus in 1878 was as follows: Each administrative district of Cyprus was governed by a body composed of five Muslim and two Christian members. Judicial Tribunals had five members. A *Kadi* presided over two Christian and two Muslim members. This probably did not make much difference to wealthy Christians as there are reports that all members of the Tribunals welcomed bribery.[10] But ordinary Christians were not even allowed to give evidence in the Tribunals until the Tanzimat reforms.

Even in 1872, after the Tanzimat, there were only 26 Greeks in public employment in Cyprus and those were in low positions.[11]

The obverse of this was that the Muslims of the Empire did not have an autonomous *millet* representation. The Christians of Cyprus may not have been represented in anything approaching their numbers in the State institutions, but as a non-Muslim *millet* which was in a majority in this particular province of the Empire, they had an autonomous representative institution, recognized by the Sultan, not only on minor issues of representation of grievances, but also as an instrument of administration. The power of the Church was such before the 1821 massacres that in 1804 we find part of the Turkish military garrison of Cyprus rebelling against the Ottoman Governor (the *Muhassil*) and also against the *Dragoman,* the Archbishop and the Bishops. At this time the *Dragoman* was a Christian official closely connected to the Church and the *Muhassil* was responsible for taxing the Muslims as well as the Christians.[12]

The fact that popular revolts were frequently on class lines seems well established.[13] Even after the beginning of the Greek War of Independence in 1821 there were revolts on class rather than religious lines. In 1830 the Archbishop had to take refuge in the *Seray,* the Ottoman Governor's residence, to protect himself from a protest against high taxes in which both Christians and Muslims participated.[14] In 1833 there were two revolts on Cyprus. One was led by "Giaur Imam", a well-to-do Turk, and the other by a monk called Joannikios. The Giaur Imam established himself in the Bishop's palace in Paphos after evicting the Bishop and for a while controlled the whole district. Joannikios appears to have been planning to capture Larnaca and murder all its wealthy inhabitants, Greek and Turk. The wealthy inhabitants of Limassol of both ethnic groups panicked and appealed to the *Muhassil* to send troops. The two rebels planned to join forces in Nicosia. However, it is also worth noting that when troops were sent to Paphos, they attacked not the rebels, but Christian inhabitants, killing twenty of them.[15] In 1855, there were outrages of Muslim policemen and protests from the *Ulema* (the Muslim religious leader) against the reforms implied in the Vienna Protocol which would have given legal equality to the Christian inhabitants of the Empire.[16] The changes were meant to secularize and bureaucratize the Empire and replace the capitulations system. They are reported to have been opposed in Cyprus by the Orthodox Primates and the European consuls, as well as Muslim religious leaders.[17]

Partly due to the very reason that the Muslim ruling group was administrative, military and judicial, economic activities were, by the middle of the nineteenth century, concentrated in the hands of the Christians.[18] (A more detailed consideration of the relative demographic and economic position of Greek and Turkish Cypriots over the years is given in Chapter V.)

In recapitulation, it seems that the situation of ruling and subject groups in Ottoman Cyprus was as follows: By the end of the Ottoman period economic power was concentrated in the hands of Greek merchants and the Orthodox Church. But the Christian population was distinctly subject politically. Ottoman political and Muslim religious leaders opposed any increase in political power for the Christian dominant group, or even attempts to give non-Muslims citizenship equality. It is probably for this reason that in spite of their dominant economic position in Cyprus the Greek merchants were on occasion disloyal to the empire. There is evidence of solidarity between Christian and Ottoman peasants against both the ruling groups on issues of unjust or excessive taxation. And there is evidence of solidarity between the two ruling groups in, for example, keeping the tribute to the Porte at a minimum and keeping Governors who were likely to be strict in the application of Imperial edicts away from Cyprus, as well as in frustrating peasant uprisings by either Christians or Muslims or both together. On the other hand the Ottoman and Church authorities both owed their position to the Sultan and were rivals for political domination on the island. The Church attracted the loyalty of Christians as a protector against arbitrary acts of the Ottoman administration. The Ottoman administrative authority presented the Church as rebellious against the authority of the Sultan. And the Muslim religious authorities appealed to Muslims on the basis of the threat to Islam posed by the dominance of the Church or the possible political equality of the Christians.

With the coming of British rule, the relationship of the two groups to the colonial government developed in very different directions. This inevitably influenced the relations of the two ethnic groups to each other. The experience of the Turkish Cypriots can be described as downward group mobility in relation to the Greeks.[19] The political representatives of the Muslims were Islamic religious leaders without the European nationalist characteristics of the Orthodox Church. They attempted to maintain a privileged administrative and political position through their relation to the colonial power. The erosion of this position also resulted in emigration and opposition to the Greek *enosis* campaign. The protests against *enosis* were on the basis of Islamic loyalty and unwillingness to be incorporated in a Christian State. While Turkish Cypriots, contrary to what some Greek Cypriot writers imply, did have a consciousness distinct from and opposed to Greek nationalism, they did not form a *Turkish* nationalism oriented to the Turkish State until the Second World War.

The Turkish "losses" were considerable with the establishment of

British rule. Though all Cypriots remained nominally Ottoman subjects until 1914 when Britain annexed Cyprus, this did not count for much and Greek Cypriots went to Greece to fight against Turkey in 1880 and in 1897. The British colonial constitution of 1882 gave some degree of proportional representation between the two communities. The Muslim leaders protested against this and asked for equal representation for the two communities, independently of their numbers. Alternatively, it was demanded, the Muslims should be allowed to emigrate.[20] Taxation levels became the same for both groups,[21] and legal equality was established for Christians and Muslims.

On the other hand, the British Government regarded the Turkish Cypriots as "loyal" in a way in which the Greek bourgeoisie and the Orthodox Church whose secular institutions were controlled by the former was not. There are for example only two recorded occasions on which the Turkish members of the Legislative Council did not vote with the Government.[22] Turks also continued to form the backbone of the British administrative machine. In 1919 out of the twenty-six officers and 763 men and NCOs in the Cyprus police force, 420 were Muslims.[23] (At this time Muslims were roughly a quarter of the population of the island.) For the Turkish Cypriots there was thus danger from the side of the Greeks who agitated for incorporation into a non-Muslim state, and hope from the side of the British who, though having eroded the privileges of the Muslims, were a barrier to the Greeks' national aims. While the Greeks expressed their nationalism through literary production, education, political opposition and loyalty to Greece, the Turks expressed their fears of domination by the Greeks through loyalty to the British administration and Islamic solidarity. They did not forge new institutions distinct from the political institutions of the Colonial Government until after the Second World War.

The Turks of Cyprus lacked a bourgeoisie that would in a similar way to the Greek one express dissatisfaction with facets of colonial policy. There is little research on this subject, but it appears that the wealthy Turks were either landowners or administrators. Since the British Government was a protector and since there was no tradition of autonomous political organization there appears to have been little opposition to Government participation or takeover of Muslim communal institutions. The *Evkaf*, the Muslim religious foundation which financed charity and education, was, after the annexation of Cyprus, partly run by a British Civil Servant.[24] The annexation of Cyprus by Britain was welcomed by the Turkish leaders because the idea was in the air that a likelier course of action would have been the establishment of a Protectorate, followed by the handing of the island to Greece. But in fact it also seems that the Muslim leaders welcomed the severance of relations with the Ottoman Empire. Before the announcement of the Annexation, the Cadi, the Mufti and the senior Muslim *Evkaf* Councillor suggested that Britain should annex the island to free it from the intrigues of the Porte. After the annexation the same dignitaries visited the High Commissioner to affirm their loyalty and to express shame at the behaviour of the Ottoman Government which had joined the war on the side of the Central Powers. When the Mufti retired in 1927 the new Mufti was appointed by the British governor of the island. (In 1923 Cyprus was promoted to the status of a Crown Colony.) The post was actually abolished the next year. By this time though there was still a Turkish Cypriot delegate to *Evkaf,* he was appointed by the British Governor.[25]

The development of Turkish education is also instructive. There was a traditional difference between Greek and Turkish education. Those Greeks who educated their children educated them for trade or the professions. An indication of the nature of the curriculum was given in the previous chapter. In addition, the Greek Cypriot bourgeoisie was always oriented to a nationalist Greek State and its educational system. The Turks of Cyprus had neither of these characteristics.[26] Their schools catered mainly for religious elementary education and education for administrators. In fact more modern schools were also established, one as early as 1862 in Nicosia. These schools gave more emphasis to algebra, natural sciences and Turkish language in their curriculum, though religious teaching and the Arabic language were still important. But it is more significant that though secular elements were introduced into the Turkish educational system there was no opportunity for a nationalist element to be introduced. There was no *Turkish* nationalism until the early 1920's. And in any event in Cyprus the Turkish Cypriot educational system came to fall under the virtually complete control of the colonial power, in great contrast to the Greek one.

Secondary education for the Turkish Cypriots appears to have been sponsored from the beginning by the colonial government. In 1901 a government assisted secondary school for Muslim girls was established and named after Queen Victoria.[27] In 1936 there were English headmasters at both the Boys' and Girls' Turkish Lycees in Nicosia.[28] As late as 1952 it appears that most Turkish Cypriot school governing bodies applied to be declared to be "public aided". In exchange for the public aid they agreed to the British director of education appointing all the teaching staff.[29] However at this time there was a conspicuous exception. The governing body of the Famagusta secondary schools refused to apply and set up the Namik Kemal Lycee with financial aid from Turkey. There was also criticism in the Turkish press for the actions of the other school boards.[30] But this was 1952, two years after the Greek Cypriot plebiscite in favour of *enosis* and three years before the beginning of the EOKA campaign.

Culturally the Muslims of Cyprus seem to have been more vulnerable and less "touchy" than the Greek Christians. Perhaps the lack of a professional class and the nature of the educational system was less conducive to the kind of intellectual production that strongly reinforces cultural identity. With the British occupation there appears to have been an outburst of Greek publishing activity. The first Greek Cypriot newspaper was published only a few months after the occupation. The first Turkish language one was published ten years later and lasted only a few months. By 1914 about 600 books had been registered under the copyright law. Of these less than fifty were even partly in Turkish. The majority were elementary manuals of various kinds and the only one with any pretensions was an eighty page history of Cyprus.[31] By the time when Cyprus became a British Colony in 1923,

> ... a number of the wealthier and more sophisticated Cypriot Muslims ... have become increasingly anglicized, concerned as they were to prevent the cession of the island to Greece.[32]

In a sense this summarizes everything. The Cypriot Muslims were opposed to *enosis* with the Greek Christian State, but had no alternative motherland other than the Ottoman Empire, or the world of Islam. Neither were units which were able to develop nationalist sentiments.

It is true that there were frequent protests by Muslim leaders against the Greek *enosis* movement. In 1893 the *Mufti* of Cyprus, leading a deputation of Muslims, visited the High Commissioner and said that the Muslims of Cyprus were content with the British administration. Cyprus was an integral part of the Ottoman Empire, and they repudiated its being given to any other power.[33] Again, in 1902, when Cyprus was being debated in a British Parliamentary committee, a Turkish member of the Legislative Council sent a telegram to the Committee. He was opposed to the cession of Cyprus to Greece which would be "to deliver peaceful people into the hands of wild beasts and ruin and destroy them". If given up by Britain, Cyprus should be returned to the Ottoman Empire.[34] In 1912, there were riots between Greeks and Muslims in Limassol. The police killed five people and injured 134. The cause was apparently Greek Cypriot exaltation because of the Ottoman defeat at the hands of the Italians.[35] But the Muslims of Cyprus appear to have been mainly thinking of preserving *British* rule when they pressed for Ottoman claims. And on occasion Ottoman claims were abandoned in favour of general Islamic loyalty. In 1912, for example, the Muslim members of the Legislative Council prayed that in the event of a change in the political situation of the island, the island should either be ceded to Great Britain or to Egypt. (The political situation of the island at the time was that it was administered by the British while under nominal Ottoman sovereignty.)[36] In 1919, after the British annexation of Cyprus and the termination of Ottoman sovereignty, the Muslim leaders of Cyprus sent a message to the Agha Khan protesting against agitation in Greece and Cyprus in favour of *enosis*.[37] The Cypriot Muslim leaders welcomed what appeared to be confirmation of the fact, through the Annexation, that Cyprus would be given neither to Greece nor to the Ottoman Government, but remain British.

The formation of the Turkish Republic, if anything, appears to have estranged the Turkish Cypriots. The relations of the British Government with the new Turkish Republic were less than friendly. Lloyd George had supported the attempt by Greece to annex part of Anatolia in 1922. In fact Britain and Turkey were close to war at this time. London was also suspicious of Ataturk's good relations with the Soviet Union. The Turkish Cypriot leadership, political and religious, were also opposed to the secular reforms in Turkey, which in Cyprus were only very gradually and voluntarily adopted. On the other hand the final establishment of British jurisdiction in 1923 led to some emigration of Cypriot Muslims from Cyprus. This was supported by the Republican Turkish Government itself. The Treaty of Lausanne included a clause allowing Cypriots to opt for retaining their Turkish nationality if they left Cyprus for Turkey within two years. By 1927 5,000 had gone to Anatolia. But by 1928 many had returned. It is hard to ascribe significance to this emigration as far as the Turkish Cypriots are concerned. It seems that many went there to occupy lands left by the Armenians and Greeks of Anatolia. Others who were literate and young went to take advantage of job opportunities in the Republic. Many who had exercised their option to retain Turkish nationality decided not to emigrate after all, presumably because they had only exercised this option as a precautionary measure in case of radical changes of British policy on Cyprus. In any event only a total of 9,000 Turkish Cypriots, of a total population of 62,000 at this time, exercised the right at all. What is significant is that the Turkish Government was anxious for emigration of Turkish Cypriots to Turkey to be facilitated and the British Government appears to have preferred the retention of a strong Turkish community in Cyprus on the assumption that this would be politically useful.[38]

Another indication of the fluid nature of the allegiance of the Cypriot Muslims at this time are the events of 1931. The Greek consul in Cyprus became for the Greek Cypriots the symbol of the *enosis* movement. He was received everywhere with rapturous expressions of Hellenic nationalism.[39] He had to be recalled by the

Greek Government after protests by the British authorities. In his memoirs he recalls that at about the same time Cypriot Muslim influentials incited the British Government of Cyprus to expel the Turkish Consul because he was a "supreme Kemalist and nationalist".[40] So it would seem that nationalist elements were at work among the Cypriot Muslim community at this time, but that neither the leadership nor the mass were particularly receptive.

There is scant information on the early stages and development of Turkish Nationalism among the Turkish Cypriots. One account[41] gives the beginning of Turkish nationalism as the educational reforms of Ataturk in the 1920's. The account implies that the revolutionary transition from religious to national and political education in Turkey was exactly paralleled in Cyprus and that Kemal was just as much a national hero among the Turkish Cypriots at this time as he was among the mainland Turks. The argument smacks of the nationalist penchant for moving the origins of nationalist fervour as far back as possible in history. Ataturk's reforms were most certainly not immediately followed by the Cypriot Turks and were only adopted gradually and voluntarily. In any event Turkish Cypriot education was in the hands of the British. It is however likely that starting with the twenties mainland nationalist ideas arrived in Cyprus, partly through school books and perhaps also through university graduates from Turkish universities.

National consciousness of being Turks came to the intellectuals in the thirties and became widespread after the Second World War.[42] During the 1931 uprising by the Greek Cypriots against British rule both the leaders of the Cypriot Turks and of Turkey welcomed the repressive measures taken by the British Government against Greek Cypriot nationalists. In spite of this the Turkish Cypriots were not exempted from the measures. During the thirties the Turks in Cyprus felt less alienated from Kemalist Turkey since after the Treaty of Montreaux in 1936 Turkey moved to the West and relations with the Soviet Union worsened, "so no Cypriot Muslim felt ashamed to call himself a Turk".[43] By 1939, though still loyal to the British, the Cypriot Turkish intellectuals were strongly influenced by the political and social ideas of the Turkish Republic. Given this, the fear of *enosis* which had always existed among the religious leaders of the Cypriot Turks acquired a new facet. And there was more to be afraid of than ever after the War. The Civil War in Greece and the possibility of Greece becoming communist was an alarming prospect for a community with a religious, conservative leadership. There were also allegations in the air that the Turks of Rhodes and Cos, islands incorporated with Greece after the war, were being discriminated against. The stage was set for the eruption of Turkish nationalism.

Intellectuals identified with the Turkish Republic. And Greek Cypriot nationalism was becoming more intense.

The development of Turkish nationalism in Cyprus between 1943 and 1955 can be signposted by the names of the main political organization of the Turkish Cypriots at different times. In 1943 the "Cyprus Turkish Minority's Association" was established. In 1945 Dr Kuchuk organized the "Cyprus Turkish National Party". In January 1947 this party expressed the opinion that if the British left Cyprus the island should "go back to Turkey".[44] In 1955 the name of the party was changed to the "Cyprus is Turkish Party".[45] In 1948, when Greek nationalist agitation was near its climax, Turkish nationalism strengthened in response. About that time the Turkish Cypriots began organizing demonstrations to express opposition to *enosis.* From one of these a telegram was sent to the Turkish Prime Minister, saying,

> The fifteen thousand Turks have decided unanimously to reject the Greek demands for Union of Cyprus with Greece and for autonomy. They believe that union and autonomy would have as a result the elimination of the Turkish community.[46]

This was also the time when the Turkish Cypriots began to acquire an autonomous political organization. In contrast to the Greek Cypriots, the Turkish Cypriots cooperated with British Government initiatives towards self-government. At least they did so to the extent of developing communal representation. A Government-appointed Committee of Turkish affairs recommended in 1948 that the office of Mufti be restored. It was, the same year, but this time as an elected office rather than one filled by an appointee of the Governor. A candidate of the Turkish National Party won over a candidate from Turkey on a platform of gaining control of *Evkaf* from government-appointed delegates. They were replaced by elected representatives of the community.

The office of Mufti however was not apparently conducive to political activity and loyalties, for the secular political organization led by Dr Kuchuk, a doctor of medicine, became the main Turkish Cypriot representative institution. According to an interview he gave in 1971, it was in 1955 that things were really organized among the Turkish Cypriot community politically.

> Although the nucleus of the first Turkish Cypriot political party was organized in 1942, it was not until 1955 that the Turkish Cypriot community became politically active. Within the next three years, a community political structure was developed as a result not only of efforts of Turkish Cypriot leaders to oppose Enosis, but also of

encouragement from British and Turkish officials who were seeking to safeguard their countries' strategic interests.[47]

In 1971 Dr Kuchuk said that the original claim was that the whole of Cyprus should become part of Turkey, but that this claim was subsequently moderated to partition along the thirty-fifth parallel. (A line including a considerably wider area than the current Attila line which gives Turkey 40% of Cyprus.) However, it seems that these demands alternated with the old demand: that the British should stay. KITEMP, the main Turkish Cypriot organization, circulated pamphlets in 1955 demanding the removal of Greek teachers from Cyprus, the separation of the Church from politics, the forbidding of the raising of the Greek flag and also demanding that the British stay in Cyprus.[48]

Real intercommunal bitterness, however, only followed the escalation of violence between the two communities and the involvement of Turkey in the conflict. The British Government contributed considerably to both in the years between 1955 and 1958.[49] As mentioned in Chapter I the British Government solicited the interest of Turkey in the strategic value of Cyprus and in the representation of the interests of the Turkish Cypriots. Locally, it seems that there was no hindrance to Turkish citizens helping the organization of the Turkish Cypriot nationalist movement. The "Cyprus is Turkish Party" was organized with the help of a Mr Hikmet Bil who arrived for this purpose from Turkey.

> The Cyprus Government raised no objection to the new party or its title when it was announced, and no questions were asked of Mr Bil, a foreign national concerning himself with colonial politics.[50]

At the same time, aid from Turkey for the organization of a Turkish Cypriot underground organization was provided. This was named Volkan, subsequently to become The Turkish Resistance Organization (TMT). In contrast to EOKA it remained legal throughout the intercommunal clashes of 1957 and 1958.

The leaders of EOKA, no matter how unrealistic in other ways, were initially careful to keep the Turkish Cypriots out of the violent conflict. The British administration formed an "Auxiliary Police Force", staffed entirely with Turkish Cypriots whose job was to counter EOKA activities. Naturally one of the Auxiliary policemen were soon killed during an EOKA attack. Lennox Boyd had already dropped his hint about partition, and it had already been taken up by Menderes and had been propounded for a few months in Cyprus through the press and Radio from Turkey. The death of the Turkish policeman was followed by a series of Turkish Cypriot riots, which confirmed the new British and Turkish diplomatic slogan that "Turkish and Greek Cypriots cannot live with each other."

There is at least one serious journalistic opinion on record that the British authorities subsequently exhibited partiality amounting to encouragement for Turkish Cypriot demonstrations and riots in opposition to *enosis* and in favour of *Taxim*, partition.[51]

In May 1958 for example there were after an explosion outside the Turkish Information Office in Nicosia riots by Turkish Cypriots. In a town then under a State of Emergency, the British army allowed the riots to continue for three hours before intervening. During this time a curfew was imposed on Greek Cypriots only. Lennox Boyd told a journalist soon afterwards, "you could not come down too hard on people who had always been so loyal and stable".[52] He added that Turkey had as much reason for strategic anxiety over Cyprus as Britain would if the Russians were about to take over the Isle of Wight.[53] Soon after the end of the riots British troops arrested a number of Greek Cypriots and dropped them near a Turkish village outside Nicosia. Nine of them were killed. By the end of July 1958 TMT had succeeded in ousting the Greek population of one of the ethnically mixed suburbs of Nicosia. The State of Emergency and the presence of 30,000 British troops seemed no barrier. In June 1958 twenty-five Greeks were killed by TMT attacks. (Four Turks were killed.) In July, fifty-five Greeks were killed. But the zenith had been reached. EOKA started retaliating. Thirty-five Turks were also killed. This "civil war" stopped abruptly after the U.S. promised economic aid amounting to 359 million dollars to Turkey and Menderes appealed for calm.[54]

The consequences of these events were very difficult to reverse. By 1958 General Grivas, the leader of EOKA, was speaking of the Turkish Cypriots being his third enemy, the other two being the British and the communists. Turkey was officially demanding the partition of the island between Greece and Turkey. TMT existed as the Turkish Cypriot Counterpart of EOKA. It was just as nationalist and anti-communist, but not anti-British. Though Turkish Cypriot nationalism developed partly as a reflection of Greek Cypriot nationalism, it had a different content which was due to the different social position of the Turkish Cypriots in Cyprus.

EOKA and TMT had very similar policies in relation to Greek Cypriot and Turkish Cypriot communists. For reasons to be discussed in a subsequent chapter, the EOKA campaign to dislocate communist organization among the Greek Cypriots failed. The parallel TMT campaign was virtually a complete success. All Turkish Cypriot communist clubs were forced to close down or were burnt. Some of the communist leaders were assassinated for criticizing TMT and *Taxim* and others had to take refuge with the Greek Cypriot communists.[55]

## The Turkish Cypriots

The violent peak of intimidation followed a May Day parade in 1958 in which Turkish and Greek workers participated together. On the same day the left wing Turkish Cypriot sports and cultural club in Nicosia was burnt. (No one was arrested by the Colonial Government.) Also on the same day Dr Kuchuk made a speech condemning communism and cooperation with the Greeks. On 22nd and 24th May a Turkish Cypriot trade unionist and a journalist were shot. On 27th May TMT pamphlets took credit and warned left-wing Turks to renounce their organizations publicly if they wanted to live. By the beginning of July some more murders or attempts against leftists followed. Hundreds of Turkish Cypriots withdrew from the left-wing trade unions and peasant organizations in which they cooperated with the Greek Cypriots.[56] During that year the separate Turkish trade unions increased their membership from 1,137 to 4,829.[57] The complete dislocation of the communist movement contributed to lack of differentiation in the Turkish Cypriot community already lacking a bourgeoisie and made it more easily controllable by TMT.

This lack of political articulation was in sharp contrast to the Greek Cypriot community. EOKA and the Greek Cypriot nationalist movement were oriented to Greece. The Church had indeed a dominating position in the Greek Cypriot community. But even at the peak of the EOKA campaign, the Greek Cypriot community was not monolithic. EOKA's attempts to impose such monolithic unity were resisted, at least to some extent, by the bourgeoisie and by the communist party, AKEL. Ultimately, the political leadership of Grivas, the EOKA military commander, was rejected. (This is discussed in Chapter VI.) These political groups had the capacity to articulate their own interest, apart from a leadership linking them directly to Greece. Even before independence, international representation took place independently and in parallel with Greek Government representation. Here there were seeds for "regional" differentiation. No matter how imbued with Greek nationalist ideas, Greek Cypriots were politically organized in a way that was capable of furthering interests distinct from those of the Greek State.

By contrast, the Turkish Cypriots hardly had a bourgeoisie and no differentiated political parties. They were initially completely dependent on the colonial government. It would be quite easy for this dependence to be transferred without internal resistance to the Turkish State. Particularly so at times when they might feel that they were in danger from the Greek Cypriots.

It is not remarkable that the Turkish Cypriots' terrorist organization should try and sever the economic relations of the Turkish Cypriots with the Greek Cypriots. It was a reasonable tactic in view of its aim, which was separation and perhaps also reversal of the dominant economic position of the Greek Cypriot business group.

What is remarkable is that they were helped in this by the Greek Cypriot underground organization. In 1956, through a pamphlet, EOKA ordered Greek workers in one of the British bases not to travel there in a Turkish-owned bus. In 1958 the political wing of EOKA tried to "solve the problem of the cooperative Bank". The problem was that in this bank "there was more than one million sterling of Greek deposits, and through this the bank was continually reinforcing the Turks".[58] This could only have reinforced the TMT campaign, which initially aimed at Cypriot Turks "buying Turkish", and after 1963 became a plan to establish a separate Turkish Cypriot economy.[59] Resentment against the more affluent Greeks may well have become one of the bases for the inculcation of Turkish nationalism and separatism.

The factors which contributed to the independence of Cyprus in 1959 have already been discussed. The settlement had many problems, and some of the constitutional and political problems have been extensively discussed in their own right.[60] The concern here is mainly to show the implications of the Zurich Republic for feelings of group identity, and the implications of the ways in which Cypriot Greek or Turkish group identity was felt.

The form of independence which Cyprus received in 1959 was so hedged about by international limitations and internal immutable constitutional provisions that it is best described as "limited independence".[61] However what were limitations on independence for the majority of the population, the Greek Cypriots, were safeguards for the Turkish Cypriots. Since they were safeguards "more extensive perhaps, than any ever written into a constitution for the protection of a minority community",[62] they were also symbols of the Turkish victory against Greek nationalism. Since the aim of the Greek Cypriots was *enosis,* the Turkish Cypriots regarded independence, with a guaranteed form of power sharing for them, as a victory for themselves. The Zurich Republic was an entity to which they could commit their allegiance. The Turkish Cypriot leadership had been opposed to any form of independence as well as to *enosis.* But once the form of independence had ensured a substantial share of power to the Turkish Cypriot leadership, matters appeared in a different light. Its view now became that EOKA had been struggling to dissuade Greek Cypriots from accepting self-government. "Greek Cypriots were killed by EOKA in order to silence the vast majority of Greeks who were ready to accept self-government", was Mr Denktas' view in 1974.[63] In this view the Turkish Cypriots had also fought against colonialism since "the Turkish Cypriots looked on *enosis* as a change of colonial masters for the worse".[64] The leadership immediately began to prepare the defence of the position the Turks had gained as a community. Even before the formal declaration of independence they started importing arms with which to ensure what had been gained. On 19th October 1959 a Turkish motorboat, *Deniz* was sunk by its Turkish crew when the British mine-sweeper, H.M.S. *Burmaston* tried to intercept it off the north-west coast of Cyprus. The British were able to salvage two cases of ammunition before the boat went under. Two other boats had been intercepted earlier, but their cargo had been dropped overboard before a search could be made.[65]

For the Greek Cypriots, by contrast, Zurich was a defeat. The Turkish Cypriots, who, apart from their occasional protests, were apparently an insignificant quantity politically, had suddenly acquired an altogether disproportionate importance. They, the Greeks, had fought against British rule, while the Turkish Cypriots had helped the British. From a religious minority they had become co-rulers of Cyprus. They were also arming. There was no knowing where this would stop. As one Greek Cypriot writer put it,

> ... All that the Turks had to do was to stick to their privileged position, granted to them by the constitution in such a way as to make mockery of the principle of a unitary state.[66]

There is no doubt that the Zurich Republic, no matter what its shortcomings, provided some of the preconditions for the development of "Cypriot consciousness", a post-colonial rather than European nationalism. These processes are discussed in the next chapter. But these were not the only processes. Paradoxically, the independent Republic also strengthened some nationalist tendencies among both communities along traditional lines.

In a sense the problem lay in the factionalist conflicts which seem to be a fairly universal concomitant of independence.[67] For Cyprus the processes of these conflicts have not been studied in detail.[68] But their outlines are fairly clear. What is very significant however is that these conflicts were tinged with elements relating to the international status of Cyprus. These elements were connected with Greek and Turkish Nationalism on the one hand, and with Cold War issues on the other.

The simplest factionalist conflicts had to do with the allocation of jobs and economic resources. When the British left Cyprus the proportion of Turkish Cypriots in the various grades of the civil service starting with the most senior grade were: 26%, 19%, 20%, 18%, 17%, 25%. The proportion of Turkish Cypriots in the population was 18.5% according to the census of 1960. According to the newly established constitution, the proportion at all levels had to be raised to 30% within five months of independence. The issue was a bureaucrat's nightmare. The civil service was already well staffed by tenured people. In addition, at a time of economic recession and unemployment, those Greek Cypriots who had fought the British expected some recognition in the form of government employment. The Greek Cypriot Civil Servants Association organized protest demonstrations against the application of an article of the constitution which would have hurt their promotion prospects. The Turkish Cypriot leaders argued that the Greeks had managed to manoeuvre themselves into high administrative and executive posts during the British Occupation, retained these, and used them to block promotions or appointments of Turkish Cypriots. Two thousand Civil Service appointments were appealed against in the Supreme Court between 1960 and 1963. There was a danger of factionalization among the Greek Community between Makarios, the political leader of the *enosis* campaign and Grivas, its military leader. This meant that from the point of view of the Greek Cypriot leaders it appeared that the fewer dissatisfied ex-EOKA fighters existed, the less the likelihood of civil strife. On the other hand Turks naturally resented the appointment to the Civil Service of ex-EOKA fighters. (As a matter of fact many established Greek Cypriot Civil Servants also resented this.) But the issue caused continual friction, in which it seemed that to be a Greek or a Turkish Cypriot was relevant to your opportunities and that the opportunities of one group diminished as those of the other increased. In spite of this, progress was made towards the application of the constitutional provision. But not in five months. In fact even by 1963, the 30% level had only been reached in the highest grade. The proportion of the Turkish Cypriots in the various grades, starting from the highest was: 33%, 27%, 26%, 23%, 18%.[69] The constitutionally unyielding target which was so hard to reach in practice was a constant reminder to a young man aspiring to be a civil servant that he and his community were in competition with the other community for these appointments.

A similar problem developed with the allocation of development aid. The constitution provided for communal chambers for the cultural affairs of Greek and Turkish Cypriots respectively. They were mainly concerned with education, religion and family law. The Greek leaders argued that the part of development aid of about 30 million sterling which Cyprus received between 1960 and 1963 which would be used for such purposes should be allocated in proportion to the population of the two ethnic groups. This would have involved a proportion of 20:80. The "Communal Chambers" were financed from taxes raised by each community separately. The Turkish community was not only smaller, but also poorer. They naturally claimed that this allocation would perpetuate lower standards in their communal institutions. The President eventually agreed for the foreign aid allocation for the Turkish Cypriots to be raised to 28.5%, but the Turkish Cypriot leadership was still dissatisfied.[70] Political conditions among the Greek Cypriot leadership and the aims of the Turkish

Cypriot leadership were not such as to be conducive to a realistic policy of integrating the Turkish Cypriots. Had it been possible to use the carrot of economic aid instead of the stick of political out-manoeuvring things might have developed rather differently in Cyprus.

The other issues of conflict involved not only internal arrangements on the island, but issues of the international alignment of Cyprus, nationalist or Cold War. If, as the Greek Cypriots suspected, and as the *Deniz* incident might be taken to confirm, Turkey was planning to partition Cyprus when the opportunity arose, it was necessary to resist the application of constitutional provisions or other demands of the Turkish Cypriot leadership which tended in this direction. The establishment of the Republic meant that four sovereign states were now involved in the island. The Treaty of Establishment between Britain and the Republic of Cyprus provided that Britain should retain sovereignty over two areas of the island as bases. The Treaty of Alliance between Cyprus, Greece and Turkey involved the stationing of Greek and Turkish troops on Cyprus. The Treaty of Guarantee between the Republic of Cyprus, Britain, Turkey and Greece gave all the latter countries rights of intervention in the Republic of Cyprus either jointly or singly, if the independence, territorial integrity, security or constitution of the Republic of Cyprus were threatened. (For the sole purpose of restoring the *status quo*.) For the Greek Cypriot majority who had been fighting for *enosis*, the provisions allowing the stationing of Turkish troops on Cyprus and giving rights of intervention to Turkey were worrying indeed in view of Turkey's frequently proclaimed aim of partitioning Cyprus. Since the main bridge of Turkey into Cyprus were the Turkish Cypriots, it was hard to dissociate consideration of their rights from consideration of incursions of Turkey into Cyprus. The constitutional rights of the Turkish Cypriots involved among other things a Veto by the Turkish vice-president of Cyprus on matters of finance, foreign affairs and internal security. The constitution provided that 40% of the police-force and the army should be composed of Turkish Cypriots. It also provided that in the main towns there should be separate Greek and Turkish Cypriot municipal authorities, responsible for areas of predominantly Greek and Turkish settlement respectively. These provisions of the Constitution were immutable in perpetuity, under pain of being "guaranteed" by one of the powers involved.[71]

These provisions may be seen in the light of a minority's need to have guarantees of some form of power sharing. Power sharing may involve disproportion in terms of numbers if the economic and political status of the minority is to be secure. The Greek Cypriots however could not see the provisions in this light. They saw them in association with Turkey's newly acquired rights on Cyprus and its previous claims as the thin end of a partitioning wedge. Take the municipalities issue as an example. The actual provision initially seems more disadvantageous to the Turkish than the Greek Cypriots. As a smaller and poorer community they would have to duplicate services which would otherwise be mainly financed by the majority. But the Greek Cypriots could easily imagine that any concession of territorial authority to Turkish Cypriots would be used to seal off territory to be made into areas of military build-up and later used in an effort to dissect Cyprus into Greek and Turkish parts. Separate municipalities had been part of the "Macmillan Plan" for Cyprus which the British had threatened to implement unilaterally in 1958. They were, in this plan, part of a scheme by which Greek Cypriots would acquire Greek nationality in addition to the British one. After seven years of rule by an administrative Council which included representatives of Greece and Turkey, Britain would "share sovereignty" of Cyprus with Greece and Turkey.[72] The Turkish Cypriots did nothing to dispel these fears.

> Conscious of Turkey's power at their back and Turkish troops on the island itself, they were intransigent in claiming their full rights as a separate community, even where these rights were unworkable in practice or seen to conflict with the interests of the state as a whole.[73]

The final problem involved not only "sectarian" and nationalist conflict, but also the different Cold War alignments by the leaders of the two communities. President Makarios' early identification with the Afro-Asians was a matter that his vice-president, Dr Kuchuk, strongly disagreed with. The Turkish Cypriot vice-president also disagreed with the expansion of trade with Socialist countries and the development of close relations with Nasser's Egypt.[74] Since the Zurich Republic had satisfied the Turkish Cypriot leaders and since it was a "NATO solution" this was natural. Besides, it has already been mentioned that communism had been much more successfully combated among the Turkish than the Greek Cypriot community.

The difference in Cold War orientations between the two political leaderships became very explicit on occasion. Makarios has recalled that when, after the establishment of the Republic, the Egyptian ambassador arrived, Turkish Cypriot vice-president Dr Kuchuk, would not agree to his accreditation unless diplomatic relations with Israel were also established. Makarios obtained Nasser's consent for his ambassador to remain while the Israeli one was also accredited.[75] This difference in Cold War alignments was to become very explicit when intercommunal fighting broke out in 1964. Mr Denktas has put himself on record as disapproving of Makarios' rejection of a "NATO peace-keeping force" for Cyprus in 1964. (Makarios insisted on a force under the auspices of the U.N.)[76] At the conference in London held by the Guarantor powers and representatives of the Cypriot ethnic groups soon after the outbreak of fighting in 1964, Mr Denktas is reported to have expressed the opinion that 35% of the Greek Cypriots were communists or communist supporters who intended to turn Cyprus into another Cuba.[77] At about the same time, Dr Kuchuk, the Vice-President of Cyprus appealed to President Johnson to keep Cyprus from being turned into another Cuba by "Communist armed infiltration". He accused the President of negotiating with the Russians in violation of the Cypriot constitution which gave him a veto over foreign policy.[78]

One of the most explosive ingredients in the situation was that the friction between the two ethnic groups took place in the context of a heightened level of public exhibition of nationalist symbolism. Ironically, independence meant that the most determined advocates of Greek and Turkish nationalism came to power.[79] The Government, the police and the civil service were to a large extent staffed by the leaders of the two ethnic nationalist movements. For both communities, Greek and Turkish nationalism could be expressed openly and was frequently expressed officially. For the Greek Cypriots it meant that services could be held for EOKA heroes, at which ministers of the government of the Republic could be heard speaking on the continuation of the struggle for *enosis* until its successful conclusion. Radio, television and newspapers could report these and other nationalist events in full. This had not been possible with the state-run radio and censored newspapers of the last period of British rule.

Since for the Turkish Cypriots Zurich was in many ways a victory, they were more restrained. But Mr Denktas, who was reputed to be the leader of TMT,[80] did become the President of the Turkish Communal Chamber. What is perhaps more significant was that this was the first time in the educational history of the Turkish Cypriot community that they were in control of their own educational system. As in the case of the Greek Cypriots it resulted in an educational system identical to that of the mainland motherland.[81]

The nationalisms of the two ethnic groups naturally fed each other. The leaders planned for the time when the Republic would break down and there would be a free-for-all for territory that would become Greek or Turkish. As early as the beginning of 1963 TMT began organizing a secret army according to the Greek Minister of Defence at the time. In April a member of the Turkish General Staff went to Cyprus to study conditions there. According to the same source, a clear plan was prepared by the Turkish General Staff and the Turkish Cypriot leadership which involved occupying and holding militarily five enclaves, three of them in the main towns, but all of them lying apparently north of the thirty-fifth parallel.[82] In April 1963 the Greek General staff prepared a plan under the code name of "Pyrsos" to help the Greek Cypriots when such aid was needed. However the plan was based on the assumption that large-scale air and naval action would be impossible.[83] In August 1963 "The Organization of Greek Cypriot Patriots" was founded under the command of the Minister of the Interior, Georkadjis. There were also other weak Greek groups which were formed under the leadership of ex-EOKA splinter group leaders. These groups had no contact with each other (and some were actually hostile to each other), or with the main force.[84]

When nationalism and armed preparation coexist, it is difficult to tell what is a precautionary measure and what is part of a planned scheme. The occasion for the beginning of armed clashes was a proposal by the President to the Turkish Cypriot vice-president for a revision of a number of points in the constitution which gave the Turkish Cypriots power disproportionate to their numbers. The Greek Cypriot leadership put forward the proposals without previous military preparation. It was not immediately clear whether this was ineptness or an indication that what was in fact aimed at were peaceful negotiations for a readjustment of the constitutional provisions which would still safeguard the share of the Turkish Cypriots in State power.

# CHAPTER IV

## Sources of Cypriot consciousness

That Cyprus would at some stage be incorporated with Greece had been regarded as natural, not only by most Greek Cypriots, but also by others. The views of some British politicians have already been mentioned. In the years that followed the war the international communist movement also took this view. However, tactical British moves in the United Nations and in Cyprus complicated the problem of "decolonization". Initially, the Cyprus problem was a dispute between Britain, a colonial power which was reluctant to leave one of its colonial territories on the one hand and the main subject ethnic group of Cyprus on the other. In the 1950's the problem became transformed into a dispute between two allies of the North Atlantic Treaty Organization, Greece and Turkey. The colonial power, Britain, moved to the position of mediator. The senior partner of the alliance, the United States, became increasingly involved.

This transition complicated the Cyprus problem. So long as the problem was one of "decolonization", the lines of conflict were clear. On the one side were the Greek Cypriots determined to shake off the control of the colonial power in order to be incorporated with Greece. On the other hand was the imperial power whose strategic interests favoured control of the territory. When Cyprus became a NATO problem the aims of the imperial powers became more complex. The imperial aim remained constant. This was the securing of the strategic use of Cyprus and the denial of the island to the opponent, the Soviet Union. But another problem intruded now. This was the necessity to save the Alliance itself from disruption through the rival claims of Greece and Turkey on the island. The control of Cyprus by the Alliance would have been a simple matter had there been no dispute within the Alliance as to who should exercise this control. The type of independence which was granted to Cyprus was a compromise not just between the Cypriots and the colonial power, but between the interested parties within the Alliance.

The problem for the Alliance became that the Cyprus Government after independence grasped the levers which statehood made available and used them in ways which threatened the total escape of the island from the Alliance. This is a crucial process in the current phase of the Cyprus problem. It has made the conflict between Greece and Turkey over Cyprus rather different from any conflict which has previously existed between the two States over a disputed territory. True, there are in Cyprus elements of a "Hundred Year War of Ottoman succession". But there are also strong elements of the type of conflict that is engendered by disputes between the Cold War Opponents. Cyprus came into conflict eventually not only with the imperial powers and Turkey, but also with Greece. The coup and the invasion of the summer of 1974 represent a severe setback to the full decolonization of Cyprus. The setback was administered by the two countries which had influence over political movements and ideologies in Cyprus itself, that is, Greece and Turkey.

This chapter will describe those tendencies which led to the development of a "regionalism" in the relations between Greek Cypriots and Greece in spite of the intense Hellenic nationalism that the former had been fired with in the 1950's. The next chapter will describe the very different tendency in relations between Turkey and the Turkish Cypriots, and the consequent problem that was posed for the Greek Cypriot leadership if the demand for the recognition of two equal ethnic groups in Cyprus were to be accepted.

The line of thought of this chapter depends quite heavily on the fact that Greece and the Greeks of Cyprus, even though linked by an intense nationalist consciousness were in different positions in the lines drawn by Cold War politics. Cyprus tended to ally itself internationally with other colonial, newly independent or socialist countries in order to achieve independence from colonial rule and at a later stage to eliminate limitations on its independence. It is not necessary to attribute intrinsic virtue to socialist and non-aligned countries within the terms of this argument. It is enough to bear in mind that at the time of the anti-colonial movements the socialist countries were powerful alternatives to the colonial powers and that they were countries which were hostile to these same powers.

Greece by contrast was in the Western sphere of influence. Until 1947 it was in the British sphere and after that within that of the United States. A strong leftist resistance movement grew during the Second World War. But at the end of the war, the imperial power alignments allowed it to be crushed in the first U.S. sponsored "counter-insurgency" operation.[1] The civil war resulted in the establishment of the theory and practice of anti-communism as an important ideology of the Greek state.[2] But it also resulted in the readiness of the Greek State to accept the NATO Alliance, which it entered in 1951, two years after the end of the civil war, as an essential safeguard against a future resurgence of internal subversion. The internal threat appeared to be inextricably connected with the threat of attack from the northern borders. The Alliance which safeguarded Greece against such an attack included Turkey.

For the Cypriots by contrast the "communist danger" was largely incomprehensible. In an interview with a British journalist in the early 1950's Archbishop Makarios explained that people in Cyprus saw communism much as British working people viewed their trade unions, that is as a way of improving their working conditions and living standards.[3] The main enemies of the Cypriots appeared to be not the Russians but Britain, the country which ruled them against their will. The United States, despite its declared anti-colonial principles apparently lent support to Britain. This was not the only fact. Cyprus after independence prospered economically to such a degree that the Statehood that had been thrust on its inhabitants could be seen in a more sympathetic light. These main processes were the basis of a differentiation between Greece and the Greek Cypriots. By contrast, for reasons already discussed, the Turkish Cypriots remained politically monolithic, anti-communist and tied to Turkey.

The term "Cypriot Consciousness" is used in this connection because it is one which has been used in Cypriot politics. But it must be noted that the term was mainly used by the opponents of the phenomenon. Its manifestation remained largely on the level of diffuse awareness and in individual expression of views. In fact Chapter VI examines Cypriot politics with the aim of explaining why this was the case, and why "Cypriot Consciousness" never became structured and expressed as a political ideology. There is an apparent paradox in the fact that while the international and internal preconditions for the emergence of a "Cypriot Consciousness" were strongly present, the consciousness itself, though widespread as individual opinion and though it was incorporated in many actions of the Government, remained publicly unexpressed as an ideology which was binding on any political group.

Greece, as a marginal and relatively underdeveloped Mediterranean country, has for years been dependent on the dominant imperial power of the Mediterranean. Before the Second World War this country was Britain. It is not surprising that Greek Governments proceeded gingerly in any practical pursuit of the realization of the national aim of incorporating Cyprus. (The same applied to the Dodecanese islands, also inhabited by Greeks and ruled by Italy.) In 1931, after the anti-British riots in Cyprus, Venizelos, then Prime Minister of Greece explained that:

> No matter how deep the response which the national wishes of the inhabitants of these islands finds in the Greek soul, it is impossible for the Greek State to undertake support for their realization, or to tolerate that its territory be used to organize a systematic reaction against the peace of these islands. Crucial and more than crucial interests of Greece impose the necessity of undisturbed friendship with Great Britain and with our neighbour, the great Mediterranean power, Italy ... In fact we have the right to demand of the Greek inhabitants of these islands that

59

they be less egoistical ... Only in the case in which Great Britain were pursuaded that Cyprus would in no way be useful to it, or that it could secure this usefulness through holding only a small part, would it be possible that it might listen to the national prayers of the Cypriots, under the condition that the relations of the population to the sovereign power would be restored to such normality that it could not be supposed that the latter bowed to force.[4]

Metaxas, the dictator of Greece during the late thirties, never mentioned the Cyprus problem.[5] The re-establishment of a Royalist Government in Greece after the war was heavily dependent on British military support, as was the struggle of this government to defeat the left wing movement in Greece. In accord with Cold War alignments, the Greek Government concerned itself with territorial claims against Bulgaria and Albania. Even a man like A. Kyrou, the diplomat of Cypriot descent who earlier had played such an important role in pursuing *enosis* and would do so again subsequently, was, at this time, against the public raising of the question.[6] The Communist Party of Greece accused the Government of expansionism because of its territorial claims against its northern neighbours and at the same time accused it of betrayal in the case of Cyprus. The Greek Communist Party also demanded expansion into Eastern Thrace which belonged to Turkey.[7] When in 1950 the Church in Cyprus organized a plebiscite in favour of *enosis,* the Greek Government refused to accept the volumes in which the signatures had been entered.[8] In March 1951 a meeting of all party leaders in Athens agreed that the Cyprus Question should be promoted within the framework of Anglo-Greek friendship and expressed willingness to have British bases in Cyprus and elsewhere in Greece.[9] When the Greek ambassador to the U.N. first made some comments on the Cyprus issue in the General Assembly, it was done in such a way that it provoked the thanks of the British ambassador in Athens for "their politeness and friendly formulation".[10]

In 1947 Britain decided to withdraw military support from Greece, the Truman doctrine had been enunciated and the United States was becoming Greece's main protector. In 1948 King Paul of Greece told an American journalist that Greece desired the union of Cyprus with Greece and that far from this interfering with the British bases in Cyprus it would lead to Britain and the United States being given bases in Crete and elsewhere in Greece.[11] It has already been mentioned that when Greece raised the issue of Cyprus in the United Nations, the Greek Ambassador to the organization believed that in this Greece had the support of the United States. It was not that Greece had acquired autonomy from its ally. The ally had changed.

Greece had to pursue the policy of incorporating Cyprus with one hand tied behind its back, or to use George Papandreou's later, and more dramatic metaphor in speaking to the mayor of Nicosia,

> Greece breathes with two lungs, one British and the other American, and cannot suffocate for the sake of the Cypriot problem.[12]

Yet Greek diplomatic history is scattered with examples of antinomies in policy because of the contradiction between national aspirations and "careful" government policy in relation to the important ally of the time. In 1931, for example, at the time of Venizelos' statement directing the Cypriots to be law-abiding, a committee was formed in Athens under the Chairmanship of an ex-president of the Republic with the purpose of furthering the cause of Cyprus. And in 1950, when the Greek Government refused to accept the volumes of the plebiscite, they were accepted by the President of the Greek Parliament and by the King. Those not immediately responsible for Government policy did not have to renounce national claims and exactly toe the Alliance line.

The initial steps of Archbishop Makarios in pursuing *enosis* along a line opposed to the policy of the Greek Government must be interpreted in this spirit. In 1951, the year in which he became Archbishop, he tried to press the Greek Government to take the Cyprus issue to the U.N. with the threat that if the Greek Government did not do so, he would ask the Syrian Government to appeal for Cyprus. He also exercised pressure on the Greek Government through appeals to Greek public opinion. In 1952 he called a "Pan-Cyprian National Congress" and demanded that the Greek Government bring the Cyprus problem to the first U.N. General Assembly.[13] By 1953 he was treading what must have seemed subversive ground to Greek conservatives. In a speech delivered in Church he announced:

> Greek-British friendship ... is unacceptable on the side of the Greek People if this is one sided and in its name the freedom of Cyprus is strangled. And we consider the statements of the Greek Government from time to time that the problem will be solved within the terms of Greek-British friendship as deceit. ... In our attempt to gain our freedom we will stretch out our right hand and our left hand in order to accept any help which is offered from East and West.[14]

The problems for the Greek Government increased as it became apparent not only that Britain was unwilling to be friendly over Cyprus, but also that the United States would not support Greece in the United Nations. In fact the United States took the lead in blocking discussion of the Cyprus problem in the U.N. between 1954 and 1958.[15] In 1955 Queen Frederica was writing to General Marshall about "anti-Americanism and fear of renewed Russian plans in Greece".[16] In fact the Left was gaining in elections, and anti-NATO opinion gained adherents. At the same time strains between the Greek Cypriots fighting for *enosis* through all means and Greece, aiming to maintain the equilibrium of its alliance, increased. When the British called the London conference in 1955 for discussions with Greece and Turkey, Makarios held a press conference and argued that Greece should not attend the conference unless Britain recognized the right of self-determination for Cyprus immediately.[17] The Greek Foreign Minister curtly told the Cypriots that it was inconceivable to think that they could direct Greek foreign policy.[18]

So evident were the inhibiting influences on Greece of her alliances that even Grivas, the anti-communist military leader of EOKA in Cyprus, argued for a neutralist Greece. In August 1958 in a letter to the Greek Foreign Minister he argues that Greece should "risk everything", including the Alliance. He points out that Greece should not allow Turkey to be the only one to play the game of threatening to leave NATO in order to strengthen her claims on Cyprus. Greece's adherence to the alliance is sentimental and does not serve the real national interests of Greece. In fact, it does not even form a barrier to "communist penetration" in Greece, but rather reinforces it because of disappointment with the Allies.[19]

The Greek Foreign Minister was not swayed by such arguments and the road to the Zurich agreements was near its end. The Greek Foreign Minister may have been realistic in his estimation of the facts in his reply to Grivas. Turkey was of enormous significance to the West. A neutral Greece would not be such a worrying gadfly to the West. There were pressures from "outside the alliance" for Greece not to leave it. (This is a probable reference to Yugoslavia.) The Turkish Government itself was willing to compromise since it feared the possibility of a Labour Government in Britain. Labour favoured self-determination for Cyprus.[20] But the crowning argument was that,

> Important Conservatives and unfortunately important Labourites, are of the opinion that if there is significant turmoil in Cyprus, Britain must state that it will keep the Bases and invite the Turks to occupy the northern part of Cyprus and the Greeks the southern part ...[21]

There is no avoiding the fact that this unpalatable situation and its resolution has to be forced on the Greek Cypriots by Greece. Alliance cohesion and avoiding war and the partition of Cyprus required that the Greek Government pressure the Greek Cypriots into accepting the Zurich agreements. The Cypriot delegation invited to London with Makarios to sign the agreement which had already been reached by the Greek and Turkish Foreign Ministers had to be dealt with by the Greek Foreign Minister. One of the members of the Greek Cypriot delegation, a political representative of EOKA,[22] wrote to his chief about "shameful behind-the-scenes activities", so that in spite of initial universal opposition by the Greek Cypriots to the agreements, in the end only the leftists and a handful of nationalists maintained their opposition. The Cypriot delegation, he writes, was bluntly told by the Greek Foreign Minister that if the Zurich agreement were rejected, "Greece would no longer support us in any kind of struggle." He also appeals to Grivas not to hold Makarios responsible for the agreements. Grivas' own comment is that,

> The Greek Government agreed with Britain and Turkey whose interests it mainly supported at the expense of the interests of the Greek Cypriot people.[23]

When the Cyprus crisis of 1963 arose the differences of interest between the Greek Government and that of Cyprus developed sharply. This was because the Cyprus Government had already exercised for three years an independent foreign policy, and because this policy had tended towards non-alignment. As has been mentioned, the crisis started with the proposals for a revising of the constitution. The Turkish Cypriot leadership has firmly claimed that these proposals aimed at breaking down the constitution of Cyprus and ultimately at achieving *enosis*.[24] There is little doubt that *enosis* was still favourably regarded by some proportion of the Greek population of Cyprus. There is also little doubt that a substantial faction of the people who had led EOKA were in favour of such a solution at the time. But the course of the conflict quickly showed the Greek Cypriots that the two aims, which might have seemed but two aspects of one, that is, keeping Turkey out of Cyprus and Union with Greece, were in fact contradictory. The contradiction was made manifest by the Acheson Plan.

Soon after the beginning of the conflict the Government of Cyprus fell exclusively into Greek Cypriot hands. In the first days of the conflict it became apparent that the Cyprus Government could not renounce the Zurich and London agreements without provoking an immediate invasion by Turkey. An invasion by Turkey also seemed likely if the intercommunal clashes which began in December 1963 continued. But from the outset the Government resisted the idea that the conflict should be settled by the guarantor powers or within the context of the NATO alliance. "Makarios aimed to tactically exploit the competing Soviet and American interests and to 'internationalize' further the Cyprus problem by putting it before the U.N."[25]

Of course, there was a large area of community of interest between the Greek Government and that of Cyprus. The prevention of an invasion by Turkey was an important common aim. But due to their different international orientations, the Greek and Cypriot Governments came to differ considerably as to how this should be done. Most of the differences came from the fact that the Greek governments were bound to keep an eye on the effect of the conflict on the NATO Alliance. But there was also the basic fact that Cyprus, even though controlled by Greek Cypriots, was a separate state. Even apart from Cold War politics it was not possible to have interests which were identical in all respects. Concessions to Turkey which seemed small to the Greek Government seemed unthinkable to Greek Cypriots who could not tolerate a territorial alteration to their island. There was also the problem that, contrary to the Greek one, the Cyprus Government was not imbued with dread of either the Soviet Union or an internal communist threat.

For Greece, its Alliance and its national interest was once more in opposition, as it appeared to have been in the late fifties, and at least one Greek Prime Minister, George Papandreou, showed signs of being aware of this. While he was Prime Minister between November 1963 and September 1965 he fluctuated in his policy in such a way that differences between Greece and Cyprus were kept under control. But also he is likely to have earned a reputation for being "unreliable" among the State Department experts, a reputation which must at least partly account for the sanguine attitude of the U.S. to the gradual destruction of democracy in Greece between 1965 and 1967.

Immediately after the beginning of the crisis at the end of 1963, a conference of the Guarantor Powers was called in London. The Cyprus Government was strongly opposed to it since it tended to move the Cyprus problem once more into the corridors of NATO. At the conference the Greek Prime Minister was reported to have emphasized his anxiety to keep the Cyprus problem within the bounds of NATO, and by the end of the month the Greek Government had agreed, albeit "against its better judgement", to a NATO force intervening in Cyprus.[26] The force was frustrated by President Makarios' insistent refusal, even under persistent attempts at persuasion by U.S. Under-secretary George Ball, but also by the reluctance of France and Germany to agree to such a force. But even at the end of January the Greek Foreign Minister was stating that:

> It is not in the interests of either Greece or Turkey for the Cyprus Question to be taken to the United Nations ...[27]

The reason for the Greek Government's and generally NATO's concern to keep the issue outside the U.N. was that this would immediately involve the Soviet Union in attempts to solve the problem. Greek governments, apart from a short period of wavering on the part of George Papandreou, were opposed to the Cypriots accepting Soviet support whether diplomatic or more substantial. Foreign Minister Costopoulos had gone on to say in the interview just quoted, which was given to a Turkish newspaper,

> Greece and Turkey have no territorial claims ... on our two countries is based the defensive system of the Balkans, the Middle East and the front against the common threat from the North.[28]

This was a caretaker Foreign Minister during a brief interlude in the Papandreou administration. But the return of a Papandreou Government did not produce an immediate change in concerns. His Foreign Minister stated to the *Washington Post* in March 1964 that,

> Greece's position under Papandreou considerably reduced the danger of the establishment of Soviet influence in Cyprus, and minimized the danger of the creation in the Eastern Mediterranean ... of a Soviet base which would have been an equally great danger for Greece and Turkey. We could not tolerate such a fact.[29]

This at a time, when the Greek Cypriot newspapers appeared to make it clear that the main barrier to a Turkish invasion of Cyprus were Soviet warnings against such a move.

In August, when after intercommunal clashes in Cyprus the Turkish air force had bombed Greek Cypriot positions and villages, the Greek Foreign Minister told the Turkish newspaper *Milliet* that "Naturally Greece is worried about the Soviet offer of aid to Cyprus."[30] Three days earlier, the Cypriot Foreign Minister had said in Athens that "Greek aid to Cyprus does not make Soviet aid redundant."[31] There was a report at this time that the Soviet Union had offered Cyprus thirty million dollars in credit on condition that the Cyprus Government would continue its insistence on self-determination,[32] a fact which, if it resulted in an independent Cyprus rather than in an "Acheson type" solution, would tend to demilitarize Cyprus as far as NATO was concerned. Makarios was reported to be under pressure from Greece to refuse help from the Soviet Union. The Cypriot Foreign Minister had been to Athens four times in two weeks, and the Greek Foreign Minister was in Cyprus for the same purpose.[33] The Greek Government hoped for a solution along the lines proposed by Acheson,[34] whereas the Cyprus Government insisted on independence. *Enosis* based on the Acheson plan was what Greek and United States political leaders favoured according to one report since *enosis* "would be likely to spare the Western Powers the hazards of a future communist takeover in an independent Cypriot State".[35] A Cypriot-Soviet agreement had been signed at this time. George

## CYPRUS

Papandreou's Centre Union Government was now giving some support to the Cypriot line. He had agreed to the Cypriot Foreign Minister visiting Moscow, a fact to which his own Minister of Defence was strongly opposed.[36] In May 1965 his own and Makarios' positions seemed to converge. At a meeting of the Crown Council in Athens, Makarios offered to proclaim *enosis,* if Athens supported him and were prepared to face the consequences which would inevitably follow a unilateral declaration of *enosis.* Athens would not take on such a responsibility. Papandreou acknowledged that to achieve *enosis* a price would have to be paid to Turkey. If this price were too high new constitutional arrangements for an Independent Cyprus should be sought.[37] The Greek Prime Minister was himself planning to visit Moscow later in the month. (The visit was cancelled due to an apparent Soviet swing to Turkey's position on Cyprus.)[38] This was one of the issues which led to a sustained effort by the Greek King and Right to split his government. The Royalist and Right wing newspapers which had expressed the position of the Greek Government virtually uninterruptedly since the war, and would soon do so again, were expressing concern that after the Cyprus-Soviet agreement the mainland Greek troops which were now in Cyprus might "in case of a conflict, suddenly find themselves fighting side by side with Russians or Arabs".[39]

The line which the United States pursued at this time (and probably uninterruptedly since), was that the Cyprus problem should be solved by direct negotiations between Greece and Turkey. To the Government of Cyprus this represented an abolition of its sovereignty. This was no mere legal problem. A solution agreed between Greece and Turkey would involve either "double *enosis*", partition, or a "condominium" between the two governments over Cyprus. Naturally the Cyprus Government was opposed to both. Both would be much worse than the Zurich-London Republic as far as the Greek Cypriots were concerned.

Greek governments took a more sanguine view of such a possibility. In July 1964 the Greek Prime Minister was in Washington and, while he refused a direct meeting with the Turkish Prime Minister, he agreed to Greek and Turkish representatives meeting in Geneva under nominal U.N. and in fact American mediation to discuss the Cyprus issue. The idea for the partition of Cyprus that emerged at this meeting was not unacceptable to the Greek Prime Minister, if one can rely on the published version of his written views on the subject. Writing to Dean Acheson, and referring to Acheson's warnings of the threat of communist takeover in Cyprus he says:

I agree absolutely with your view that this threat creates a common interest between Turkey and Greece which is greater by far than the exact lines which we draw on a map.[40]

But Papandreou was aware of the fact that he did not control the Government of Cyprus. He points out in the same letter that his Defence Minister had just returned from Nicosia. He had merely succeeded in postponing the projected visits of the Cypriot Foreign Minister to Moscow and of Makarios to Cairo. Makarios had told the Greek Defence Minister that he not only rejects the establishment of a Turkish base in Cyprus (according to the Acheson Plan) but he would also work for the abolition of the existing British bases. Papandreou goes on to point out that the climate in Cyprus is very negative to Turkey (which had threatened to invade Cyprus), NATO (whose dominant partner, the United States, favoured partitioning the island), and Greece (which had not counterattacked when the Turkish air force had bombed Cyprus).

*Enosis* for most Greek Cypriots was now identified with the Acheson Plan. The worry began to be expressed by prominent Cypriots that so strong were the alliance interests of Greece, that it would come to some understanding with Turkey to deceive the Greek Cypriots into abandoning their statehood. This would involve renunciation of any protection they could achieve through non-alignment and through the U.N. The then President of the House of Representatives said in August 1964:

> If union with Greece is to take place first and then Greece is to negotiate with Turkey what the rights of the Turkish community in Cyprus are going to be and whether there will be a Turkish or NATO base in Cyprus, then this is an unacceptable proposition.

This would amount to

> an attempt to force the solution of the Cyprus problem within the Western Alliance and to deprive Cyprus of the support of countries outside the alliance.[41]

A few days later Makarios stated that he would welcome the "unconditional" union of Cyprus with Greece.[42] This was a reference to the distinction he wished to make between *enosis* and the various forms of condominium of Greece and Turkey over Cyprus which were at this time being served as *enosis*. The Cypriots were worried by reports[43] that the Greek Government was favourably disposed to the Acheson Plan, and statements such as that of the Turkish Foreign Minister to the effect that "some interesting ideas" had been produced during the Geneva talks.[44]

The differences in interests and orientations of the two states were at times expressed as struggles to influence each other's policies. The Cypriots were opposed to the London Conference of December, 1963 since it squarely placed the Cyprus problem in the context of NATO rather than the U.N. At the next Greek-Turkish conference over Cyprus, in Geneva during the summer of 1964, the Cypriot position was stronger as the Soviet Union had already expressed its support. At the end of August it was reported[45] that Makarios persuaded the Greek Government to withdraw from the negotiations, which were based on various versions of the Acheson Plan, by promising to suspend negotiations with Moscow. In fact, the Greek Prime Minister and the Cypriot President made a joint communique to the effect that the Cyprus issue would go to the U.N. as soon as the Geneva negotiations were suspended.

The differences between the two states at this time had the germ of what would develop into the "National Centre" controversy. That was the issue of whether Athens had precedence in decision making on Cyprus over Nicosia. At the end of August 1964 the Greek Prime Minister wrote to the Cypriot President expressing the essence of the "National Centre" view. Cyprus, he pointed out, could not determine Greek foreign policy. There were now Greek troops on Cyprus and Greece would defend Cyprus in case of attack by Turkey. If there is any disagreement the opinion of Athens must be accepted because it carries responsibility for all of Hellenism.[46] Makarios replied to Papandreou about six months later. He says that he would never seek to draw Greece into a war against her will. But he refused to accept the Greek Government's political initiatives if they led to compromises which were unacceptable to the Cypriot point of view. He mentions one such initiative. He claims that the caretaker Greek Government in February 1964 tried to impose on him the Ball plan for a NATO peace-keeping force in Cyprus.[47]

The differences between the two governments increased after the dismissal of the Papandreou Government. After all, it was partly because of his wavering on following the Alliance line that Papandreou was regarded as such a threat by the Greek Right, the King and the U.S. representatives in Athens. And the epicentre of the conflict was the control of the means of violence in Cyprus. This issue was interconnected with the issue of whether Cyprus should obtain Soviet aid. Such aid would be largely used to strengthen the autonomous defensive power of Cyprus and would be used to safeguard its independence. By contrast aid from Greece would tend to lead to military control of Cyprus by Greece and tend to whatever form of *enosis* was possible under the strategic circumstances.

In the summer of 1964 the Cypriot parliament, now composed entirely of Greek Cypriots, passed three bills intended to strengthen the Cypriot armed forces, which at this stage were largely based on voluntary recruitment. The bills introduced conscription, merged the police and the gendarmerie, and enabled the Government to buy heavy arms. It has been claimed that Greece as well as Turkey opposed these bills.[48] In August, when the Cyprus Government was pressing for an interruption of the Geneva talks, there were in Cyprus rumours which found their way into newspapers that the Greek forces in Cyprus would conduct a coup and proclaim *enosis* on the basis of the Acheson Plan.[49] The next month the Greek Minister of Defence was in Cyprus to dissuade the Cypriot Foreign Minister from his planned trip to Moscow to negotiate economic aid and arms purchases, on the grounds that the involvement of the Soviet Union would counter attempts at *enosis*.[50] There is a report[51] that the first Greek Prime Minister after the fall of the Papandreou Government stated that the Greek troops in Cyprus "were there to impose the policy of the Athens Government rather than to defend the island from the Turks".

The main internal means of pressure on the Cyprus Government was the return of General Grivas. He returned to Cyprus in the summer of 1964. As a symbol of the uncompromising *enosis* of the EOKA struggle he was a powerful man in Cyprus. "Greeks, Turks and Americans all counted on the Greek General Grivas to act as a counterweight. In a showdown ... Grivas and his soldiers would force Makarios to *enosis*"[52] (i.e. the Acheson Plan). The Cyprus Government had to accept the return of the General not only because of his symbolic status, but also because of its own need to have an experienced officer organize the "private armies" which were becoming difficult to control, and which had attacked civilian Turkish Cypriots. In practice, Grivas formed the mailed fist of conservative Greek Government policy in Cyprus.

Soon after his return it was rumoured that a secret organization was formed whose aim was

> to stifle communism, to suppress every move for the cultivation of a Cypriot consciousness and to strive for a revival of the Greek virtues and Greek consciousness. The organization's oath bound members to *enosis* as the only solution.[53]

In November 1964 there were rumours of a second plot to overthrow President Makarios and to proclaim *enosis*.[54] The Cypriot President tried to curtail the powers of General Grivas and put the National Guard, which had been formed on the basis of the conscription law, under the control of the Cypriot Minister of Defence. Grivas declared that he would not take orders from the Cyprus Government, but only from Athens.[55] In fact, the first post-Papandreou Government in Greece had restored Grivas, who was a reservist when he arrived in Cyprus, to active service.[56] Makarios himself accused Grivas of plotting to overthrow him in the spring of 1966.[57] By the end of the year the Cyprus Government was importing arms from Czechoslovakia.[58] The arms were not used to strengthen the National Guard against a possible Turkish invasion. They had to be used to arm the police as a disincentive to a coup by the National Guard against the Government.

These were episodes in the continuing attempt to keep the spirit of Acheson alive. Makarios, and his charismatic hold over the Greek Cypriots, as well as the communist party of Cyprus were the main barriers to this. Even they however became vulnerable when the plan for partitioning Cyprus was presented as *enosis*. Hence the method of implementation would be through the force of *Greek* Arms. A secret NATO protocol on the necessary concessions to Turkey would be made. The change in Cypriot sovereignty would initially be presented as unconditional union with Greece.[59] While Acheson tried to sell the plan to Athens, Under-secretary George Ball tried to sell it to the only man with any hopes of shaking Makarios' popularity—George Grivas.[60] One report maintains that Ball met secretly with Grivas, and gained his endorsement for a plan to unite Cyprus with Greece. Bases (presumably the British ones) would be turned over to Turkey and eventually to NATO. Makarios, who was the chief obstacle, would be ousted.[61] While the reality of a Grivas-Ball meeting has been authoritatively contested, the existence of the Acheson Plan has not. The Greek Defence Minister of the time has since written[62] that Grivas agreed only to that part of the Acheson Plan which provided for a Turkish military presence in Cyprus either through the use of the British bases, or the use of a base of a forty square mile uninhabited area south of Famagusta. Grivas did not accept either the idea of Turkish cantons, or the turning of the inhabited area of Karpasia into a Turkish military base. The Defence Minister argues that this plan was unacceptable to Turkey. Yet at the same time he insists that the Government of Cyprus organized clashes with the Turkish Cypriots at that time in order to break up the Geneva negotiations at which the plan was being discussed. The unearthing of the true details is a matter for the historian when the archives are open. But it is possible to make some comments on the known facts. It seems very likely that U.S. State Department officials were engaged in promoting the union of part of the Republic of Cyprus with Greece, and turning a smaller part into a Turkish military base. It also appears possible that Grivas was not aware of the full implications of the Acheson Plan. This would partly explain his bitterness against Makarios for impeding what he saw as *enosis*. The Greek Defence

Minister Garoufalias' imputation indicates the degree of suspicion between the Government of Cyprus and that of Greece at that time.

The last elected government of Greece, that of George Papandreou, was dismissed by the King with U.S. encouragement[63] in July 1965. Between then and the establishment of the military dictatorship in April 1967 relations between the Cypriot and the Greek Governments deteriorated further. In May 1966 the Greek Stephanopoulos government announced its intention to start a secret dialogue with Turkey on Cyprus. In fact, there is a report[64] that by December of 1966 a protocol was signed in Paris between the Greek and Turkish Foreign Ministers. The Turkish Foreign Minister according to this protocol insisted that Cyprus should be independent, or alternatively that a form of condominium should be established by the two countries. The Greek Foreign Minister insisted on "a form of *enosis*". The Greek Minister agreed that Dhekelia, one of the British bases, would be made available for Turkish security in case of an agreement. The Turkish Minister demanded full sovereignty for that base, but the Greek Minister said that he could not answer immediately. Experts of the two Governments would discuss arrangements for the self-government of the Turkish Cypriots in the areas where they were in a majority. The agreement would be accompanied by an Alliance (presumably this is a reference to the maintenance of the existing Treaty of Alliance), and agreements on the economy, tourism, trade and fishing. Nothing developed further since the Greek Government fell from office a few days later.

These diplomatic manoeuvres were of course not public at the time. But it is certain that the distrust of NATO and that aspect of Greek foreign policy which was connected with the significance of the Alliance which possessed Cypriot Government and diplomatic circles also seeped into public opinion.

As early as October 1964 Makarios complained to the Greek Defence Minister that the Greek army officers in Cyprus were criticizing his policies. The Greek Defence Minister admonished Makarios in turn that there should be concerted campaign in Cyprus in favour of *enosis*. The Defence Minister notes that during the days of a visit he made to Cyprus "anti-*enosist* propaganda which had started the day after the establishment of the Cypriot State" abated, only to resume immediately after his departure. He implies that such propaganda was even conducted by the State-controlled Radio, and the Government-influenced newspaper. Greek officers were discredited and called "kalamarades". (Literally "pen-pushers".) The contribution of the Greek Government to the defence of Cyprus was minimized. Every statement of the Russians, Nasser, or the non-aligned countries in favour of Cyprus was praised.[65] He continues with the intriguing suggestion that the anti-*enosist* propaganda was initially conducted with the covert cooperation of British agents.[66] The Cypriots, for their part, were concerned with more indirect symbolism. The Greek Defence Minister received a letter from the Cypriot Minister of Interior. The Cypriot was concerned about two "delicate issues" connected with the Greek army officers. One was that they spent dollars and the other was that they smoked American cigarettes. Both facts were "not in accord with the sharply anti-American feeling here".[67]

In April 1965 Mr Garoufalias has further bitter reminiscenses about Cyprus. A Cypriot newspaper attacks him personally and another Minister, Stephanopoulos. They were accused of bringing pressure on the Cypriots to accept the Acheson Plan, of preventing the importation to Cyprus of defensive anti-aircraft missiles and of financing an anti-Makarios newspaper within Cyprus. In the article it was demanded that those two Ministers be tried by a special court. Garoufalias was informed of this article by telegram by the Greek Ambassador in Cyprus, who adds the information that the article was inspired by the President of the House of Representatives, Mr Clerides. Makarios had refused to make a clear condemnation of the article.[68]

Within Greece itself, a political faction under the Prime Minister's son, Andreas Papandreou, supported most of the positions of the Cyprus Government (as well as many reforms in the internal affairs of Greece and its international alignments). This faction was anathema both to the Greek establishment and to the U.S. agencies in Greece.[69] Three days after he was dismissed from his father's government as part of an attempt to bridge the Centre and Moderate right forces in Greek politics, he visited Cyprus where according to the Greek Defence Minister and presumably to his chagrin, he was received "with great honours".[70] By 1966 there were attacks on President Makarios in the right wing Athens press for his disobedience to the "National Centre", his opposition to *enosis*, and his retention of a Foreign Minister who applied a non-aligned policy.[71]

Relations between the "National Centre" and Cyprus had now been deteriorating for almost ten years.

> It must be remembered that the prestige of Athens began to fall in the eyes of the Cypriots from the time of the EOKA struggle and the compromising attempts of Karamanlis and Averoff. This fall was partly held up during the months of Papandreou's government, though the contradictions of the Centre Union's leader gave rise to many issues in Cyprus. But (the fall) resumed rapidly from the moment when the "apostates" came to power and has never stopped since then. Among the

Cypriots the conviction took increasingly deeper root that the interests and aims of Greece were not the same as their own.[72]

The policies of the Greek Junta, which followed the "apostates", do not represent a discontinuity in substance. But they do differ substantially in methods and in the degree of the vulnerability of Cyprus, once the great restraining factor of Greek public opinion was removed.

It is obvious that the difference in international orientations which developed due to the separate histories of Greece and Cyprus had a considerable influence in differentiating the two States. The abstract hankering for *enosis* of the Greek Cypriots was tempered. For the struggle for incorporation with Greece had indeed been abstract. It developed out of internal political conflicts and conflicts with the colonial power and out of the Greek cultural identity of the Greek Cypriots. But it involved very little knowledge of Greek society or a realistic estimate of the consequences of incorporation with the Greek State. With the beginning of Cyprus' independent statehood, social processes operated to induce a more realistic estimation of the process of incorporation with Greece. In a sense this resulted in economic and cultural differentiation of the Greeks of the island from their cultural motherland.

This chapter started with a consideration of the differentiation of Greece and Cyprus in relation to their position in international alliances and indicated the kinds of strains that developed between the two states and their public reflection. But this is not all. The separate historical development of the two societies had other consequences. Some are interconnected, but they can be conveniently discussed as four main problems. The existence of a legal communist party in Cyprus is one. The second is the separate development of Cypriot institutions and its specific history of British colonialism. The third is the creation of vested interests in independence among various groups of the Cypriot population. Fourthly, there is the fact that the attitude of the Greek Cypriots to the Turkish Cypriots was not necessarily analogous to the attitudes and relations of mainland Greeks to mainland Turks.

The development and political significance of the communist movement in colonial and post-colonial Cyprus is discussed in Chapter VI. For reasons which are fairly obvious, but which will subsequently be spelled out, the communist party AKEL, though nominally subscribing to the ideal of *enosis* at some time in the indefinite future was strongly in favour of cooperation between Greek and Turkish Cypriots, and of strengthening the independence of Cyprus. After the eruption of intercommunal conflict, this party which had the support of almost a third of the Greek Cypriot population, played a significant part in opposition to an Acheson-type solution to the Cyprus problem. Apart from anything else, *enosis* would mean that Cypriot communists would become part of a State whose governments had spent the last decade attempting to eliminate all traces of Leftism. But in a sense, the problem of the Cypriot communists may be placed in a broader historical perspective. The existence of AKEL, a legal party in Cyprus, was part of the liberal British political heritage, one which differentiated Cyprus from mainland Greece.

The fact is that

> Since 1191 when Cyprus was detached from Byzantine Hellenism, until today, Cypriot institutions, with the exception of religious and educational ones, have never been identical with Greek ones.[73]

An analysis by a Greek Cypriot intellectual,[74] which appeared in Cyprus in 1964, places the problem in its framework. It is true that the Greeks of Cyprus have the same intellectual and cultural tradition with that of the Greek State. This is obvious if cultural aspects of the Greeks of Cyprus are compared, allowing for regional variations, with those of Greeks of other areas. But the development of Cyprus in different historical contexts since the early Byzantine era has introduced differences. Perhaps of more immediate importance was the introduction of Anglo-Saxon institutions and links with the Metropolis by the British colonial administration. The writer does not go into details. But what he has in mind is fairly evident. Cyprus had a British-organized Civil Service in contrast to a German-organized one imposed on an Ottoman society which Greece had. In Cyprus there was a flourishing cooperative movement for credit supply and disposal of agricultural products in which some of the most active participants at grass roots level were communists. This in contrast to false starts and ineffectiveness in the mainland cooperative movement. Educated Cypriots knew English and many of them had been educated in British universities. Political polarization between Left and Right was never as extreme in Cyprus as it was in Greece. Communists sat in the House of Representatives and on government committees connected with welfare, labour and development. The well-known "individualism" of mainland Greeks was, in Cyprus, tempered by the fact of the successful imposition by the British of certain norms of "citizenship" and cooperation.

In addition, there was the economic divergence. Greece had been crushed by a Nazi occupation and subsequently a Civil War. Cyprus had hardly experienced the war and after the war the development programme initiated by the British in order to reduce the Cypriots' hankering for *enosis* had considerably increased the standard of living.

The writer[75] estimates that in the mid fifties income per head in Cyprus, at 160 pounds sterling, was roughly double that of Greece. This is a substantial difference reflecting itself in differences in domestic material ways of life.

When Greek Cypriots for the first time came into contact with large numbers of mainland Greeks with the arrival in Cyprus of Greek troops in 1964, more subtle problems operated. As in other culturally Greeks areas, the regional vernacular speech of Cyprus has considerable variation from, for example, the version of Greek used on the State-run radio in Greece.

Since many of the Cypriot elite were educated in British universities rather than Greek ones, they combined educated cosmopolitanism with, in terms of Hellenic culture, regional provincialism. A Greek Cypriot psychiatrist and nationalist, analysed the ambivalence in the feelings which resulted in this way.[76] (He was concerned, in 1965, to eliminate "psychic barriers to *enosis*".) He points out that Cypriots have feelings of inferiority in relation to mainland Greeks. The Greek Cypriot feels that he lacks something in comparison to the mainland Greek. It is likely, he points out, that this "lack" comes from the difference in linguistic usage. Cypriots have a different, and to mainland Greeks, "heavy"-sounding accent, with variations in vocabulary and syntax. This makes it difficult for a Greek Cypriot to converse freely with a "kalamaras". Cypriots who adopt the "pan-Hellenic" mode of speech are subjected to joking about their imitating "kalamarades". The Cypriot pronunciation "is something like a barrier which prevents the individual from expressing his psychic world, even his abilities and talents". Cypriots, especially of the middle and upper middle class, react to these feelings with a haughty emphasis on their cosmopolitanism, their superior university education in European universities other than those of Greece, and a general emphasis of the superiority of Cypriot society to Greek society.

This cultural variation must not of course be overemphasized. For example had union with Greece followed the transition from British colonialism, Cypriots would soon have adapted to mainland Greek culture, or at the most retained a "Cypriot" accent as a domestic alternative in some strata of the population, much as the Maniates and Cretans did for example. But this difference acquires an increasing significance in combination with statehood, institutional differences and the creation of vested interests among various groups in independence.

It has been indicated that in the fifties there was a sharp divergence in the standards of living of Cyprus and Greece. After independence Cyprus became the recipient of foreign aid which, in proportion to its size and population, was considerable. Between 1961 and 1966 it received grants from the United Kingdom amounting to almost thirteen million pounds sterling. It received aid in commodities from the U.S. amounting to three million sterling. And it received another nine million from the International Bank, the U.N. Special Fund, West Germany and the Council of Europe.[77] In combination with the expenditure from the British bases, the beginnings of tourism and development planning conducted by a fairly efficient Civil Service, there was a "take-off" certainly in profits, but also in standards of living for most of the population. One example of the rapid economic advance of Cyprus after independence was agriculture; a notoriously slow sector to develop. The value of agricultural production increased by 70% between 1961 and 1968.[78] Income per head, which in the mid 1950's was about 160 pounds sterling per head, had crawled to 171 pounds per head at the time of independence.[79] In the first three years of independence it shot up to 250 pounds per head.[80] It was to continue increasing steadily and at a high rate, so that just before the Turkish invasion in 1974 destroyed the Cypriot economy, it stood at 535 Cypriot pounds per head.[81]

As in any similar situation in a capitalist economy, the group which benefited most from this economic advance was the bourgeoisie. Since the advance in the Cypriot economy came primarily from an influx of wealth from abroad, and since, in spite of considerable development, it also resulted in enormous increases in consumption, the mercantile bourgeoisie of Cyprus achieved enormous windfall profits. Their position and profits depended on the possession of franchises to import mainly British but increasingly more diversified products. It seems that this group were quite open to argument in favour of the independence of Cyprus. They were in 1964 "the target of an intensive communist propaganda focusing on the theme that *enosis* would turn them into provincial agents of Athenian business lords".[82] The same Cypriot nationalist psychiatrist who has been previously mentioned points out that one of the "psychic barriers to *enosis*" is that merchants are afraid that they will lose their franchises to "kalamarades". One merchant, he writes, said to him, "and then I will become the employee of the general representative in Athens and merely get a proportion of the profit. We can still be Greeks without *enosis*."

Also at the time the impression existed[83] that Civil Servants of the Cyprus Government were concerned about their job and promotion prospects, since they supposed that in the case of *enosis* the highest posts would be filled by mainland Greeks. These concerns among various groups of influential Cypriots seem to have been widespread enough to provoke a response in the Greek Foreign Office. The *Times* of London reported that the problem was interpreted as a communist drive against the age-old aspiration of the Greek Cypriots for *enosis*.

An *enosis* Committee was formed in the Greek Foreign Office. The job of the committee was to counter the "communist propaganda drive" by preparing a detailed plan for *enosis* which would provide for the problems of eventual integration. It was intended that representatives of the Greek Cypriots would be invited to Athens and assured that their interest would not be harmed if Cyprus came under Greek administration. In October 1964 a group of Greek experts was already in Nicosia to seek the views of Greek Cypriot businessmen. It was intended that other missions would follow to study the problems of banking and agriculture. The issue here (in Athens), wrote the *Times* correspondent,

> is no longer whether Archbishop Makarios himself genuinely desires *enosis* or is scheming to keep the island independent. It is whether, if *enosis* were agreed upon as a lasting solution or were offered as a choice under self-determination, it would be accepted by the majority of the Greek Cypriots.[84]

The final source of Cypriot consciousness is also derived from the bourgeoisie, but must be discussed separately since the views of the situation involved also concern the Turkish Cypriots. It differs from that favouring independence on the basis of immediate interests, in the sense that it is a much more pervasive and developed view of the world that existed among professionals, businessmen and senior civil servants, even during the British period. It is in a sense a composite, among the most highly aware sections of Cypriot society (apart from the AKEL leadership) of all the aspects of the sources of Cypriot consciousness previously discussed. It represents the enlightened but failed bourgeois alternative leadership in the politics of Cyprus to the Church and the traditional intellectuals who controlled the educational system. The continuity of this way of thinking has not been studied historically, but it seems that there was a section of the Greek Cypriot merchant and professional groups who for example favoured at least some of the British attempts at educational reform in the 1930's. The notable characteristic of this way of looking at the world is the lack of nationalist rhetoric, concern with practical problems of economic development and political stability and awareness of the need for a peaceful *modus vivendi* for the Greek and Turkish Cypriots.

There was an attempt to give this political position an organised form when, at the initiative of a prominent businessman and with the cooperation of other businessmen and professionals, the "Social Progress Society" was formed after the Second World War. It advocated the acceptance of the offers of a constitution for self-government which the British were making as ... "through a process of evolution we would become masters in our own house, and finally united with Greece if we wanted to".[85] The other main aim of the society, besides the development of constitutional processes of self-government was to achieve close cooperation between Greek and Turkish Cypriots. The Society published a newspaper for three years, in a vain attempt to influence the nationalist leaders and public opinion. Lanitis, the same prominent businessman who had taken the initiative with the Social Progress Society was again expressing this tendency in 1963, before the breakdown of the constitution and the intercommunal conflict. Essentially he was urging the development of a Cypriot consciousness and awareness of the interdependence of Greek and Turkish Cypriots, the economic benefits to be derived from independence and the crucial importance of political stability for prosperity. It is worth mentioning his main points as they are as valid in 1979 as they were in 1963.

He accepts that the Zurich constitution has imperfections, but points out that Cyprus came to that largely because of the "*enosis* and only *enosis*" position of the Greek Cypriot leaders. But at least "it makes us masters in our own house". As for the 70:30 proportion, "The rule 70:30 in an inverted way says that there will be so many more Greeks employed in private industry and trade than Turks. If this was objectively expressed in the agreements, the Turks would probably be in revolt." The really damaging provisions of the constitution are those that are divisive of the Greeks and the Turks, he goes on. Above all this is the case with the institution of Communal Chambers which are a financial burden and divide the country through a constant stirring of nationalist feeling. The Greek and Turkish Cypriots are one people. The Greek Cypriots as the majority have the responsibility for strengthening cooperation. The less our friendship towards the Turkish Cypriots, he points out, the more they will turn to Turkey, whereas with cooperation it is easy to change the worst aspects of the constitution. Symbolic acts are important. It is necessary to give less emphasis to the celebration of Greek national holidays and more to Cypriot ones.

Already, he points out, we face economic disruption in, for example, the collection of taxes due to our political upheavals. He points out dire economic consequences if the path of sectarian conflict and nationalist demonstrations is continued. But the political consequences are the most worrying. The present cleavage, he points out, will sooner or later turn into hate. The result will be open conflict and the leaders of both communities will lose control of the situation. The exercise of power will be in the hands of irresponsible gunmen or the enraged mob. Eventually we may end up having a communist regime or a war between Greece and Turkey.

As an addendum, he meets criticisms which were made of his

articles. He points out that the Greek Cypriots could afford to engage in nationalist celebrations at the time when Cyprus was a British colony and responsibility for government was in British hands. "Now ... we are an independent people and must exercise self-control if we are to survive." We do not have to be united with Greece politically because we are Greek culturally. He lists examples of multi-ethnic states and language groups which form more than one state. In any event if we are not independent we will loose both our international standing and membership of international organizations and the advantages of foreign economic aid.[86]

These views were common among Greek Cypriots. After all, they were more or less the views of AKEL, and the majority of workers belonged to trade unions which supported it. The majority of Civil Servants and businessmen would also have expressed some or all of these views. However, the ones quoted appeared in print. This was very rarely to be seen outside the Greek and Turkish language left-wing newspapers. The question is why, given the widespread existence of these views as individual opinion and as the political opinion of the biggest single party in Cyprus, they were not much more widely articulated ideologically. They did not enter the political process as overt ideological determinants of the actions of the Cyprus Government. Why, in other words, did the Greek Cypriots not become capable of reconciling their Greek cultural identity with loyalty to an independent State in such a way that the state was supported and strengthened by the ideologies of organized political movements and parties? A more specific part of the same question, is why the political and economic reintegration of the Turkish Cypriots into the economy, society and political processes of Cyprus took so long to achieve after the intercommunal clashes of 1963-4, in spite of the fact that the policy of the Government of Cyprus was to preserve and strengthen the independence of the island?

# CHAPTER V

## *Relations between Greek and Turkish Cypriots and the problem of bicommunalism*

The Greek Cypriots, it was shown in the previous chapter, developed strong elements of independence from the cultural motherland. At the end of the last chapter two questions were posed about the weakness of the Cypriot political processes in reaching a "post colonial nationalist" situation. The first question was connected with the ideological articulation of independence from Greece, the second with relations to the Turkish Cypriots. The latter question will be tackled in this chapter. To show the difficulty of integrating the Turkish Cypriots into Cypriot society is to show the integration of the Turkish Cypriot leadership with Turkey. To rephrase the question, the issue becomes that of explaining why the Turkish Cypriot community was drawn into dependence on Turkey, particularly in view of the traditional rural coexistence of the Greek and Turkish Cypriot population on Cyprus. Of course, part of the answer has already been given in Chapter III in the discussion of the development of Turkish Cypriot nationalism and the brief analysis of the consequences of the Zurich Republic on inter-ethnic relations. Here the issue will be examined more schematically, making a reference to events already discussed in the previous chapters where necessary.

The common fate and solidarity of Greek and Turkish peasants during the Ottoman period has already been referred to. Here some further elements of the traditional rural coexistence of Greek and Turkish Cypriots will be mentioned, as they form the backdrop for understanding the complex political events which determined the increasing separation and conflict between the two groups.

Evidence has been offered of a substantial number of conversions from Christianity to Islam during the Ottoman period.[1] This being the case, it would explain the substantial similarities in patterns of life, other than religious life, of the two main ethnic groups of Cyprus. The edges of the two groups must indeed have been quite blurred, even culturally, if one takes into account in addition two facts. One is that until very recent years there were virtually whole villages of Greek-speaking Muslims; secondly, that there were various phenomena of "dual religious allegiance"[2] and degrees of religious syncretism, on the part of Muslims which only lapsed with the development of nationalism.[3]

But perhaps the most important elements in the traditional coexistence of Greek and Turkish Cypriot peasants are the inextricably interdependent patterns of economic and ritual relations. Indeed so inextricable are they that they survived until just before the invasion in 1974, and for all we know may, to some extent continue in areas where the traditional settlement pattern has been allowed to stand. From personal enquiry in the Karpasia area of Cyprus I know of two elements of economic interdependence and two elements of ritual interdependence existing in 1974 which are likely to go back indefinitely into the past.

Perhaps two of the most important economic institutional patterns of traditional Cypriot society are the merchant intermediary relation to the peasant producer, through which the merchandise of the peasant was marketed and credit was provided by the merchant to the peasant. These patterns survived until 1974 in the interstices of the cooperative movement. In 1974 there were still Greek Cypriot intermediaries buying from Turkish Cypriot peasants. Secondly, the share-cropping pattern, whereby surplus land of one family was combined with surplus labour of another, seems a well-established though in recent years declining pattern. But even in 1974 there were instances of share-cropping arrangements between Greek and Turkish Cypriots.

Ritually, in traditional society weddings and coffee shops have been important indicators of who belongs within the given social entity. Again from oral reports in Karpasia I know that in cases of weddings in Greek villages, there was an established ritual way of inviting a whole neighbouring Turkish village. The family conducting the wedding would place a large candle in the Mosque of the Turkish village. This was an open invitation. Then there is the case of coffee shops. They are so important as indicators of belongingness that in many villages Greek Cypriot leftists and rightists have separate coffee shops and rarely, if ever, patronize the coffee shop of the politically opposite side. Yet in numerous mixed villages, even in 1974, Greeks and Turks sat in the same coffee shop.

It has been described how during the whole period up to its abolition, Greek Cypriot and Turkish Cypriot leaders disputed in the Legislative Council and that the Turkish Cypriot leaders often counter-petitioned the Greek claims for *enosis*. But it seems that it was only on rare occasions that such differences affected the pattern of traditional rural coexistence. At grass roots the patterns of traditional coexistence have never been totally disrupted. Even at the most critical times there have been surprising indications of this.

In March 1965 while occasional intercommunal violence was still continuing, the U.N. mediator, Mr Plaza said in his report:

I am reluctant to believe, as the Turkish leadership claims, in the "impossibility" of Greek-Cypriots and Turkish-Cypriots learning to live together in peace. In those parts of the country where movement controls have been relaxed and tensions reduced, they are already proving otherwise.[4]

Brigadier Harbottle, who was Chief of Staff of the United Nations Force in Cyprus (UNFICYP), describes relations between Greek and Turkish villagers in Ayios Theodoros in the following way. The village was the scene of fighting between the National Guard and the Turkish Cypriot Fighters in the middle of November 1967. Within a day or two of the fighting he writes,

I suppose the most heartening sight of all was to see the way in which the two communities of Ayios Theodoros picked up the threads of their old relationships and life together. The Greek villagers, who had opened their doors to the Turkish women and children at the height of the battle, now lent a hand in the restoration work, and it was not long before social contacts were being resumed. One should never be surprised at anything in the Near or Middle East, but even the most experienced ones among us were mildly astonished when at the height of the international crisis in December it was reported that members of both communities in Ayios Theodoros were sitting together in the same coffee house, not only exchanging conversation but Christmas gifts—a sign that whatever the rest of the world was doing, they at least were determined to get relationships back to normal and to live in quiet accord with their neighbours.[5]

This was no out of the way case. In the same book[6] Brigadier Harbottle describes the way in which in the summer of 1967 Greek and Turkish Mukhtars in the Paphos district cooperated with the help of UNFICYP to make it safe for Greek and Turkish Cypriot villagers to move about the country roads.

Most Cypriots have heard first hand accounts of assistance by Turkish to Greek Cypriots and the other way round during the events of July and August 1974. But it is more impressive to see it put in print by a neutral observer. Again it is Brigadier Harbottle, who was interested enough to visit Cyprus to see for himself after the Turkish invasion in 1974. He wrote after his visit:

The myth of deep animosity between Greeks and Turks is one that has been perpetuated by those who seek to convince their fellows and world opinion that the two communities cannot live together; but it is a myth long overdue for exploding. There are too many examples of people in mixed villages and mixed communities living amicably as neighbours; of Greeks and Turks working together in factories and the fields; of cooperation together over community issues. One would imagine that such relations would have been severely or badly mauled as a result of recent events, but no, the cooperation and coexistence remains as firm as before. Many are the examples during the fighting where human relations and standards of civilized behaviour have triumphed over ethnic differences, requiring a degree of courage of the persons concerned.[7]

Given this background of coexistence, the increasing dependence of the Turkish Cypriots of Cyprus as an organized entity on Turkey does not intrinsically follow from the ethnic and cultural facts of the language and religion of the Turkish Cypriots. The first point to be looked at is the timing and nature of the involvement of the Turkish State in the affairs of Cyprus.

The peak of the Greek Cypriot *enosis* agitation could not have come at a less propitious time as far as international conditions were concerned. Not only did it coincide, as has been mentioned, with a British need for a last ditch stand to retain imperial territory in the Eastern Mediterranean, but it also coincided with the accession to power in Turkey, for the first time since Ataturk's reforms, of a government not produced by the Republican Peoples Party, Ataturk's party. In 1950 the Democratic Party under Menderes came to power, representing a policy in many respects counter-revolutionary to Ataturk's reforms. The National Pact of Ataturk had defined Turkey as the territory of the Turkish Republic and had renounced irredentist claims to territory formerly under the rule of the Ottoman Empire.

The sole exception to this during Kemal's rule over Turkey had been the case of the Hatay, where a sequence of moves captured an area not inhabited by a majority of Turks for Turkey. It is interesting that there are recent hints in the Turkish press that Cyprus was the other exception to Ataturk's policy. Hatay started in 1921, with specially guaranteed rights for the Turkish minority as a territory of French-Mandated Syria. In 1937, when Syria became independent, the Hatay was given internal self-government, linked with Syria with a customs union and with Syrian responsibility for foreign policy. After disturbances were caused by some of the Turkish inhabitants of the territory because the League of Nations-prepared registers showed them to be in a minority, Turkish troops entered the territory to police it. New electoral registers were drawn up showing the Turks in a majority. In elections in August 1938, conducted in the presence of Turkish troops, a majority of Turkish representatives were elected. They declared an independent Republic which became part of Turkey in June 1939. An anti-axis alliance was signed between France, Britain and Turkey the same year.[8]

It has recently been claimed that Ataturk had the same fate in mind for Cyprus. It has been hinted by an American social scientist writing in a Turkish journal that ...

> ... Turkey, while officially divorced from the island's internal affairs, may have been monitoring developments there rather more closely than is generally acknowledged.[9]

There has been a more explicit indication in a newspaper in the Turkish-occupied part of Cyprus. In a comment on the occasion of the 37th anniversary of Kemal's death, the newspaper reminisced that he once pointed out to some officers with whom he was on manoeuvres that in case Turkey was ever occupied and the Turkish army was resisting only in the South, Cyprus would provide the only channel for reinforcements for Turkey, provided it was not in enemy hands. After the annexation of the Hatay in 1939 a Turkish Cypriot intellectual asked Ataturk about Cyprus. The answer was reported to have been: "Its turn will come."[10]

Whatever may or may not have been the concern of the Turkish foreign office, army and secret services with Cyprus, it was only after British encouragement of Menderes, and his coinciding economic problems within Turkey, that the Cyprus problem was turned into a Turkish national issue, nationally and internationally.

Since that time, the actually formulated demands of Turkey in Cyprus have been remarkably constant. The fact that the Turkish Cypriots are a minority of the population of the island has generally been overlooked as irrelevant and attempts made to counterbalance it by two arguments. One was the overwhelming strategic importance of Cyprus to Turkey, particularly if the island were to fall into communist hands. The second argument, the "bicommunalist" one, is that for historical reasons dating to the Ottoman Empire the Turkish Cypriots are not a minority of the whole population of Cyprus counted as individuals, but are a corporate unit, and thus equal in aggregate with the other corporate unit forming the population of Cyprus, the Greek Cypriots. However, the overwhelming consideration was strategic.[11]

In 1954 and 1955, at the London Conference, Turkey seems to have favoured the maintenance of the *status quo* in Cyprus, with some internal autonomy granted so long as it was understood that this would not lead to self-determination or to *enosis*.[12] Though "Taksim", partition, was the slogan of Turkish nationalism in Cyprus, Turkey does not appear to have put forth or negotiated for the subdivision of Cyprus between Greece and Turkey, except for a brief period in 1964. Partly this must have been because "Taksim" could only have been accomplished *after* an opportunity had arisen for a forced shift in the population of Cyprus in order to make a "Greek" and a "Turkish"

Cyprus demographically possible. But there may have been other, equally sinister, considerations.

At the London conference, called by the guarantor powers after the outbreak of fighting in Cyprus in 1964, the proposal was put forward officially, apparently for the first time, for Cyprus to be split in two. A form of partition which would at least nominally, maintain Cyprus as an independent state was the first choice, and "double *enosis*" was the second choice. At the NATO Foreign Ministers conference in The Hague in May 1964, the visualized form of a Cypriot Federation was spelt out by the Turkish Government.

The Turkish Cypriots would be concentrated in one geographical area and the Greek Cypriots in another. The area "given" to the Turkish Cypriots would be 38% of the island. This would involve a line of subdivision very similar to that created by the Turkish invasion forces in July and August 1974. The lines would extend from Yialia on the north-west coast through the centre of Nicosia to Famagusta. It was suggested that twenty or twenty-five thousand families would have to "move" for this plan to be realized. (Ten years later when the experiment was actually realized, the number proved to be closer to forty thousand.) Each Federal State would be allowed to have direct cultural and economic relations with Greece and Turkey respectively. The federal government would have responsibility for foreign affairs, defence, monetary policy, public utilities, ports, airports, passport matters and criminal legislation and jurisdiction. There would be unrestricted movement for products between the two areas. The two ethnic groups would be represented in the legislature, the ministerial council and the civil service in the proportions of 70:30, and in the army and police by 60:40. The president would be Greek and elected by the Greek Cypriots, and the vice-president Turkish and elected by the Turkish Cypriots.[13] The plan was apparently a re-establishment of the Zurich Republic constitutionally with the addition of partition.

This plan was first given a public airing when the Turkish Cypriot leader Mr Kuchuk presented it to the U.N. mediator in 1965, with the added proviso of the free movement of citizens of Greece and Turkey to the respective zones of Cyprus with a pass system.[14]

During the summer of 1964 it seems that the Turkish Government did consider the formal ending of the independence of Cyprus as visualized by the Acheson Plan. But as early as October 1964 it was reported to have reverted to the position of "federal independence".[15]

It seems that on every occasion when it has been made public, the Turkish Government position has, since the 1964 proposals, remained constant, until the invasion in 1974. For example at the Evros talks, held between the Greek Junta and the Turkish Government in 1967, the latter rejected any kind of *enosis* and insisted on some kind of "reinforced" Zurich type independence.[16] Though the phrasing is

85

quite vague, in January 1974 the Ecevit coalition government signed a protocol on Cyprus which essentially provided for the same position.[17] It is not surprising that Turkey has not, as is generally believed and as appears from Turkish nationalist slogans, steadily pushed for the partition of Cyprus between itself and Greece. The main concern for Turkey in Cyprus has been strategic, rather than that of the protection of the Turkish minority. Even in 1965, the Turkish Government position as expressed to Gallo Plaza, the U.N. mediator, was that

> any settlement firstly must maintain the equilibrium of territorial interests in the eastern Mediterranean and especially as between Turkey and Greece ..., and secondly, must ensure the security and well being of the Turkish Cypriot community.[18]

This being the case, "double *enosis*", with a Greek presence in the southern part of Cyprus was only slightly less objectionable than *enosis*. On the other hand, a "federal independence" with the Turkish Cypriot part of the island closely connected to Turkey would have many advantages and many potentialities for the future. Not the least of the advantages was the fact that it enabled the claim for an actual partition of the island to be phrased in terms that were relatively acceptable to the socialist and non-aligned countries since it nominally preserved the independence of the island.[19] On the other hand, in communicating in the direction of NATO the emphasis was on the fact that the largest Greek Cypriot party was communist and that the Turkish Cypriot community should be strengthened to counter its influence.[20] But an independent federal Cyprus, with the Turkish part dominated by Turkey, has potentialities for the takeover of the whole of Cyprus which partition between Greece and Turkey does not.

The Turkish proposals for "federal partition" involved an uprooting, not only of Greek, but also of Turkish Cypriots. In fact, as the events of 1974-5 showed, a higher proportion of the Turkish Cypriot population had to move in order to conform to the line of partition than of the Greek Cypriot population. Also, there was no intrinsic reason for the Turkish Cypriots to be concerned with the strategic considerations of mainland Turkey. Their falling in with mainland Turkish arguments was not automatic. It had to do with various forces which operated during the last twenty years, some of them being neither spontaneous nor unforeseen.

The factors in the political development of the Turkish Cypriots as a group which were discussed in Chapter III are relevant to understanding the development of a monolithic political structure for the community, initially dependent on the colonial government. This dependence was readily available to be transferred to the Turkish

State. However, two characteristics conducive to these developments have not been fully elaborated. One is the demographic position of the Turkish Cypriot group within the Cypriot population and the other is the economic position. These will now be sketched before moving on to the consequences of the intercommunal conflict in 1964-7 and their contribution to the separation of the two communities.

The economic position of the Turkish Cypriots is important in discussing inter-ethnic relations from two points of view. On the one hand, it contributed to the lack of differentiation of the Turkish Cypriots as a group and made their control by TMT easier. On the other, it resulted, particularly after 1963, in a standard of living which was on average considerably lower than that of the Greek Cypriots.

The first point to make about the economic position of the Turkish Cypriots is that it had deep historic roots in their position in the Ottoman Empire. The only economic history of Cyprus during the Ottoman period[21] describes how between the Ottoman conquest of Cyprus in the sixteenth century and the eighteenth century, a native bourgeoisie developed for the first time in Cyprus. The preconditions were created by the expulsion by the Ottoman administration of Venetian agents and Jews settled in Cyprus as traders. Initially, the opportunity was offered of low-level positions in the Ottoman or Church administration. Corruption allowed the accumulation of some capital with which to enter the grain or wine trade.

Greek Cypriots were, for the first time since the twelfth century, allowed to enter trade. The previous Venetian rulers had reserved trade for themselves. The Ottomans did not, reserving for themselves military and administrative careers.

The Christian traders were additionally reinforced by the establishment of European consulates in Cyprus, who extended their immunity to their Greek-Christian employees. The latter could then expand their trading activities to lending money to the Cypriot peasants.

> Thus, in several ways there grew up during the Turkish regime a small but influential class of native Cypriot merchants such as had not existed since the Byzantine era, men who occupied themselves usually in commerce, but who possessed surplus funds which they could risk in tax-farming, invest in town and country real estate, or lend to impoverished peasants desperately trying to pay their taxes and support their families until the next harvest ... Hardly any of them, ironically enough, belonged to the Moslem community that claimed political control of Cyprus.[22]

The situation hardly seems to have changed during the period of British rule. We have figures for 1901,[23] at least insofar as professional enterprise is concerned. At that date there were 32 Greek medical practitioners, 5 belonging to other ethnic groups and no Turkish Cypriot ones. There were 28 Greek registered chemists, 1 Turk and 10 belonging to other ethnic groups. There were 42 Greek advocates, 7 Turks and 5 others. There were 8 Greek and 1 Turkish newspaper. By contrast, in the police force there were 281 Muslims and 387 Christians. At this time the Turkish Cypriots composed roughly a quarter of the population of Cyprus.

In 1963, only three years after the departure of the British and before the outbreak of intercommunal troubles, we have statistical evidence for the economic position of the two groups. There seems little doubt that production in most sectors was in Greek Cypriot hands. The Turkish Cypriots were then 18% of the population of Cyprus. The value added to the main agricultural crops by Turkish Cypriot producers was 12%. Only 11% of manufacturing establishments employing over five persons were in Turkish Cypriot hands and their proportion of gross value added to manufacturing was 2%. Only 2% of income tax was contributed by Turkish Cypriots (31% was contributed by Greek Cypriots and 67% by "others", mainly foreign mining companies).[24] Only 3% of imports and 0,2% of exports were in the hands of Turkish Cypriots.[25]

What this means is that the Cypriot bourgeoisie was still Greek rather than Turkish Cypriot. Of course it also means that there was a higher incidence of wealthy individuals among Greek than Turkish Cypriots. For example only 15% of the registered owners of motor vehicles were Turkish Cypriots.[26] But it did not mean that the Turkish Cypriots formed an inferior economic caste. It is true that in 1961 the average per capita income of Turkish Cypriots was 20% lower than the average for Greek Cypriots. It was £130-5 as compared to £160-6.[27] But this was natural given the high incidence of businessmen and professionals among the Greek Cypriots and did not mean for example that a Turkish Cypriot worker or peasant was poorer than a Greek Cypriot one. The fact that Turkish Cypriots had been until a couple of years previously members of the same trade unions as the Greeks is a sure indication that this could not have been the case.

On the other hand Turkish Cypriots remained, encouraged by the provisions of the Zurich constitution, disproportionately concentrated in government employment. In the public service 25% were Turkish Cypriots and in the army and police, 36%.[28]

The second precondition to understanding the political relations of Greek and Turkish Cypriots in depth is the demographic relation between the two groups over time. It can be presented in figures in three short tables.

1570 was the year of the Ottoman occupation of Cyprus. It is estimated that half the population was lost during the fighting and

## Relations between Greek and Turkish Cypriots

Table 1. Greek- and Turkish-speaking population of Cyprus 1570-1960 (in thousands).[29]

|        | 1570 | 1572     | 1777     | 1881     | 1931     | 1960       |
|--------|------|----------|----------|----------|----------|------------|
| Greek  | 150  | 85       | 60       | 138      | 277      | 442        |
| Turkish| —    | 20(19%)  | 20(25%)  | 45(25%)  | 64(19%)  | 105(18%)   |

Table 2. Percentages of Greek and Turkish Cypriots living in all urban areas and percentage contribution to the population of Nicosia.[30]

|         | % Urban | | % in Nicosia | |
|---------|------|------|------|------|
|         | 1881 | 1960 | 1881 | 1960 |
| Greek   | 13   | 32   | 50   | 77   |
| Turkish | 25   | 40   | 50   | 23   |
|         |      |      | 100  | 100  |

Table 3. Number of villages in Cyprus according to whether Greek, Turkish or mixed.[31]

|         | 1881 | 1931 | 1960 | 1970 |
|---------|------|------|------|------|
| Greek   | 342  | 358  | 392  | 444  |
| Turkish | 114  | 84   | 117  | 110  |
| Mixed   | 342  | 252  | 114  | 48   |
|         | 798  | 694  | 623  | 602  |

subsequent events. The figures for 1572 are hotly debated by historians, for the appearance of 20,000 Turks in Cyprus within two years of the conquest would represent the settlement of a considerable number of Asia Minor Turks. The opposite school in the controversy holds that a considerable proportion of the contemporary Turkish Cypriots are descendants of Christian converts to Islam. In fact the debate does not concern us. What is relevant is that the figure is substantially accurate for the eighteenth century. Whether they are descendants of the Ottoman military force or converts from the local Venetian and Greek population, they were settled in a highly dispersed fashion throughout Cyprus, forming the "ethnographic fruitcake" that Cyprus was to be until 1975.

The proportion of Turkish Cypriots in the population declined, largely because the Treaty of Lausanne and the policy of the Kemalist government of Turkey encouraged them to emigrate to Turkey.[32]

Turkish Cypriots have always proportionately been more urban than the Greek Cypriots reflecting their ruling class position and, later, preference for administrative positions. But their proportion in the population of the capital falls considerably during the course of British rule as Greeks develop increasingly commercially and as they gain in administrative positions in the civil service.

The demographic and economic position here presented confirms the political analysis of previous chapters. It indicates a picture of an ethnic group given to a tradition of urbanism and administration, of statism that is, rather than entrepreneurial activity, traditionally highly interspersed with the majority group. It is interesting that there was a trend for the mixed villages to decline in number, long before any intercommunal incidents. (Table 3.) The likeliest explanation is that mixed villages contained groups of people from each ethnic group that were too small to support communal institutions, particularly a school, and were the victims of urbanization or movement to larger villages. They do not represent a natural trend in separation between Turkish and Greek Cypriots, because, as shown in Chapter III, these trends were accompanied by integration in the developing urban economy as is indicated by the consolidated trade union movement which was only split by the political pressure of TMT.

A community that was economically dependent to a large extent on state institutions, numerically a minority, with its left-wing political movement eliminated by the nationalist organization oriented to Turkey and possessing a highly anti-communist leadership was obviously one capable of turning into a "strategic" one, quite reminiscent of the Sudeten Germans in relation to Nazi Germany. But before 1963 there was a severe limitation to this, and that was the interspersed nature of the Turkish Cypriot settlement pattern in Cyprus. This presented obstacles as to the means by which partition could be imposed and territorial control of part of Cyprus could be acquired. It also presented barriers to an exclusive control of the mass of the Turkish Cypriots by its anti-communist, Turkish oriented leadership.

This is why the intercommunal conflicts of 1963-7 are probably the most tragic events in the history of Cyprus. The main consequences of the events of this period were two. That by 1965, the Republic of Cyprus had removed many of the internal constraints on its independence, and appeared to be having success in removing the international ones. But 1.6% of the area of the republic was controlled by the "Provisional Turkish Cypriot Administration", and contained almost a half of the Turkish Cypriot population.[33] In terms of relations between the ethnic groups the most important consequences of the events between 1963 and 1967 was the vertical extension of separation to the mass of Greek and Turkish Cypriots.

There is no doubt that, as a minority in every area of Cyprus, the Turkish Cypriots were in a weaker position and there was a natural impetus to concentrate in order to avoid the fighting, a normal reaction of a civilian population. It is also remarkable that the fighting was limited to areas close to Nicosia and Larnaca, until the "freedom of movement agreement" on the 9th January 1964 enabled Turkish Cypriot political and TMT leaders to visit villages all over Cyprus and to describe the fighting near the capital. By the middle of February fighting had spread to Paphos and Limassol; by August 350 Turkish Cypriots and 200 Greek Cypriots had lost their lives. Another 45 Turkish Cypriots and 15 Greek Cypriots were to loose their lives during the intermittent incidents until 1967.[34]

The germ of fear among Turkish Cypriots (which must have been quite similar to the germ of fear among Greek Cypriots) was reinforced by their unwitting "trojan horse" status. Since they were the bases of a possible Turkish invasion, it was inevitable that government security measures would reflect on the mass of the Turkish Cypriots, whether favouring an invasion from the mainland or not. Thus, for example, Turkish Cypriots were searched at police check-points.[35] Those that were in areas militarily controlled by the leadership were subject to the hardships of the embargo on strategic goods placed by the government for a few months. And most seriously they were terrorised by the incidents of attacks against civilians by Greek Cypriot armed groups which evaded the control of the Government until the formation of the National Guard brought them under government control.

On these facts was built the institutionalization and enforcement of separation by the Turkish Cypriot leadership. Turkish Cypriots who had fled the fighting were forbidden by their leaders to return to the Government-controlled areas. A Canadian U.N. officer in Cyprus notes that in late 1964 refugees who wanted to return were threatened and some were even murdered.[36] Greek Cypriots were not allowed to enter the enclaves controlled by the leadership, but nor were Turkish Cypriots allowed to leave them.[37]

In early December 1964, the U.N. Secretary General reported that in Cyprus,

> The situation is complicated by evidence made available to UNFICYP that certain non-normal conditions are being kept in existence by measures applied by the Turkish Community to its own members.[38]

The nature of these conditions is indicated in an order issued by the Turkish Cypriot leaders on the 18th December 1964. It was brought to the attention of UNFICYP and the U.N. Security Council and, as published by the Government of Cyprus, reads:

> Turkish Cypriots not in the possession of a permit are prohibited to enter the Greek sector.
> 1. Those who disobey the order with a view to trading with Greek Cypriots should pay a fine of £25 or be punished with imprisonment.
> 2. A fine will be imposed on:
> (a) Those who converse or enter into negotiations with Greek Cypriots or accompany any stranger into our sector.
> (b) Those who come into contact with Greek Cypriots for any official work.
> (c) Those who appear before Greek Cypriot courts.
> (d) Those who visit the Greek Cypriot hospitals for examination or in order to obtain pharmaceuticals. ...
> ......
> 4. A fine of £25 or other severe punishment and one month's imprisonment or whipping should be imposed on those who enter the Greek Cypriot sector:
> (a) for promenade
> (b) for friendly association with Greek Cypriots
> (c) for amusement. ...[39]

Presumably this order was among the evidence which the Secretary General of the U.N. had in mind when he wrote in his report on the 11th March 1965 that

> The Turkish Cypriot policy of self-isolation has led the community in the opposite direction from normality. The Community leadership discourages the Turkish Cypriot population from engaging in personal, commercial or other contacts with their Greek Cypriot compatriots, from applying to Government offices in administrative matters, or from resettling in their home villages if they are refugees.[40]

There is no intention to minimize the actual incidents of unjustified attacks against Turkish Cypriots during the period of 1963-7. (Unjustified attacks against Greek Cypriot civilians also took place. But since the Turkish Cypriots were fewer, as the casualty figures indicate, they got the worse of it.) But what I would like to show is that even in 1964 and 1965, and increasingly after that, there was a reintegrating trend, arising spontaneously in relations between Greek and Turkish Cypriots, which was resisted by the Turkish Cypriot leadership largely controlled by Turkey, and indirectly by the Greek Junta, which unfortunately controlled the Greek Cypriot armed forces. The point is that far from there being an intrinsic cultural incompatibility between Greek and Turkish Cypriots, even after events such as those of 1963-7, there was a trend towards reintegration which was the object of active political resistance.

This reintegrating trend from the side of the Turkish Cypriot group was evident on the political level, on the level of the return of refugees and on the economic level. On the political level, a series of incidents indicates the repression of integrative trends by the Turkish Cypriot leadership, or at least the atmosphere prevailing within the Turkish Cypriot ethnic group now indubitably organized as a community. The murder of Kavazoglu in 1965 is significant. He was a journalist and trade unionist who attributed the separation of the Turkish Cypriots to the leadership's policy and to imperialism.

Evidence of internal political processes in the Turkish Cypriot community is hard to come by. Fortunately we have one study which shows the general structure and lines of opposition to the leadership's policy, the level of involvement of Turkey, as well as the magnitude of opposition to the leadership between the years 1968 and 1974. The "critics of the leadership", among whom the most prominent name is that of Mr Berberoglu, argued that the leadership's policy on the refugee question (there were estimated to be approximately 20,000 Turkish Cypriot refugees after 1964) was retarding a permanent settlement and prolonging the dispute. The leadership would not allow the return of refugees until after a political settlement. They encouraged the return to only 16 villages. On another issue, a mainland Turkish military officer was attached to each area controlled by the Turkish Cypriot leadership. His job, the Canadian writer reports, was to support the administration, if it followed the policy guidelines of Ankara, and to help the administration's efforts to maintain a united communal front. Berberoglu argued that they suppressed critics of the leadership. Though the maintenance of the closed areas were only made possible by an annual grant of £10m from Turkey, there appears to have been a chronic shortage of cash for the administration. (Incidentally budgets were never published or subjected to legislative approval.) The critics of the administration argued that more money could be made available for development purposes by reducing the Turkish Cypriot Fighter strength, by allowing the refugees to return to their homes, and by a closer cooperation with the Cyprus Government, so as to gain more of the U.N. development aid and to reduce the unnecessary duplication of services. They were in general critical of the leadership's line of general non-cooperation with the Government until there was a political settlement.

. The Republican Turkish Party was formed in December 1970 with Mr Berberoglu as chairman. In March 1971 he announced that he had more than 2,000 signed membership applications. This is an enormous number given that civil servants and fighters were not allowed to be politically active. And the majority of adult males were dependent for their jobs on the "Administration" and through the

# CYPRUS

Administration on Turkish economic aid. In a population of 120,000, there were 20,000 Fighters[41] and 9,000 civil servants.[42] Mr Berberoglu appears however to have been prevented at the last minute from testing his strength at the polls against Mr Denktas at the 1971 vice-presidential elections.[43]

In spite of the leadership's discouragement, the Cyprus Government's measures had some effect in the return of Turkish Cypriot refugees. In April 1964 the Cyprus Government had announced that it would help Turkish Cypriots resettle in their villages and pay recompense for any damage they had suffered. By 1971 2,000 Turkish Cypriots had returned to 22 villages which were under government control.[44] By the beginning of 1971 government sources were estimating that by the end of the year 6,000 Turkish Cypriots would be returning to their homes and were taking measures to repair houses in 21 villages.[45]

But reintegration was also taking place on a very significant level, the economic one. In 1970 the Turkish Cypriot labour force was composed of 45,000 people. Of these 33,000 were full time labourers. Five thousand of them were employed in Greek enterprises outside the Leadership-controlled enclaves. 4,000 Turkish Cypriots worked as seasonal labourers, and of these 3,000 were employed by Greeks. Eight thousand working Turkish Cypriots were self-employed. Of these, 5,000 had cooperative relations with Greek businessmen.[46]

Before turning to the issue of why these reintegrative trends did not receive a political seal by 1974, a further problem must be looked at in some more detail. That is a consideration of the economic implications of the separatist movement for the mass of the Turkish Cypriot population. For their indubitably poor economic position served both as one of the arguments for Turkish military intervention in 1974 and, equally importantly, for U.S. support for this intervention. On 13th August 1974 when overwhelmingly powerful Turkish forces were already on Cyprus and preparing to extend the area under their occupation, the State Department issued a statement containing the following incitement:

> We recognize the position of the Turkish community on Cyprus requires considerable improvement and protection.

There are three distinct questions to be asked of the position of the Turkish Cypriots in the Cypriot economy. One is an indication of their position, a comparison to the Greek population. This has been done, up to the time of the beginning of intercommunal incidents in 1963. The second is an explanation of the worsening of this position after 1963. The third, is an examination of the likely consequences for the mass of the Turkish Cypriots in their attitude to the Greek Cypriots and the Government.

94

After 1963 the economic difference between the two ethnic groups widened considerably. In 1971 it was estimated by a U.N. economist[48] that the average per capita income of Turkish Cypriots was 50% lower than that of Greek Cypriots at £150 compared to £300. The Turkish Cypriot leadership has implicitly claimed that this was due to Cyprus Government discrimination and withholding of services from Turkish Cypriots as a group.[49] There has been no thorough investigation of these claims. But the evidence that exists makes it appear unlikely. If one takes four examples, one can see how the process by which the mass of Turkish Cypriots acquired a lower standard of living operated.

Firstly, there was the attempt of the Turkish Cypriot leadership since the late 1950's to impose a "buy Turkish campaign", and since 1963 to build a separate economy.[50] Economically, this attempt, based on a population of 100,000, is bound to lead to a lower standard of living. Turkish Cypriots were deprived of the economies which buying in the integrated Cypriot economy would have involved, both through the limitations on movement and through the placing of intermediaries between the Greek and Turkish market. There was also in some cases attempts to set up Turkish Cypriot separate industries and facilities.

In other cases, the problem was the claim of exclusive control of people and areas by the Turkish Cypriot Leadership. For example, the leadership has claimed that since 1963, the Cyprus Government has withheld payments of social insurance benefits to eligible Turkish Cypriots on the pretext that the claim could not be verified, whereas the leadership claims "this could be carried out very easily through UNFICYP".[51] A study by an American political scientist of the role of United Nations Force in Cyprus contains a passing reference to the problem of social insurance payments to Turkish Cypriots. Success in re-establishing the programme, he points out, was quite limited,

> ... in large measure because the Turkish Cypriots have been unwilling to admit the government's legitimacy by allowing government insurance officers and welfare workers to carry out the requested inspections and verifications, even under UNFICYP escort.

For this statement he quotes three reports of the U.N. Secretary General.[52]

Another case is instructive. It was claimed by the Leadership that the Cyprus Government body, the Grain Commission, which buys all grain marketed in Cyprus, paid Turkish Cypriot producers 20% less than it paid Greek Cypriot producers.[53] The Canadian investigator previously cited mentions this fact, but also points out that the reason did not lie in an intention for Turkish producers to receive a lower price. Grain purchases by the Government grain commission were mediated by the Turkish Cypriot Cooperative Bank. Since the Cooperative Bank owed a sum of money to the Grain Commission, the sum was cut in instalments from the lump payments to the Turkish Cooperative Bank.[54] If the Bank, which engaged in many activities other than purchasing grain, chose to pass this on in the form of lower prices to Turkish Cypriot producers, it is true that to the producers it would appear that the Government was discriminating against them.

Until 1969 Turkish Cypriots received almost no benefit from aid to Cyprus from the U.N. Development Programme (UNDP). This was because the leadership insisted that it receive aid from the U.N. directly, which was refused. Of course individual Turkish Cypriots could apply to the Cyprus Government for participation in UNDP-financed projects. But the leadership put pressure on Turkish Cypriots to discourage them from applying.[55] We have seen that one of the demands of the Turkish Cypriot opposition was that the leadership cooperate with the Government so that Turkish Cypriots would receive the benefits of the UNDP programme.

Postal services were disrupted because government officials were barred from entering Leadership-controlled areas. Where postal services existed in mixed villages and in towns, Turkish Cypriots were prevented by the leadership from using them.[56]

Examples where Turkish Cypriot farmers, businessmen or whole villages suffered as a result of the leadership's separatist policy could be multiplied. But only one more case will be cited, that of village roads and water supplies. There is no doubt that there was a higher incidence of villages inhabited by Turkish Cypriots with inadequate streets, rural roads and water supplies. No doubt Turkish Cypriot villagers suffered from this lack. There were two conditions for the Government undertaking to provide these facilities to villages whether Greek or Turkish. One was that the village did not owe any money to the Government. This was a legal impediment to Government subsidies in many Turkish Cypriot villages, as the withholding of recognition from the Government by the Leadership certainly extended to withholding money owed. The second point worked on a purely informal level. Facilities such as village water supplies and streets were only financed to the extent of half the cost by the Government. The rest was paid for by the village itself, allocating the expense to the working inhabitants according to their means. Many authorities in villages in the Government-controlled areas were reluctant to tax their fellow villagers in this way. District Officers often had a hard job of persuasion before many villages acquired roads and water supplies. Of course they had no access to doing this in enclaved villages.

The significant point is that it is unlikely that the Turkish Cypriots were able to diagnose the reasons for their deprivation in these ways. It is quite likely that they attributed it to discrimination on the part of the Greeks, especially since this was the line of their leaders. And the Cyprus Government failed to find ways of overcoming the exclusive control of the Leadership in order to bring the mass of the Turkish Cypriots into fuller integration with the Cypriot economy. But in conditions where their leaders had disrupted the Turkish Cypriots' links to the Cyprus Trade Union movement and its protection, had isolated them from contact with Greek Cypriot businessmen and government officials, attempted to build a separate mini-economy and insisted on receiving benefits of government programmes through its own intermediary agency and territorial control, this task would have been difficult indeed for the Cyprus Government. Whether the effort was made to a sufficient degree is an important issue of self-examination for the Greeks of Cyprus.

But making the effort would have meant a major transformation of Cypriot society. Cyprus has a free market capitalist economy. Such economies are not notably susceptible to political measures for the economic amelioration of special groups. (The most important capitalist economy in the world has not itself been notably successful in dealing with such problems.)

The Turkish Cypriots had been outnumbered in the fighting of 1964-7. The fighting had driven them to accept the concentration, limitation of movement and monolithic direction of a leadership dependent on mainland Turkish military and economic support and the separatist control of the Turkish Cypriot population for the maintenance of its position. This in turn had led to their exclusion from the prosperity which Cyprus enjoyed between 1964 and 1974. The opposition movement within the Turkish community could be effectively discouraged by the leadership, on the basis of the need for unity in the face of the majority. And the line of the leadership, the line of Turkey, was the exclusive line presented to the Greek Cypriots both in the intercommunal talks and in the Greek Cypriot press.

By contrast, the Greek Cypriots, having apparently succeeded in many respects in their political aims of removing the constraints imposed in 1960, having achieved economic prosperity and being internationally represented by the Cypriot State, were in a very different position. Led by the President, they largely accepted that *enosis* was impossible and that their relations with Greece would be one of brotherly independence. The internal problem was largely solved for the Greek Cypriots. But their *political* dealings with the Turkish Cypriots were placed in cast iron constraints because of the political threats posed by Turkey on the one hand, and the Greek dictatorship on the other. They were also by no means helped by the

97

fact that some of the Western Powers distrusted the president who embodied this situation.

The problem for the Government of Cyprus was how to reintegrate an ethnic minority which had to a considerable extent been moulded as a separate state entity and whose leadership demanded a legalization of this position. This chapter will conclude with a consideration of how this problem was reflected in the "inter-communal talks" on Cyprus between 1968 and 1974. However, it must be added here, though it will only be shown in subsequent chapters, that the Cyprus Government was confronted with two further problems, which made this political task virtually impossible. One was the problem of the Greek Dictatorship. The meaning of its policy on Cyprus is highly opaque. Here it will be noted that it consisted of pressures on the Cyprus Government to make concessions to the Turkish Cypriots, while at the same time subverting the institutions of the Republic in favour of Hellenic nationalism. The second problem which the Cyprus Government had to face, on the evidence available, was that the Western Powers did not favour the process of the intercommunal talks as a means of political accommodation for the Cyprus problem. They appeared to favour a solution which would come from an agreement between Greece and Turkey. One probable reason for this is that such a solution would be likely to weaken the independence of a non-aligned Republic with leftist tendencies in the Eastern Mediterranean. The Greek dictatorship and Turkey, as well as their "national" interests in Cyprus, had an anti-communist orientation. In the years between 1971 and 1974, the Greek Dictatorship, the Turkish Government, the Hellenic nationalist extremists on Cyprus and the Turkish Cypriot Leadership were all virtually saying the same things. But this is for the last two chapters.

The demand for the initiation of intercommunal talks between the Greek Cypriots of Cyprus and the Turkish Cypriot Leadership had come from Turkey in the 1967 crisis. The agreement followed an attack by the Greek Cypriot National Guard on a strategically placed Turkish Cypriot village. The National Guard at this time was under the control of General Grivas, a General of the Greek army on active service. He had stated that he accepted no commands from the Cyprus Government, but only from the Greek one. On numerous occasions[57] he had acted on his own initiative and to the embarrassment of the Cyprus Government. However, on this particular occasion the incidents had built up over a period of time as a consequence of a mainland Turkish officer in command of a local Turkish Cypriot armed force impeding the passage of police through the village. The attack seems to have had the sanction of the Cyprus Government and the U.N. appeared to agree that the Turkish actions had impeded freedom of movement.[58]

The result of the fighting which followed however was a military confrontation between Greece and Turkey. With the mediation of U.S. Under-secretary Cyrus Vance, an agreement was reached between the two countries, the major provision of which was that Greek troops on Cyprus would be withdrawn within forty-five days. Though the Cyprus Government at this time refused to be bound by a clause in the agreement to disband the National Guard as well, this resulted in a major change in the military balance of power on Cyprus. But it also seemed to represent a major change in the attitude of the Greek military dictatorship. The controlled Greek press had until recently been attacking those in Cyprus who

> do not believe in the sanctity of the struggle and the pessimists who do not consider *enosis* possible.

and the

> category of supposed *enosists*, including those who present such groundless conditions and subversive preconditions, that *enosis* becomes problematic.[59]

The Greek troops, apart from officers commanding the National Guard, were withdrawn from Cyprus by January 1968. By the summer, the Greek Foreign Minister, Mr Pipinellis, had communicated to the Cyprus Government his view that *enosis* was absolutely impossible, as the recent events had shown, and would probably never be possible without reciprocal concessions to Turkey. Cyprus could not be assisted effectively by Greece in the event of an invasion. It was too far away for effective air cover and would find itself at the mercy of the Turkish air force. Finally, he indicated that the U.S. had pointed out to the Greek dictatorship that a Greek-Turkish war over Cyprus would provide the pretext for an irreversible Soviet intrusion into the area. The U.S. would do nothing, either in the event of a Greek-Turkish war or in case Turkey invaded Cyprus.[60] The removal of the Greek troops had also removed any justification for a Turkish military intervention at this time.

From the Cypriot point of view, President Makarios stated on the 12th January 1968 that *enosis* was no longer possible. Though it had been the desired aim for the Greek Cypriots, this aim had now to be replaced by what was possible. And what was possible was a regime of independence to be arrived at through negotiation with the Turkish Cypriots.

The talks started in auspicious circumstances. On the 12th March 1968 the Cyprus Government made proposals to the U.N. Secretary General aimed at constitutional revision in Cyprus which would reintegrate the Turkish Cypriots. Cyprus was to remain an independent Republic. The Cyprus Government accepted that the Turkish Cypriot position in the structure of the state would be a matter of negotiation, that is it was agreed by the Government that they would have a special position as a community and would not merely be guaranteed minority rights. There would be proportional representation in the civil service and political institutions and a special ministry of Turkish affairs.

At the first meeting of the negotiators for the two ethnic groups in Beirut in June 1968 Mr Denktas acknowledged that the Zurich constitution had contained unjust provisions for both communities. As examples of unjust provisions for the Turkish Cypriots he gave the provisions which had been the subject of such unbudging insistence in 1960-3. He said that the provision for separate municipalities imposed a heavy financial burden on his community. The provision for overrepresentation of the Turkish Cypriots in the civil service deprived the Turkish Cypriot community of young, able and educated persons in the private sector. He agreed to the elimination of these clauses if the Greek Cypriot side was to agree to some degree of local autonomy for the Turkish Cypriots. At this stage the claim for local autonomy seemed no more than a claim for the strengthening of the institutions of local government as he accepted that these powers and functions would be exercised subject to laws passed by the House of Representatives.[61]

At this stage the gap between the two positions seemed easily within the range of possible bridging. However this gap over the next six years during which the talks dragged on with interruptions, became a chasm. Only a summary of the issues involved need be indicated here. Firstly, it must be made clear that agreement was reached on numerous issues which had been the subject of dispute in the Zurich Constitution. It was agreed by November 1973 that veto powers of both the President and the Vice-President should be abolished; that the necessity for concurrent and separate majorities for representatives of the two ethnic groups for certain kinds of legislation should be abolished; that the separate Constitutional Court should be abolished and merged with a High Court composed of 6 Greek and 3 Turkish Cypriots; and that on a wide range of issues, the House of Representatives should divide into a Greek Cypriot and a Turkish Cypriot branch in order to legislate; Ministers of the Government and officials would be in proportion to the Greek and Turkish Cypriot population.[62]

The issue of disagreement, and the one on which agreement of the two sides seemed an increasingly tenuous possibility, was that of "local government". It is necessary to examine this issue a little more closely, for it was for years the crux of the Cyprus problem. It was an issue moreover on which the Cyprus Government made successive concessions, under pressure from all sides, and with increasing reluctance. At the beginning of the intercommunal talks the Greek Cypriot negotiator had regarded it as a natural assumption that, as in any system of local government, the local authorities in urban and rural areas where the Turkish Cypriots were a majority of the population would be Turkish Cypriot. In the "package deal proposals" of the Cyprus Government in November 1970, it was conceded that Turkish Cypriot villages could be grouped together for purposes of administration (even though these villages could not be contiguous due to the ethnic settlement pattern) to form *areas* of Turkish local government.[63] By the middle of 1973, it was agreed further that the two branches of the House of Representatives previously mentioned, the Greek Cypriot and the Turkish Cypriot ones, would be the bearers of central coordination and supervision of Greek and Turkish Cypriot areas respectively.[64] This was a move that was quite close to a federal arrangement.

The Turkish Cypriot positions however seem to have always kept ahead of Greek Cypriot concessions. The initial position of Mr Denktas seemed to be a far cry from the demands for partition of 1964 and 1965. It is true that from the beginning a demand for some kind of local autonomy was made. However, it was initially accepted that this autonomy would be subject to the laws of the Republic as legislated by the House of Representatives as a whole. But by the end of the first phase of the talks in 1968 the demand had intruded itself for this local autonomy to include police and judicial functions. In the course of the talks, the Turkish Cypriot position became an increasingly strong demand on three points: increasing territorially defined powers for the Turkish Cypriot community, increasing degrees of autonomy for the Turkish Cypriot community from the central organs of government, or rather an increasing tendency to demand that the Government of the Republic be composed of the central organs of local government for the two communities, and finally a demand for an increasing participation of Greece and Turkey in the affairs of Cyprus.

In April 1971, in reply to Mr Clerides' package proposals, Mr Denktas claimed that the powers of local authorities should be subject only to judicial and not to governmental supervision. He also demanded that the Greek Cypriot side stop using the word "unitary" in describing the resultant Cypriot state.[65] At the first session of the "reactivated communal talks", reinforced with the participation of Greek and Turkish constitutional experts in June 1972, Mr Denktas stated that the Turkish community should have such powers that it would become completely self-sufficient.[66] In proposals in December 1973 he demanded regional autonomy of such a degree for the

Turkish Cypriot community that it would be able to contract directly with foreign states in relation to financial and technical aid.[67] Two months previously, the Turkish constitutional expert had stated in an interview that he had suggested that the Turkish Cypriots should have rights of carrying on forestry work and water prospecting and drilling autonomously.[68] By June 1974 Mr Denktas was stating that:

> As an administration with regional autonomy we shall have administrative, legislative, executive and judicial powers. These powers will be used within the limits of Turkish municipalities and villages.[69]

These demands for separation based on territorial control and autonomous Governmental functions came accompanied by demands for an increasing participation of Greece and Turkey in the affairs of the two communities. In 1972 Mr Denktas wrote:

> Greece and Turkey are the motherlands of the two communities in Cyprus. In fact Greece and Turkey are in Cyprus through their own communities.

and described as "an unrealistic appraisal of the situation" the view that

> ... the Cypriots must find a peaceful solution to their problems on the basis of independence without outside interference.

And he added:

> Who are the Cypriots? In the absence of a nation of that name, Cypriots are (and continue to be) the extension of Greece in Cyprus through Greek Cypriots, and the extension of Turkey in Cyprus through Turkish Cypriots. How can it be said that attempts to settle the problem with the active help of Greece and Turkey is outside interference in the affairs of Cyprus ...
> Turkey and Greece can settle this problem in 24 hours and it is high time they did so, once and for all.[70]

In view of these positions and the previous positions of Turkey, the Cyprus Government had considerable misgivings that a settlement in the intercommunal talks would only be a stage on the path of partition. The ingredients were all there. Separate authority, territorial control and the demand for the involvement of Greece and Turkey. The main obstacle, said the Cypriot president in March 1973

> ... which slows down the progress of the talks is the issue of local Government. We are prepared to accept, to a certain degree, a form of

local Government, but not to such an extent that might lead to cantonization or federation. Such a settlement could at a later stage lead to partition. ...[71]

In spite of these fears and problems, the concessions made by the Turkish Cypriot side on the issues of the veto powers and reinforced representation and the concessions made by the Greek Cypriot side to the increasing demands for autonomy by the Turkish Cypriots appear to have led to a near agreement in November 1973. At least at this time optimism was expressed by both President Makarios[72] and Mr Clerides, the Greek Cypriot interlocutor.[73] These statements, however, as well as the judgement of a legal expert who has examined the documents relating to the intercommunal talks, to the effect that virtually all was over by the end of 1973 but the signing,[74] are puzzling. Though there was a wide range of agreement on many issues, there were still outstanding a number of crucial problems. These included such vital issues (that is vital for the survival of Cyprus as a state) as the organization and control of the police and army, the establishment of a unitary judiciary, the establishment of municipalities and a definitive list of powers of the Greek and Turkish Cypriot branches of the judiciary.[75] The agreement on other points was of no significance in the absence of agreement on these points, or at least was only significant procedurally and as a declaration of intent on the points on which agreement had been reached.

It is at least conceivable that the statements of optimism at this time were in reality appeals to those interested in a solution outside Cyprus to credit the island with a little more time. In November 1973 there were indications of U.S. pressure for a rapid conclusion of the intercommunal talks, accompanied by the threat that the U.S. would not necessarily find it "desirable or possible" to prevent a Greek-Turkish war over Cyprus.[76]

The full significance of the position of the U.S. at this time can only be seen in relation to its policy towards the Greek Junta, its relation to Turkey, its strategic difficulties in the eastern Mediterranean and its attitude to the Cyprus Government and the intercommunal talks. This has to wait for the last chapter.

## CHAPTER VI

# Greek Cypriot politics: the paradox of enosis after independence

One of the most important elements contributing to the idea of partitioning Cyprus was the propagation of the *enosis* ideology by those who had most to lose by such a solution—the Greek Cypriots. Though this outcome was unintended by virtually all who adhered to the ideology, it was in some ways recognized by some people and pointed out, but went unheeded on the whole, indicating that even recognition is not enough protection against the unforeseen consequences of our actions and beliefs, since the actions and beliefs are determined by other forces than the teleological perception of their consequences. This problem is even further complicated by the fact that symbols, in which many actions and ideologies are expressed, have different meanings for different groups. *Enosis* meant something very different to a Greek Cypriot businessman and a Turkish Cypriot official; the latter could not be expected to understand that what the businessman meant by "*enosis*" was not intended as a threat to him. What the two respectively meant by *enosis* is only comprehensible by reference to their historical experience and current relationships to groups in their own communities.

For the observer, the problem may pose itself as follows: since the configuration of international power made the achievement by the Greek Cypriots of incorporation with Greece impossible, and since all classes and political elites were deriving great economic and other benefits from independence, why did the apparently suicidal slogan of *enosis* continue to be an important expression of political orthodoxy? The answer to the question must lie in the bases and meanings it acquired in the relationships of different Greek Cypriot groups among themselves, and, as a community, with others, and must include other meanings that the overt one of incorporation with the State of Greece. The significance of the *enosis* movement and its persistence in a latent form as well as its militant resurgence can not be understood apart from its articulation with strategic interests in the eastern Mediterranean. It cannot be understood apart from the fact that while having a stable emotional appeal for the Greeks of Cyprus, its international significance changed from a movement by a colony to rid itself of British Government to a movement by an independent uncommitted state to dismember itself between two members of the Atlantic Alliance.

Though in the sense of a practical pursuit of the incorporation of Cyprus with Greece the idea was not entertained by any figure in the Cyprus Government after 1967, its presence was very significant indeed in the course of events in Cyprus. Its presence as an over-arching ideology prevented the development of political ideologies more in accord with the objective situation of the Cypriot State, which might have contributed to the resolution of its political problems.

It is true that, as described in the previous chapter, the position of the Turkish Cypriot leadership and of Turkey made it difficult to incorporate the Turkish Cypriots into the Cypriot State. But the political processes within the Greek Cypriot group were not favourable in their consequences for the resolution of the problem. The *enosis* ideology in recent years was not an expression of an intention to join Greece politically. But its dominance made the clear and public expression of the problems confronting the island impossible. No ideology found expression in Cyprus making the reintegration of the Turkish Cypriots a positive aim. There was no open articulation of a pro-independence ideology. Public political statements were loaded with the symbols of Hellenic nationalism associated with the *enosis* ideology, which as a practical aim was virtually universally acknowledged to be impossible.

It is quite clear that these ideological characteristics cannot be explained by the internal processes of Greek Cypriot politics alone. It must be said at the outset that this state of affairs was directly encouraged by the Greek Junta, and to varying degrees, whether directly or indirectly, by NATO and by the United States and even by the Turkish Cypriot leadership. But it is useless to point to these facts without identifying the vulnerability of Greek Cypriot politics to such intervention. The significance of trying to explain why the Greek Cypriot political process did not succeed in overcoming the emotional attractions of Hellenic nationalism and the *enosis* ideology lies precisely in the fact that the ideology could become the second Trojan Horse for Cyprus. For not only did expressions of Hellenic nationalism further consolidate the alienated position of the Turkish Cypriots and their susceptibility to separatist control, but also the fanatical bearers of the ideology of *enosis* become the direct, if unwitting, instruments for the invasion of Cyprus by Turkey. In this chapter then, the intrinsic weakness of Greek Cypriot political processes will be examined, leaving as far as is possible, for the next chapter discussion of the encouragement which the forces tending to the dissolution of the Republic received from outside.

The significance of the *enosis* ideology in Cyprus is more easily comprehensible if one bears in mind some of the most significant enosis central power about church.

elements of the career of the nationalist movement in Cyprus. This indicates that while its symbolic manifestation and psychological appeal was fairly constant over the years, its social significance varied considerably at different stages.[1] Its initial motivating force as a political movement had been bourgeois protest against unjust colonial taxation and inadequate political representation. It continued as a call by the Church for unity around itself rather than any other political agency, and most significantly, AKEL, the communist party. In its encounter with AKEL, the *enosis* ideology came to symbolize anti-communism. Thanks to British manoeuvres in the 50's, it also acquired elements of anti-Turkish meaning. It has already been pointed out that it fully identified the sense of Greek cultural identity with belongingness to the Greek Nation and the pursuit of incorporation with the Greek State. The point is that the multiplicity of meanings which it incorporated made it readily accessible to a wide variety of political groups.

In addition, as has been indicated in Chapter II, it acquired in the 1950's, the socially detached, messianic character of a religious symbol. It became psychologically engrained through education, association with the Orthodox religion and punishment at the hands of the colonial power. It must be remembered that the adult generation who were the constituents of a President following a non-aligned policy in the 1960's were the schoolboys who had experienced baton charges and worse at the hands of British troops and Turkish Cypriot auxiliary policemen in the 1950's in the cause of *enosis*. And some of the elder statesmen had been persecuted in the cause of *enosis* in 1931.

This capability of taking on a wide range of social meanings, combined with universal psychological appeal, is important in understanding the uses to which the *enosis* ideology could be put and the problems which it could involve.

The second important ideological characteristics of the Hellenic nationalist movement is very hard to explain without some familiarity with modern Greek culture. However, briefly it can be said that Greek culture is bifurcated into an official, "high culture" which is characterized by formalism, rigidity, authoritarianism, and since the civil war, intense anti-communism, and a popular, non-official culture of the literary and artistic worlds. The real contacts of Cypriots with Greek society were largely through two channels: the educational and the military. Both institutions (in spite of serious attempts to alter this situation in the educational system) are in Greece primary bearers of the official culture.[2] The school-teachers who had absorbed this official culture from the Greek university system naturally achieved prominence during the EOKA struggle against the British. Their narrow horizons, scholastic attitudes, political lack of realism and religious fervour in matters "national" hardly changed with the independence of Cyprus and their elevation to positions of authority in the educational system of the Republic. Far from it, in an independent republic where serious counter-trends were evident in the business world, the civil service and the communist party, they defined themselves as "the true believers" and the guardians of the purity of the Greek Cypriot soul. They decisively influenced the cultural life of the Republic, since their natural niche was the Greek Communal Chamber, which was responsible for Greek Cypriot educational and cultural affairs. The cultural dominance of this group of people, or rather their dominance over the means of dissemination of culture, contributed decisively to preventing Greek Cypriots from thinking realistically about their political problems, including the fact of the logical separability of sovereignty and cultural identity. When subsequently in this chapter reference is made to the lack of challenge to the *enosis* ideology, in practical terms the reference is to the content of the educational system, "serious" newspapers and journals, and national celebrations which this group of traditional intellectuals presided over. In spite of widespread private deriding of their attitudes, no serious political attempt was ever mounted against these bastions of political black magic.

This chapter then, is an attempt to rationally explicate deeply non-rational patterns of human behaviour. The Hellenic nationalist slogan of *enosis*, probably like any other emotionally held slogan, proved to be dangerous in its consequences. In this case it was because it could not be rejected in the public political process even though it was clear that it could no longer mean what it had originally meant. This, in Cyprus of the last ten years, made rational political discourse virtually impossible. The slogan could be manipulated to purposes quite different or even opposed to its overt meaning. Its overt meaning could be taken up at opportune moments to justify actions bearing no relation to it. In other words, it reduced politics to chaos.

These facts can only be regarded as factually contradictory to the real development of "Cypriot consciousness" among the Greek Cypriots if two facts are overlooked. The first fact is that the reiteration of the tenets of official Greek culture and Hellenic nationalism was the main peg on which a small group of political ritualists hung their high status and not the habitual manner of thought of the mass of Greek Cypriots. Far from it, these expressions were regarded as ritual and separate from everyday life by most people. But secondly it must be remembered that ritual does create real emotions. And these emotions may be contrary to both habitual patterns of thought and action and to rational reflection. To put it simply, any Cypriot businessman who knew that his business might collapse in the case of union with Greece and who habitually planned on the basis of the continuing independence of Cyprus, might also be stirred by the nationalist oratory which passed for political commentary in many public contexts.

The main factors entering the dynamics of the Greek Cypriot political process and making the renunciation of the symbols of Hellenic nationalism extremely difficult can be interpreted as products of the interaction of the main political forces in Greek Cypriot politics. Here an explanation will be sought for the paradox of a policy of independence in practice and of adherence to the *enosis* ideal in theory, by examining the interaction of the communist party of Cyprus with the Church of Cyprus, the development of political factions out of EOKA, the social and political position of the Greek Cypriot bourgeoisie and the factor of mainland Greece in Greek Cypriot politics. It is the interaction of these factors which created a kind of ideological paralysis in Greek Cypriot politics.

The conditions of the anti-colonial struggle in Cyprus created a sequence of political situations, which resulted by the 1960's in paradoxical postures both by the Church of Cyprus and the Communist Party of Cyprus. What is important as an end result in the position of the communist party of Cyprus by the time just before the coup and the Turkish invasion was its degree of docility, and acceptance of the line of the President of Cyprus, Archbishop Makarios. It also involved a weak position in relation to the problem of Hellenic nationalism and the Turkish Cypriots. The political force which one would have expected to take the most militant ideological and practical position in favour of the development of post-colonial nationalism in Cyprus seemed highly reluctant to do so. This was to a very large extent the result of the historical position in which AKEL had been placed through its non-participation in the anti-colonial struggle.

The communist party of Cyprus had, at various times since its foundation in 1926, held different views of what the anti-imperialist aims of the Cypriots should be. From its foundation until 1933, when it was declared illegal by the colonial government, it followed a left, united front from below strategy, arguing for the unity of Greek and Turkish Cypriots against the colonial government and against the Ethnarchy. In December 1931 the communist party (KKK) issued a manifesto, which in contrast to the bourgeoisie and the Church, rejected the slogan of *enosis*. It supported instead the immediate satisfaction of the economic demands of workers and peasants. It expressed opposition to the nationalist leaders and their "counter-revolutionary slogan" of *enosis*, called for a united front against imperialism of the toiling Turks and Greeks and posed as an ultimate aim a "free workers and peasants Soviet Republic of Cyprus".[3] At the beginning of the Second World War, the colonial government legalized political parties in Cyprus, which had been banned since 1933. A popular front party, AKEL, was then formed. Virtually from its inception AKEL adopted the aim of *enosis*, engaged in militant trade union and anti-colonial actions and still opposed the leadership of the Church in the anti-colonial struggle.

The time during and just after the war was a period of very strong gains in electoral support for AKEL. At the first municipal elections to be held after the legalization of parties, in 1943, AKEL won in two of the six main towns. In 1946 the party gained electoral control of four of the main towns. AKEL had become a very significant political force indeed, with a possibility of wresting the leadership of the anti-colonial struggle from the Church.

There are indications that what AKEL meant by *enosis* at this time was not precisely the same thing as what the Ethnarchy meant. This is not crystal clear, because AKEL appears to have followed a fluctuating policy on the "national issue" which was probably the result of the conflict between the aim of electoral popularity and its diagnosis of the political factors in the colonial situation. AKEL leaders had always indicated awareness of the problem of the Turkish Cypriots. On the other hand they aimed to appeal electorally to the nationalistically fired Greek Cypriots. But certainly there are indications that AKEL meant "We are ultimately in favour of *enosis* but ...", ironically a position similar to that adopted by the Archbishop in the 60's.

Twice before the beginning of the EOKA campaign, AKEL leaders had supported the aim of *enosis* before an international communist audience. These occasions were in 1947 and in 1954 at the conferences in London of the communist parties within the sphere of the British Empire. The reasoning was similar on both occasions, and quite different from the reasoning of the Ethnarchy. *Enosis* was a progressive aim since it would remove Cyprus from the British Empire and eliminate its potential use as an Imperial base in the Middle East. The majority of the population was in favour of incorporation with Greece. The fact that Greece was a "monarcho-fascist" regime was irrelevant since this regime was imposed by external force and would soon collapse. In 1947 a conference resolution supported the AKEL position in favour of *enosis*.[4] In fact, during the next year, in Cyprus, AKEL agreed to discuss British constitutional proposals which would have led to self-government, not immediate *enosis*. Negotiations failed partly because of the position of the Greek communist party which argued that the Cypriot communists should not be negotiating for constitutional changes at a time when they, the Greeks, were conducting an armed struggle[5] against the same foe.

In 1951 AKEL cooperated with the Ethnarchy in conducting a plebiscite in favour of *enosis*. The essence of the difference became the leadership of the struggle. In 1954 the AKEL secretary general pointed out that AKEL was not asking for a constitution but for union with Greece. But he condemned the "traitorous policy of the monarcho-fascist government" in Greece, and the "so-called Ethnarchy in Cyprus". He supported a united patriotic front to achieve *enosis*, but under the leaderships of AKEL, rather than the Church.[6] However, during the same year, at the AKEL party congress, the view that *enosis* would soon be achieved was rejected as ridiculous and misleading.[7]

In spite of AKEL's full support for *enosis* and in spite of its acceptance of the "no compromise with the British" position, AKEL condemned EOKA when it started the anti-British armed struggle in 1955 at the same time as the Greek Communist Party did so. At this time AKEL completely rejected the tactics of EOKA as anti-Leninist and as substituting tactics of individual terrorism for mass struggle.[8] The left wing trade union organization expressed its opposition to EOKA on the grounds that it would separate Greek and Turkish Cypriots.[9] AKEL maintained this opposition for some time, and in May 1956 the party addressed itself to all Cypriots, Greek and Turkish, left wing and right wing and appealed for a democratic mass struggle against the colonialists and not for a factional struggle which seemed to lead to civil war.[10]

Once again, however, AKEL was not able to maintain a courageous, and essentially correct, position once it had taken it. The pressure appears to have once again come from the Greek Communist Party, which after a purge of its leadership in 1957, and in contrast to its initial position, supported the EOKA struggle.[11]

It is an apparent paradox that in spite of their opposition to EOKA, the AKEL leaders had been interned by the colonial power in November 1955. In view of the fact that AKEL had formed a bridge between Greek and Turkish Cypriots, and in view of previous and subsequent British policy, the reasons for their internment would be an interesting topic for research once the colonial archives are open. On their release in 1957, and apparently after a party split, AKEL admitted that its estimation of the character of EOKA as a trap to eliminate communists and to further the imperialists' plans had been an error, but justified its opposition to the armed struggle on the grounds that the positions of the Greek, U.S. and British Governments and the "Turkish factor" made the possibilities of success of an armed struggle very small.[12]

It is likely that these fluctuations were based on several objective problems which AKEL had to face. One was that *enosis* was already an established ideology, on which the leadership of the Ethnarchy was based. The Ethnarchy may have feared AKEL's electoral position. But AKEL was also probably worried that the Ethnarchy's ideological strength posed a problem to its own electoral position. In the May 1949 elections, which closely followed AKEL's participation in the

110

British constitutional conference, it lost all but two of the towns it controlled.

AKEL also appears to have been aware that, though support of *enosis* was an internal political necessity, the possibility of its immediate achievement was very small in view of the importance of Cyprus in British strategic considerations and in view of the Turkish factor. Being the strongest organisation which bridged the two ethnic groups of Cyprus, it must have been peculiarly conscious of the problem. Hence the position of AKEL had pragmatic consistency in its opposition to an armed struggle, agreeing to consider the possibility of a gradual transition of seeking to integrate the Turkish Cypriots. But all this was pursued under the ideological umbrella of *enosis*.

However, the fact that an armed struggle did take place without AKEL participation had drastic long-term consequences. AKEL lost the possibility of decisively influencing events during the course of the armed struggle or after independence. It was forced to seek an alliance with the Church leadership largely on the Church's terms. This alliance has lasted until 1978 with only a short interruption. The question of the political position of AKEL in the course of events in Cyprus since 1955 is of major importance. Firstly, because it is the oldest, largest and only bureaucratically organized Cypriot party, and secondly, because it is a communist party, that is a party that might have been expected to play a major role in the development of "post-colonial" rather than Hellenic and Turkish nationalism in Cyprus. Right wing nationalist critics have accused AKEL of being treacherous for this reason. But what is more significant is the more socially oriented criticism of left wing critics.

The most important criticism, by an ex-member of AKEL[13], points out that the consequences of AKEL's non-participation in the anti-British armed struggle have been: that it weakened the party's ability to subsequently oppose the Zurich agreements; that it lost support from the youth, the intellectuals, the middle farmers, the white collar workers and the petite bourgeoisie; that AKEL's non-participation in revolutionary activity made Cypriot revolutionaries available for the leadership of "any socialist charlatan" and that it gave communists the reputation of being deficient in their contribution to the national cause. This is no doubt all plausible. But whether AKEL had the political scope for acting differently from the way it did is not so easy to establish. Nor is it easy to establish that AKEL participation in EOKA would have had purely positive consequences. As it is, AKEL can claim that it is a major political party in Cyprus whose members have never engaged in ethnic conflict and have never exacerbated the traditional nationalisms of the Cypriots.

There is no doubt that the position of AKEL and its room for ideological manoeuvre became extremely limited after the establishment of the Zurich Republic. The limits of AKEL's room for manoeuvre were set by two parameters. One was its own defined anti-imperialist aims in a situation where Cyprus was clearly militarily dominated by NATO powers with a claim of legal justification for intervention. The other parameter was the need to maintain its position among the Greek Cypriot majority of the population, particularly in view of its non-participation in the armed struggle. These parameters were not only limiting, but were also contradictory. In practice, both of these aims did little to develop an ideology and practice of reintegrating the Turkish Cypriots. In general the problem can be phrased as follows.

The anti-imperialist aims of AKEL involved attempts to alter the Zurich and London constitution which it interpreted as being an imperialist imposition on Cyprus. AKEL leaders must also have been aware that the party could never come to power and stay there while the guarantors of Cyprus were NATO powers. Hence AKEL's support for attempts to revise the constitution in 1963. Cyprus was still at a stage of attempting to complete its national liberation.[14] There were "reactionary and anti-democratic elements in the London and Zurich agreement". But the main objections were to the presence of British bases on Cyprus, Greek and Turkish troops, the right to use communications facilities in Cyprus by British troops and the forced Alliance of Cyprus with the "Guarantor Powers". Hence, AKEL supported the President's attempt to alter the structure of the agreements under which Cyprus became independent.[15]

AKEL was fully aware that these changes could only come about if there was a joint effort between Greek and Turkish Cypriots and pointed out that

> Anti-imperialist understanding and cooperation between Greek and Turkish Cypriots is a decisive factor for the success of the struggle of the Cypriot people for peace, economic advance, democracy and complete independence.[16]

But its practical ability to ensure this was severely limited after TMT's dislocation of trade union ties of the Turkish Cypriot working class to AKEL. It also, together with all other Greek Cypriot political factions, seems to have underestimated the degree to which the Zurich agreements had a real significance for the Turkish Cypriots as a guarantee of some degree of power-sharing in the Cypriot State, so the 1963 events were seen mainly as a

> ... revolt of Turkish extremists engineered by Western imperialists and by chauvinist elements in Ankara.[17]

112

Subsequently, AKEL could take important conciliatory positions and make valuable suggestions for re-establishing the links with the Turkish Cypriots. For example, in 1966 at its eleventh congress the party called for the creation of committees of Greek and Turkish Cypriots in mixed villages to enlighten Greek and Turkish Cypriots on the correct attitudes and policies to each other, and also for members of parliament and government officials to actively propagate and enlighten people on the nature of the Government measures for reintegrating the Turkish Cypriots.[18]

AKEL also attempted, where conditions allowed, to maintain and rebuild contacts with Turkish Cypriot Trade Unionists. In the 1966 and 1967 party congresses, Turkish Cypriots from the United Kingdom and Turks from Bulgaria came and attempted to form a link between AKEL and Turkish Cypriot workers in Cyprus.[19] Also, until 1974, PEO, the left wing trade union organization, maintained relations with the Patriotic Union of Turkish Cypriots. This was a Turkish Cypriot trade union organization partly composed of Turkish Cypriots who had been members of PEO before they were forced to secede in 1958, and also of elements of the Turkish Peoples Party formed by the social democrats Hikmet and Gurkan who had been assassinated by Turkish Cypriot right wing extremists in 1962. They were mainly active among the Turkish Cypriot workers who worked in the government controlled areas, but they also maintained some degree of underground organization within the enclaves controlled by the Turkish Cypriot Leadership.

More than any other Greek Cypriot political force, AKEL saw the necessity for cooperation betweeen Greek and Turkish Cypriots. At the thirteenth party congress in April 1974 the secretary general of the party reviewed the tragic state of separation that was gradually being established between the communities, especially the youth, and also saw the need for measures by the Greek Cypriots to reestablish contact.

> In order that the Cyprus Turkish youth may be detached from the destructive chauvinist policy (of their leadership) it should be given the opportunity to know the advantages of the policy of cooperation with the Greek Cypriots. And it is exactly here that against the policy of non-cooperation the policy of all-sided cooperation for the benefit of the people should be arranged.

Programmes of resettling the Turkish Cypriot refugees, road-building and disposal of agricultural products, could "by proper handling attract the broad mass of the Turkish Cypriots away from chauvinist influences towards closer cooperation with the Government and the Greek Cypriot side". Such programmes of cooperation would create a favourable climate for the success of the intercommunal talks and would also contribute to the development of democratic and progressive forces within the Turkish Cypriot community.[20]

AKEL leaders, if criticised on being deficient in their role as bearers of a post-colonial nationalism in Cyprus, will point to such facts as the ones cited in the previous pages as an indication of AKEL's conciliatory and constructive role in relation to the Turkish Cypriots. But these positions were never militantly maintained by AKEL. Since 1957, and with one exception, AKEL not only largely accepted an identity of aims with the Church of Cyprus, but also acquiesced to the leadership of the Church. Ideologically what this meant was a definition of Cyprus as being at a stage of pursuing "national liberation", and thus requiring unity between all patriotic forces. The target in this respect were the foreign bases on Cyprus and Western influences. But the ultimate aim of national liberation remained for the AKEL leaders unclear. Generally it was implied that it was that of *enosis*. On the surface this was an odd ideological stance for the communist party of Cyprus.

It seems more than likely that what the slogan of "*enosis*-in-the-distant-future" symbolised for AKEL was the need for political unity among the Greek Cypriots. This will become more easily understood when the "Grivas faction" is discussed. But the point is that ever since 1964 support for or opposition to *enosis* had acquired cold war international significance. As has already been pointed out, after the involvement of Turkey, and particularly after 1963 and the Acheson Plan, the pursuit of *enosis* essentially meant the partition of Cyprus between Greece and Turkey. Within Cyprus, there was always a small faction which, either due to ignorance or due to acceptance of partition in preference to independence, were known as the *enosists*. Both President Makarios and AKEL chose to face the danger of this minority increasing in popularity *not* by denouncing *enosis* as an ultimate aim, but rather by arguing that in the long run they were in favour of pure *enosis* (between 1963 and 1968), or that *enosis* was the desirable aim, but it was impracticable (after 1968). *Enosis*, they presumably judged, was too deeply ingrained a slogan and its renunciation by the main representative political forces in Cyprus would lead to an increase in support for the *enosist* minority.

At the eleventh congress, in 1966, AKEL described its position as follows. It condemned the rabble rousing slogan of "*Enosis* Now" which was encouraged by the imperialists and would lead to partition. It supported the broadest possible anti-imperialist unity of all patriotic forces, Greeks, Turks, Armenians the right and the left. AKEL was in favour of *enosis*, but in the long run and after various stages. "AKEL is most sincere in its support of the Government on the basis of the line of unfettered independence—self-determination—genuine *enosis* without bases, interventions or concessions."[21]

AKEL has always supported this position on the basis of the need for unity. In 1970 a party publication defended the line on unity.[22] In November 1964 according to the publication the Minister of Foreign Affairs of the Republic had said in the House of Representatives that

> ... the only weapon left in the hands of the enemies of the Cypriot aim is the division of the Greek Cypriot front. We know that agents of foreign powers are spreading seeds of divisiveness and are cultivating the soil to break up the Greek front.

These agents, according to AKEL, were those poeple who were accusing Makarios, the Left and others among those who supported the realistic patriotic line of uncommitted independence as anti-*enosists* and were projecting the slogan of achieving *enosis* through a coup, an aim which involved deadly dangers. The general secretary pointed out at this time that,

> ... wearing the mask of the *enosist* the Anglo-Americans and their agents try to conceal their real policy which is partition and the enslavement of Cyprus to NATO.

As a defence against these plots, the party chose not the renunciation of the *enosis* slogan, but the adoption of the aim in a purified form.

> What we want is national liberation and in Cyprus this means *enosis*—but we want genuine *enosis* and not of the kind proposed by Acheson.[23]

AKEL immediately commended and itself adopted the statement by Makarios in 1968, that *enosis* in its "genuine" form was no longer attainable. The party supported the aim of complete independence, in the place of the previous aim of "genuine *enosis*". Henceforth, in line with the President, *enosis* would be referred to as the "desirable" but impractical aim. As such it was still referred to by party leaders in 1971. Its use in this context clearly indicates its function. By this time, armed groups were attempting to overthrow the government claiming that *enosis* was immediately possible. The general secretary of the left wing trade unions pointed out that,

> If the people follow those whom Makarios has called imprudent and attempt through illegality and violence to achieve what is the wish of all, the catastrophe will be unavoidable.[24]

Though the retention of the *enosis* slogan for AKEL served the function of maintaining unity among the Greek Cypriots, both the unity and the slogan it was achieved under indicated a fundamental weakness in the party's position. The emphasis on anti-imperialism and national liberation and the identification of this aim with *enosis* left no more room for AKEL than for the bourgeois leadership with which it cooperated to practically mobilize and ideologically rouse the Cypriots to the need for an inter-ethnic united front within Cyprus.

There is no doubt that no matter how understandable under the circumstances, the "*enosis* in the future" slogan resulted in problems of both omission and confusion in AKEL policy. A good example of the former is that the secretary general of AKEL could write an article in 1974 on "strengthening the unity of the people"[25] where the main ideological problem to be justified was that of the support given by AKEL to President Makarios, without mention of the problem of the Turkish Cypriot population or of the ultimate aims of this support.

The confusion is indicated in the position of AKEL on the status of the Cypriot national problem. In January 1965 the Foreign Minister of the Soviet Union, Mr Gromyko, had made a statement implying the possibility of a federation between Greek and Turkish Cypriots. AKEL criticized this position. But two of the arguments used indicate a fundamental unclarity in AKEL's views of the internal arrangements in the future of the demilitarized and non-aligned Cypriot Republic which the struggle for self-determination would result in. "We start from the basic position" the AKEL statement said

> that the essence of the Cypriot national problem does not lie in the creation of a separate national entity, with a separate national conscience, but to the national restoration of the Cypriot people, which in its overwhelming majority is Greek.[26]

But while rejecting the possibility of a Cypriot entity with a Cypriot national conscience, AKEL also rejected in the same statement the existence of two national communities in Cyprus:

> The Cyprus problem is *not* a matter of two national communities, but of the Cypriot people as a whole.[27]

It is clear then that the major party of post colonial nationalism in Cyprus did not successfully further the *ideological* strengthening of the Cypriot state. The same can be said of the Government of Cyprus. But to understand the reasons for this one must understand the development of political factions out of the anti-colonial organization, EOKA, the position of the "Archbishop" as an institution rather than as a person and the impact of Greece on Greek Cypriot politics. Briefly the main shape of events can be summarized as follows. The Ethnarchy, which had partly embarked on the EOKA struggle because of the communist threat in Cyprus, gradually adopted on the "national issue" a policy which was quite similar to that of the communist party of Cyprus. This was under the impact of international circumstances. The military leader of EOKA took with him a small faction of his organization after independence which militantly opposed the policy of the Ethnarchy, now part of the Government. The Government was under continual ideological and, after 1968, armed attack from this group. It was severely limited in possible reactions because of the support for them by the Right Wing Greek Governments which controlled the Cypriot armed forces. Under the circumstances the power of the Cypriot president to follow an ideological line denouncing the nominal claim to "*enosis*-in-the-distant-future" would be to run a serious risk of hastening the coup which finally took place in July 1974. The *enosis* movement in Cyprus was basically maintained through the terrorism of the Greek Junta, its officers in Cyprus and the small group of Greek Cypriots who supported them. In the next chapter it will be shown how Western and U.S. policy strengthened exactly those irrational forces for *enosis* and opposed those forces which tended towards integration with the Turkish Cypriots and independence.

The historical position of the Church in Cyprus has already been discussed, as well as the Ethnarchic role of the Archbishop. For conservative Cypriots, the Archbishop had been the natural leader of the nationalist anti-colonial uprising, particularly since no secular political representation had been allowed to develop by the colonial government after the 1931 uprising. (The communist party and AKEL had survived with some continuity due to the techniques of underground organization which Leninist parties come to master.) In the process of the independence struggle, the position of the Archbishop was challenged by the military leader of EOKA, General Grivas. This challenge proved unsuccessful, but with time more and more bitter as the international experience of conducting the liberation struggle brought the Archbishop politically closer to the positions of AKEL.

It has already been mentioned that conditions in 1955 were unpropitious for a successful campaign for union with Greece. The attempts of the Greek Government in the U.N. came nowhere near success and received no assistance from its western allies. The British put forward the claim that Turkey's interest should be considered. The Greek Government soon realised that the course embarked on might lead to partition. And so did Makarios. Two years to the month after the beginning of the struggle, Makarios wrote to Grivas arguing

for the cessation of the armed struggle.[28] A formula for the independence of Cyprus was already considered in the place of the
original aim of *enosis*.

Grivas was not exposed either to international pressures, or to
contact with the internal Cypriot political forces due to his forced
underground confinement. He considered such thoughts of compromise as coming from Makarios only because he was surrounded
with the "decay of the towns", that is the dominant class and
intellectuals who in his view had stayed out of the struggle. Also to
cease hostilities would be to strengthen the communists who had been
arguing against the armed campaign all along.[29] His insistence on an
uncompromising continuation of the struggle brought him into conflict
with both AKEL and the bourgeoisie of Cyprus, and ultimately
tended to concentrate all important political groups under Makarios.

It was not unnatural for an anti-communist of long pedigree like
Grivas to come into conflict with AKEL. He found it easy to interpret
the non-participation of the party in the armed struggle as betrayal.
Several members of AKEL, including leading trade unionists were
executed by EOKA as traitors. Makarios appears not to have shared
this dread of communism. As early as 1952 he refused to be
intimidated by charges in the British press that he was bringing the
Church into an alliance with communists.[30] (AKEL had cooperated
with the Church in conducting a plebiscite on the *enosis* question in
1950.) In the spring of 1957 word got to Grivas that Makarios had
shown sympathy for the leftist mayors who had gone to see him to
protest against the killing of two leftists by EOKA.[31]

In the course of the struggle, at the end of 1957, General Grivas
conceived of a passive resistance campaign, the purpose of which was
to give an opportunity for mass participation in the struggle. The
campaign involved a boycott of British and British Commonwealth
goods by Cypriot merchants and consumers. Cypriot merchants were
at this time exclusively oriented to the British metropolitan market
and, in spite of the efforts of EOKA to find alternative markets, they
suffered losses, the main result of which was alienation of the
bourgeoisie from Grivas. Makarios appealed to him to halt the
campaign and deepened the rift between the two.[32]

These experiences shaped the relations between Makarios and
Grivas. Henceforth, Grivas would nurse his hurt pride as a messianic
nationalist who is willing to sacrifice all for the cause, and who is
prepared to reduce all to ashes and dust in the service of Hellenic
nationalism. Even in view of the desperate plight of Cyprus in 1959
and the danger of partition, the Greek Foreign Minister and
Makarios delayed acquainting him with the independence agreement,
for fear that he would opt for a heroic continuation of the armed fight.
He continued to be, until his death, the living, if atavistic symbol of

Grivas poisoned from outside

the Church-induced messianic nationalism of the 1940's and the early 1950's. As such the degree of "destabilization" that he could cause if his nationalist impulses were unleashed was no doubt much greater than that of any CIA agent. This fact is unlikely to have gone unobserved in Athens, Ankara and Washington.

Immediately after independence, the presidency of Archbishop Makarios was opposed by an odd coalition composed of the Democratic Party, a small group who agreed with Grivas that the EOKA struggle should continue, and AKEL, on the main grounds that the Agreements had placed Cyprus securely in the sphere of influence of NATO. As Makarios developed a non-aligned policy, AKEL support was restored, but there was never a way of satisfying the small groups who craved for instant *enosis*.

In view of the fiasco of the passive resistance campaign and the obvious military dangers of continuing the armed uprising, Makarios did not find it difficult to secure after independence the support of the bourgeoisie in the creation of a broad conservative political force, the Patriotic Front. The bourgeoisie had no political organisation independent of the Ethnarchy. The factional political structure in Cyprus, virtually until the present, with various realignments and changes of name, revolved around five men who inherited EOKA.

The two most important elements of the Patriotic Front formed around Georkadjis who became Minister of the Interior and around the Archbishop through the Church and other organizations. Georkadjis took with him from the original EOKA organization anti-communism, but not the kind of political blindness which considered the pursuit of *enosis* a viable proposition under all circumstances. Those directly linked with the Archbishop accepted the necessity for cooperating with AKEL both on the national and on the village level. The other two factions which also at this time joined the Patriotic Front are distinguished by being much smaller and by the fact that they did not staff the civil service and government of the Republic as the leaders of the first two factions did. One, led by Nikos Sampson, occupied an intermediate position between Grivas and Makarios. The other, led by Vassos Lyssarides, occupied an intermediate position between AKEL and Makarios. Grivas retired to Athens as he was forced to do so by the Agreements. But he maintained his political contacts in Cyprus and organized the final faction, the kernel of what will be referred to as the *enosist* Opposition to Makarios. The relation between this faction and President Makarios was very different, because unlike the others which were aspiring successors, Grivas actually commanded to varying degrees the loyalty of all ex-EOKA members. In other words this was no successor faction but a potentially challenging one. Until his death in 1974 Grivas remained as a pole of attraction for the disaffected and disillusioned of Cypriot society. Those who became dissatisfied with the "Makarios establishment" whether for personal or political reasons could gravitate to the *enosist* faction and dress their grievance in impeccable terms of intense Hellenic nationalism. The potential threat to the position of the Archbishop-President and the policies he represented lay in the fact that *enosis*, unlike any other conceivable political slogan, had been built in as an emotional release trigger for all Greek Cypriots who had been brought up by Greek Cypriot families and had attended Greek Cypriot schools.

Under these circumstances, all political leaders among the Greek Cypriots considered the 1960 form of independence as a temporary arrangement. In July 1960 Grivas openly stated his intention to continue the *enosis* fight and formed the Cyprus Enosist Front.[33] Later the Enosist opposition accused Makarios that he had abandoned all intentions of achieving *enosis* after 1960, but persuaded his political colleagues that independence was a new stage to *enosis*, while having no actual intention of following this course.[34] It may be that Makarios was going through the motions of preparing for a new stage of the *enosis* struggle in order to avert an armed insurrection on the part of the *enosists*.

It has been claimed that the Patriotic Front leaders prepared a staged contingency plan for the transition from independence to *enosis*. What is clear is that all Greek Cypriot political leaders, including those of AKEL,[35] supported the President's initiative in attempting to revise the provisions of the Zurich constitution, a change which by resulting in "unfettered independence" might make *enosis* possible as a next step.

The period of 1964-7 was the heyday of unity among Greek Cypriot factions. If external threats engender unity then there was a great deal to be united about. Turkey threatened to intervene four times in 1964 alone. The United States as a price for holding it off sent a succession of emissaries to persuade Makarios to accept partition under the guise of *enosis*. The post-Papandreou Greek Governments were clothing their secret talks with the Turkish Government in the same dress. These talks did not succeed probably because the Turkish Government asked for too much in exchange for *enosis*, either in Cyprus or in Greece. Yet the *enosists* led by General Grivas maintained with absolute certainty from this time on that the Cyprus Government had frustrated the Greek Governments' talks with Turkey which would have resulted in the dream of *enosis* coming true.

Why did the Government of Cyprus not at this time clearly renounce the idea of *enosis*? After all, the events of 1964 had amply shown that the Greek air force could not defend Cyprus let alone secure it for the Greek State. They had clearly shown that the pursuit of *enosis* would result in partition. This failure may certainly have been a political mistake. It might have been the lesser of several risks to have engaged in a clear and unambiguous renunciation of *enosis*. But there were several elements inducing the Cyprus Government to maintain an insistence on "unadulterated *enosis*". Firstly, there was the threat that the *enosists*, those who really believed that *enosis* was possible or partition desirable, would monopolise the emotive slogan. Secondly, there was the contradiction of a conservative government following a non-aligned policy with the internal support of a communist party and the international support of the Soviet Union. President Makarios was faced with the blind anti-communism of the U.S. press and its influence on conservative Greek politicians. This is an example:

> ... the comparison of Makarios to Castro goes beyond the fact that they both wear beards. Heedless of consequences each has flouted the interest of others, and each has appeared to be the prisoner of more extreme factions.[36]

Adherence to the *enosis* slogan was a signal that in the long run the alliance with AKEL was tactical, not ideological, and that the non-aligned policy did not imply an anti-Western orientation.

Non-alignment provided useful diplomatic support, but no military backing against a possible intervention from mainland Turkey. The Soviet practical support started waning before it had fully waxed. Makarios also prudently relied on the general deterrent effect of Greece against a possible Turkish intervention. *Enosis* symbolized a claim on the part of the Greek Cypriots to be entitled to defence by the Greek armed forces in the case of attack by Turkey.

This situation was insolubly ambiguous. Makarios in his search for the preservation of the wholeness of Cyprus and the sheer physical survival of the Cypriots fully embodied this ambiguity. This as well as his apparently infallible role as a saviour in the face of incredible odds made for his enigma and his charisma. "He knew" A. Papandreou has written after meeting him

> ... how to talk for hours without giving a hint of his value system, strategy, or tactics. He was not just a president, not just an archbishop; he was a chief, in the tribal sense. He was identified with the cause of independence and self-determination. But beyond that, he was considered by the Cypriots as the almost infallible personification of their country. Anyone who thought that there might be a solution of the Cyprus problem without Makarios' explicit approval was hopelessly out of touch with reality.[37]

There is no doubt however that the "independence in practice, *enosis* in theory" position of the Cyprus Government created severe problems in the ultimate securing of the independence of Cyprus and in reconciliation with the Turkish Cypriots. The fact that the President was the Archbishop further complicated the issues.

The Church of Cyprus does not have the hierarchical structure of the Catholic Church. The Archbishop is in fact the bishop of a certain area of Cyprus, "first among equals" of a number of bishops. The Church of Cyprus is composed of all the Bishops who together form the "Holy Synod", the only central governing organ of the Church of Cyprus. (A number of monasteries come under no jurisdiction whatsoever other than that of the Emperor of Byzantium.) There is no church bureaucracy of the Church of Cyprus. In the early fifties the Ethnarchic Council, composed of clergy and non-communist secular appointed officials, was revived to advise the Archbishop on the conduct of the liberation struggle.

What this means in practice is that the Archbishop has the capacity to represent the Church of Cyprus, partly organizationally but mainly as the collective of the orthodox clergy and laity of Cyprus, without being specifically encumbered or tied to the decisions of a Church hierarchy. This made his position rather flexible. This in many senses justifies the Archbishop's statement in 1974 that the Church as an institution, at least in Cyprus, is not intrinsically conservative, nor does it necessarily represent conservative interests.[38] The Church, though it is the oldest, wealthiest and most powerful organization in Cyprus does not, as an institution, have intrinsic interests of its own. After all, those who administer the Church neither marry and have descendants, nor are they recruited from a particular class. And in the case of Cyprus, nor are they tied to the interests of a particular class through a Church hierarchy. The Church has the capacity to alter its policies. And for many years of colonial rule, the Archbishop was the only representative figure for whom all Greek Cypriots voted. It is not surprising then that all significant political movements in Cyprus, including on one occasion, the communist party, have at some stage attempted to capture the church politically. Political crises have at some stage always expressed themselves as Church crises.

Archishop Makarios' power in Cyprus has always been great, but it has also always been delicately balanced. And without the full retention of this power he could not have followed the flexible international policy which enabled him to steer Cyprus through so many dangers. On the whole, as shown above, the policy was pragmatically consistent, the only way perhaps for the wholeness of Cyprus to be preserved for as long as it was. But ideologically it could hardly bear discussion. External political conditions forced the necessity of following a policy of "Independence and *enosis*", "non-alignment and belongingness to the western world". Internally, parties, factions and organizations had to tolerate a considerable degree of vagueness in their positions in order to be able to support the institution of the Archbishop-President and the policies which he represented.

His internal power was built on two constellations of factors. The first was that while he had the allegiance of all political groups other than the *enosists*, he was the leader of none. "I am powerful because I am weak."[39] In this sense his position was much closer to that of a monarch than of a president. His position did not, as does that of most presidents, depend on the support of a major political party. As monarch, his position did not depend on heredity, but on Ethnarchy. This carried with it both the symbolism of the Hellenism of Cyprus and of its local characteristics, its specific regional interests in relation to Greece, as well as its Greekness.

This symbolic power would perhaps have been unstable were it not based on substantial socio-economic powers. They derived from the fact of the leadership of the wealthiest single organization in Cyprus and the foundation and presidency of the state during a time of virtually uninterrupted economic growth and expansion of both the private and state economies. The power at his disposal emanated from supervision of the considerable property of the Archbishopric, influence over the use of the wealth of some of the monasteries, as well as influence over many state appointments and appointments in public corporations and the cooperative movement. But the legitimation of this material power was the symbolic power described in the previous paragraph.

This kind and degree of power had built-in constraints. From the point of view of the main problem of this chapter, the most important was the necessity for symbolic attachment to Hellenic nationalism, to a degree over and above that required by the problems already outlined. Two of the most important practical implications were in relation to the pattern of resistance to interventions on the part of the Greek Junta, and in relation to official Greek culture in Cyprus.

As will be subsequently shown in this chapter, the interventions of the Greek Junta in Cyprus were strenuously resisted. But this resistance was first publicly expressed by the Archbishop in June 1974, that is after about seven years of "secret war" between the Greek Junta and the Cyprus Government. While every Cypriot knew that Greek army officers in Cyprus were aiding illegal terrorist groups and there was widespread suspicion of their involvement in assassination attempts against the President, these were not facts in public. For Archbishop Makarios to attack the representatives of Greece in Cyprus would have been to attack part of his own symbolic essence.

123

Similarly, the structure of official Greek culture in Cyprus was never reformed. When the Greek educational system experienced some long-overdue reforms under the administration of George Papandreou in 1964-5, they were adopted with alacrity in the Greek Cypriot educational system. But with the accession of the dictators in 1967 their obscurantist counter reforms were also adopted, though with significant incidents of boycott by Cypriot teachers tolerated by the Cypriot Ministry of Education. But the phoenix found its way into Greek Cypriot schoolbooks, together with the peculiar accounts of history favoured by the colonels, including attacks on the "anti-national activities" of Makarios.

The Greek Cypriot Communal Chamber, and later the Ministry of Education, was staffed with individuals who were themselves imbued with the paraphernalia of rigid and highly idealistic official Greek culture which was transmitted to the schoolchildren of Cyprus. Significantly, in one of the few incidents of open conflict with the Greek dictatorship, in 1972, the Cypriot President sacrificed his Minister of Foreign Affairs and his Minister of Education for the sake of limiting the overt break with the "National Centre". They were critics of the Dictators' Foreign and Educational Policies respectively. Both could be stamped in terms of official Greek culture as "anti-Hellenes" much as Americans could be stamped as "un-American" during the MacCarthy era in the United States.

Greek Cypriots were quite willing to remain separate from Greece politically if culturally they could remain Greek. The problem was that their cultural links with Greece were forged through rigid bureaucracies which themselves carried two unsettling messages. One was that there was only one Greek culture, the official one. The other was that this culture said that political separation was in fact incompatible with maintaining Greek cultural identity. These ideas involved rigid limitations on the development of independent intellectual life in Cyprus and frustrated among other things the establishment of a Cypriot university. The President of Cyprus acceded to these forces for numerous reasons. Some of them were crudely violent, but one was that one of the legs on which his legitimacy stood was involved.

These are the vulnerabilities of the Cypriot Republic to subversion couched in terms of Hellenic nationalism. After all, by the time that the Greek Dictators came to power in 1967, only eight years had elapsed since the Cypriot anti-colonial movement had been in full swing for the achievement of *enosis*. With the coming of the dictatorship, a second Trojan Horse was added to that of the Turkish Cypriot Leadership. The *enosist* minority among the Greek Cypriots found themselves able to claim that they represented the Greek Government and acquired the support of the Greek officers who staffed the National Guard on the island. The motivation to join this opposition has been analysed as partly resulting from the ambiguities in the distribution of material and moral rewards to those involved in the anti-colonial struggle. In a struggle which was defined by the Leadership as being one of the whole Cypriot people, some felt at the end that they had been cheated of adequate reward for their contribution. In addition there was the problem that while ideologically Hellenic culture and education was elevated to glorious heights, in practice many graduates of the Greek university system found that their employment chances in Cyprus were fewer than those of graduates from British universities. In this context it was easy to link a sense of injustice to feelings of Hellenic nationalism.[40] But for individually disaffected individuals, there were other reasons to gravitate to the *enosist* opposition.

It was relatively easy to point to the apparent contradictions in words and actions of the President and interpret them as betrayal. The cue could be taken from the western press, from local western diplomats and from the Greek dictators. Makarios had allied himself with the communists and frustrated the age-old dream of the Greek Cypriots for *enosis*. A certain level of political illiteracy was an asset in this movement. It could then be argued that since the right of self-determination was guaranteed by the U.N., it was only the abdication from this right by the Cypriot Government that frustrated the achievement of *enosis*. In addition, it must be remembered that the communist party was a pro-government party. This meant that other than the *enosists* there was no opposition. A government in power for over fifteen years is bound to generate a certain amount of individual disaffection. These individuals could only gravitate to the *enosist* opposition. Some of the enosist agitation was generated by the unique economic-political position of Cyprus. Relative feelings of deprivation must be greater on the part of those left behind in periods of very rapid economic development. In the free market, booming economy of Cyprus, businessmen had so few barriers to their activities that even a slight frustration might result in an anti-government stance. As for the perfectly obvious future consequences of *enosist* agitation, they could be shrugged off. The enormous rate of economic development and the by-passing of previous crises could create a feeling that "they are somehow taking care of us", and an exaggerated sense of the delicately balanced necessity for the outside world to protect Cyprus from external invasion.

When the *enosist* opposition took to the polls in the presidential elections of 1968 and the elections to the House of Representatives in 1970, their strength proved to be between 5 and 10 per cent of the electorate, but they were there and they were vocal. The general position of this group was summarised in a press conference by the chairman of the political wing of the terrorist organization which formed in 1972.

The disturbances in Cyprus, he said, are caused by the resistance of the Government to the armed *enosist* groups. General Grivas has returned to Cyprus (in September 1971), in order to prevent a solution of the Cyprus problem which excludes *enosis*, or results in partition. The chasm between Grivas and Makarios was caused by the latter's abandonment of the claim for self-determination. It can only be closed by a return to the claim for self-determination which would inevitably result in *enosis*. The intercommunal talks cannot result in a solution of the Cyprus problem. Only *enosis* can provide external security and internal peace. "And anyway, this was the basis on which Greece and Turkey asked for the assistance of their allies for the solution of the Cyprus problem in 1966." "Cyprus and our people are indissolubly linked with the Western World. The Greeks of Cyprus are part of the Greek Nation. In case of war in the Middle East ... it would be unthinkable ... for Greece and Cyprus to be in different camps ... As far as the British bases are concerned, they still belong to Britain and consequently to Western defence. I do not think that the Cyprus Government can ignore this."[41]

General Grivas himself listed the preconditions for the solution of the Cyprus problem a few months later. The dangers of an anti-national solution could be met and overcome under the following conditions: when Makarios realizes that others have a right to be interested in the solution; when the Greek Cypriots act for one purpose in a united way to achieve self-determination culminating in *enosis*; when the Greek Government realizes that Cyprus is an essential part of Hellenism; when we all ask from the U.N. the right of self-determination which even blacks have; there was no possibility of a solution which would be "in accord with the wishes of all Greeks" as long as Makarios was in power because he is in favour of a solution which is in accord with his own interests (that is independence).[42] These demands and statements were accompanied by slogans and symbols of Hellenic nationalism and the development of secret armed groups which engaged in sabotage and later murder "in the service of the national cause".

It is clear, given the Cyprus Government's constraining conditions in relation to the symbols and verbal attachment to Hellenic nationalism, that these facts were highly subversive and potentially dangerous. (The crude political pressures on the Cyprus Government cannot be underestimated and will be subsequently outlined.) Under the circumstances, one can only make the judgement with hindsight. But the President and the Government took what can only appear to have been an erroneous step. Faced with a demagogic and armed attack on the Republic which used the highly emotive symbols of

Hellenic nationalism, their response was to step up their use of nationalist symbolism.

The Turkish Cypriot Leadership has published a pamphlet designed to prove that President Makarios had never abandoned the aim of *enosis*.[43] The compilers have no difficulty whatsoever in finding quotations indicating the Archbishop's attachment to Greece, and, there is some evidence, inventing others indicating his enmity towards the Turkish Cypriots.[44] (In many cases even the out of context quotations make it clear that they are on the level of sentimental aspiration rather than political intention.) What *is* significant is that the compilers of the pamphlet were unable to locate and include a single quotation from the President's speeches linking Cyprus to Greece between the 28th October 1967 and the 19th January 1970. (This is the time between the beginning of the intercommunal talks and before the outbreak of Greek Junta supported terrorism in Cyprus on a large scale.) Significantly after this, the President felt impelled to pay homage to the aspiration of the Greek Cypriots to close relations with Greece, though always pointing out that as a practical political aim it was not feasible.

For the sake of continuous presentation and in order to show that there was a local root to the *enosists* in Cyprus, originating in one small faction of EOKA but finding an emotional response in part of the Greek Cypriot population, the role of Greek governments has been abstracted up to this point. But it must be borne in mind that the *enosist* group in Cyprus might have disappeared were it not for the support and encouragement which they received from the Greek military dictatorship. The attacks of the dictators against Cyprus were the essential backbone of the *enosist* movement within Cyprus. Since the Greek Cypriot National Guard was controlled from Athens, Cyprus was permanently condemned to try to be a State without having a monopoly of force within its own borders. (And this apart from the problem of the military force of the Turkish Cypriot Leadership.) The constraints of brute force on the actions of the Cyprus Government become clear if one reviews its relation to the anti-democratic Greek governments.

No matter what his differences with Makarios, George Papandreou had ultimately agreed that *enosis* could not have been possible. At a Crown Council meeting in Athens in May 1965 Archbishop Makarios, aware of the difficult situation he was getting into and the belief in western diplomatic circles that he was frustrating *enosis*, offered to proclaim *enosis* if Athens supported him. Prime Minister Papandreou responded that to achieve *enosis* a price would have to be paid to Turkey. If the price were too high, new constitutional arrangements for an independent Cyprus should be sought instead.[45]

But this understanding, which would have left the Cyprus Government with the road to independence open was lost with the overthrow of the Papandreou Government. The caretaker Government and the subsequent dictatorship, by agreeing to discuss the "terms" on which Turkey would agree to *"enosis"*, opened the way to partition. This created direct links to other interested parties: the U.S. and the Cypriot *enosist* movement.

For Makarios, it seems that any price at the expense of the integrity of Cyprus was too high. Not so it appears for General Grivas. In July and August 1964 secret contacts were established by State Department Officials with Grivas, then commander of the Cypriot National Guard. Grivas outlined a plan for the Union of Cyprus with Greece and the ousting of President Makarios who had consistently refused a NATO base on Cyprus.

> The plan provided protection for Turkish Cypriots remaining on the island, and compensation for those willing to leave. The British base on Cyprus would be turned over to Turkey and staffed by Turkish personnel under a Turkish commander.[46]

It is not clear whether this was a "sufficient price" for Turkey. It is very likely that it was not, as the subsequent career of the Acheson Plan and the Greek-Turkish talks of 1966 indicate. What is important however is that in principle Grivas had accepted what Makarios would not accept: the division of Cyprus between Greece and Turkey. Henceforth there was a faction within Cyprus who appeared to agree with the caretaker Greek governments and with the Dictatorship. The common elements were: that the Makarios Government had encouraged the growth of communism in Cyprus; that it was creating conditions in Cyprus that led to its "de-hellenization"; and that *enosis* had been feasible in 1966, but that it has been frustrated by Makarios. It appears that a small area of Cyprus given to Turkey was a small compensation from the removal from power of the hated "priest", and the full dominance of official Hellenism in Cyprus which would remove the ambiguous cosmopolitans from government office and make communism illegal.

As indicated in Chapter IV, differences between Greece and Cyprus had developed long before the accession of the military dictatorship in Greece. And in fact, subversion against the Republic started with the Greek governments which replaced the Papandreou Centre Coalition. The main instrument at this time was the Greek military force stationed in Cyprus. At the end of 1966 the Cyprus Government openly accused the Greek one of having spies in the National Guard of Cyprus and of incompetence in handling the Cyprus problem.[47]

But the establishment of the dictatorship had at least three important implications. Tensions between the Greek and Cyprus Governments had to be kept within limits by democratic governments. Makarios for many mainland Greeks symbolized what Greek governments had never been able to do: to act independently of "protector powers", and utilize the support of the "other side" if this was forthcoming and appeared to be in the national interest. Largely for this reason Makarios was a political figure to be reckoned with in Greece itself. A press conference in Athens could be a severe restraining influence on a democratic Greek Government considering a different course of action on the Cyprus problem than the one considered the most advantageous by Makarios. With the dictatorship Makarios' access to Greek public opinion was cut off. It is significant that virtually during the whole of the seven years of the Greek Dictatorship, Greek Cypriot newspapers were not allowed into Greece. But in any event, under dictatorship public opinion has no effect.

The Greek military dictators carried with them the tradition of the Greek army which had experienced the Greek Civil War, the challenge to the power of the Right in Greek politics in the 1960's, and had been trained in cold war politics by U.S. agencies. They had come to associate democratic politics with the danger of communist subversion. General Grivas was personally an excellent example: "Give me a whip" he had said, during a pre-election period in Cyprus, "and I will show you what I can do. What are these things? Parties, para-parties, conflicting factions and para state organisations. Let them give me a whip and then we can talk again."[48]

Postings in Cyprus were sought after and "reliable" officers were more likely to get what they sought. In Cyprus they not only observed the operation of democratic processes, but also the participation in these processes of a communist party of widespread popular influence. The Government of President Makarios, far from repressing it, had adopted certain of its positions in the international politics of Cyprus. Cypriot independence looked at through the eyes of a pro-Junta Greek army officer must have seemed as a mere preliminary to a Soviet Cyprus. In view of this danger most inhibiting measures must have seemed legitimate, particularly in view of the relationship of Greece to the United States during the Dictatorship.

But there was a final and extremely important difference on Cyprus between the dictatorial regime and the previous democratic ones. This was that being extremely deficient in internal support within Greece itself, they needed to seek the support and approval of their ally, the United States, to a greater extent than democratic governments. They were susceptible to pressure from this ally to close the Cyprus problem in a manner favourable to the Western Alliance. One of the important ways by which they could do this would be by furthering what had always been regarded as the ideal solution by the higher officials of the State Department, that is the partition of the island between Greece and Turkey. In return they could receive virtually the only support which they received; that of U.S. Admirals, Generals and Vice-President Agnew who visited Greece and made lavish statements of praise in favour of the Colonels.[49] Developments immediately after the accession of the Colonels to power were in fact such that the *Guardian* aired the view that one of the main reasons for the Colonels coming to power was to "close" the Cyprus problem.[50]

The aims and methods of the Greek Military Junta in closing the Cyprus problem remain somewhat opaque. But from the main strands of the policy which was evident after its accession to power, certain aims may be concluded. The first point is that officially the Greek Junta renounced the possibility of *enosis* in private communication to the Cyprus Government after the failure of the Evros talks with Turkey. At the beginning of the intercommunal talks, the Junta's civilian foreign minister communicated his views to the Cyprus Government as follows: *enosis* was not possible as the recent political and military events had unfolded. It was most unlikely that *enosis* would ever become possible without reciprocal concessions or the agreement of Turkey. In the event of a Turkish invasion Cyprus could not be assisted effectively by Greece. It was too far away from Greek bases for effective air cover. The U.S. had indicated to Greece that a Greek-Turkish war could provide a pretext for an irreversible Soviet intrusion into the area. The U.S. would do nothing, either in the event of a Greek-Turkish war or in the event of Turkey invading Cyprus.[51] In spite of this and in spite of periodic statements by the Junta supporting the process of the intercommunal talks, the military government refused to renounce *enosis* in public. In a communication to the Secretary General of the U.N. in 1971, it was pointed out that this was because a declaration renouncing *enosis* "might be accompanied by psychological difficulties and should, if possible be avoided". It is clear that these psychological difficulties would mainly arise among the Junta's agents and supporters in Cyprus, since the *enosis* slogan was being used in order to weaken the independence of the Republic.

But the precise detection of what exactly was going on is complicated by the fact that various factions in the dictatorial oligarchy seem to have been following different policies at different times. Before 1970 it is at least conceivable that subversion in Cyprus was going on at the initiative of officers stationed in Cyprus to staff the National Guard. (Makarios' biggest mistake had been that he had not agreed to the disbanding of the National Guard after the Kophinou incident in 1967, seeing the disbandment as a threat to the sovereignty of Cyprus.) However during 1967 the Government reduced financial allocations to the National Guard, which was controlled by Greek officers, increased the appropriations for the police, enlarged the force and imported weapons for arming it. On the first of November 1968 the Cypriot Minister of the Interior resigned after pressure from the Greek Government. He had been guilty of resisting the penetration of the Greek secret services into the Cyprus Government.[52] He had also given a passport and other assistance to a mainland Greek democrat who later attempted to assassinate the Greek Dictator. A further sign of what was to come was the formation in Cyprus of the "National Front" in the autumn of 1969, demanding a cessation of the intercommunal talks, and a policy of *enosis* to be adopted. According to a report published in 1970[53] the formation of the National Front was designed in Athens as part of a plan code-named HERMES. This had as an aim the overthrowing of Makarios, the separation of Greek and Turkish Cypriots and finally the partition of Cyprus between Greece and Turkey. On the eighth of March 1970 there was an assassination attempt against President Makarios. Two weeks previously a Tass communique had been submitted to the U.N. Secretary General in which it was claimed that "reactionary elements in Cyprus are with NATO planning subversive activities", and attributed responsibility to "reactionary Greek officers who continue to hold significant positions in the armed forces of the Republic of Cyprus".[54] After the assassination attempt, an outline of the plan was handed to Makarios. It involved, after his assassination, a move of the Greek-officered National Guard for a coup.[55] It seems likely that the plan was drawn up by Greek army officers rather than the Greek Foreign Ministry. The involvement of the whole Junta government in the overthrow of Makarios had to await the agreement with Turkey, which as mentioned previously, took place in June 1971.

The Evros talks with Turkey had been unsuccessful. More than two years later, in late 1969, the Greek Dictatorship had resumed contacts with the Turkish Government over Cyprus.[56] There is no evidence that they had come to any agreement on an overall solution of the Cyprus problem, but it is conceivable that some understanding might have been reached on the desirability of removing the Archbishop from power, since the anarchy which was likely to follow might be used as a pretext for the intervention of the Guarantor Powers. This view is given some reinforcement by the sanguine attitude of the State Department to attempts by Greece to take over Cyprus. This would be expected to result in war between Greece and Turkey if there were no previous understanding. Yet when the U.S. Ambassador in Nicosia appealed to the State Department to condemn the assassination attempts against the President of Cyprus the appeal was ignored by Dr Kissinger and opposed by the U.S. Ambassador in Athens.[57] Were they in possession of knowledge not available to the

131

Cyprus Government about a Greek Turkish agreement? But this is speculation, at this stage. The situation becomes clear the next year.

To understand the Junta's policy in Cyprus during the years 1971-4, one has to understand its relationship with its allies, primarily the United States and Turkey. The Junta's "Turkish policy"

> was formulated in Athens with the aim of falling in line with American efforts to "tidy up" the whole Eastern Mediterranean sector in view of the Soviet threat and the continuing Arab-Israeli conflict.[58]

A resolution of the Cyprus problem in terms of an agreed division of influence between Greece and Turkey would be ideal in the sense that it would be satisfactory to all concerned other than the Cypriots. A large proportion of Cyprus controlled by Greece would do for the Junta's prestige, virtually any proportion would do for Turkey's strategic need to control access to its southern ports, and the U.S. would have a double gain. An irritating dispute between allies would disappear and there would be no scandal or resistance to a gradual transformation of the British bases of Cyprus into bases to be at the disposal of the U.S. for use in their Middle East strategy.

The main problem up until 1971 was that Greece and Turkey had not agreed on the terms of the division. This was finally achieved in a secret agreement during the NATO Foreign Ministers conference in Lisbon on the third and fourth of June 1971. It was not in the interests of any of the NATO partners that the intercommunal talks should succeed and result in an independent and non-aligned Cyprus, unless of course the only alternative to this were a Greek-Turkish war. If a Greek-Turkish agreement could obviate this possibility, then the liquidation of the Cypriot state could proceed without danger to the West. The agreement was preceded by some courting of Turkish public opinion by the Greek dictator. In an interview given to a Turkish newspaper[59] on the 30th May 1971, Papadopoulos had said that he believed in a Greco-Turkish federation, and that the two countries

> should convince our communities in Cyprus that we are not disposed to spoil the relations between us and quarrel for their sake; consequently they should settle their differences in a manner acceptable to us also.

The actual agreement reached at Lisbon is of course not fully known. *Pravda* reported that it aimed basically at the division of Cyprus.[60] There is no evidence that a strategy was also agreed. The agreement involved the acceptance of the validity of the Zurich and London agreements, but only apparently as far as the rights of intervention of the Greek and Turkish Governments in Cyprus were concerned. For the agreement involved also, "basic partnership principles" between Greek and Turkish Cypriots and "substantial local autonomy for them".[61]

In view of its suspicions of the aims of the Junta and of Turkey, this agreement was not acceptable to the Cyprus Government. In fact there was now more common ground between the Greek Junta and Turkey, than between the Greek Junta and the Cyprus Government. Makarios made his last visit to Greece during the reign of the dictators in September 1971. What happened during the visit is not known, though there is one report that he was pressed to accept the Lisbon agreement, but refused to do so.[62] But from this time on the war of the Greek Junta on the Republic of Cyprus became open, though on the Cypriots' side there was always a reluctance to express open hostility.

The strategy of the Junta was to use the slogan of *enosis* to weaken and if necessary overthrow Makarios. The *enosis* slogan, and the expansion of the numbers of the tiny *enosist* group and their power, was the only conceivable strategy for shaking the power of Makarios and the policy he represented. A natural instrument in this process was General George Grivas, but numerous other methods, all based on the agitation of extreme Hellenic nationalist feelings and anti-communism were used. The pressures of the Junta in general seemed to lead into two contradictory directions. On the one hand they pressed the Government of Cyprus to make concessions in the intercommunal talks, mainly on the issue of local autonomy for the Turkish Cypriots on which the Greek Cypriots were so reluctant. On the other it consistently attempted to weaken pro-independence forces and encourage groups and organisations opposed to the intercom-munal talks and fomented intense Hellenic nationalism. If this was not a matter of sheer madness, it must have been a plan to encourage the local autonomy of the Turkish Cypriots as a first step to partition. President Makarios after the July 1974 coup said that he thought that the Junta's aims in Cyprus were to extend the dictatorial system to Cyprus, to sabotage the intercommunal talks because they had a possibility of coming to an agreement which would strengthen the autonomy of Cyprus in relation to Greece, and to break his links with AKEL.[63] The aim in other words would have been to press things to the point, but not beyond, where Makarios felt weak enough to bow to the "National Centre". However much more radical measures were not out of the question if they could be achieved quickly and effectively and without Turkish hostility. As early as 1971 the Greek dictator communicated to the U.S. government his intention to remove Makarios through a coup, if he did not capitulate to the pressures mounted against him.[64] A review of the highlights of the Junta's activities in Cyprus after 1971 is necessary to bear up the points made on their general aims.

General George Grivas had been under house arrest in Athens. Two months after the Lisbon agreement it was announced that he had escaped and was in hiding in Cyprus. He announced the reasons for his presence in a pamphlet addressed to the youth of Cyprus: the Cyprus leaders, he claimed, have led Cyprus to destruction. They are unworthy of being called Greeks. The Turkish Cypriots are a "barbarian minority". In the anti-British fight of which he had been military leader, the enemy had been defeated militarily, but the cowardly political leaders of the Cypriots had compromised. The Greek Government (the Junta), were "men with strong hearts who do not tremble before enemies or caress ambiguous friends, nor do they beg for aid from the hundredfold worse tyrants of the Russian steppes who wait to tear our motherland to pieces". His aims, he said, were "to save my country from destruction". "The hour has come for the realization of the centuries old national wishes of Cypriot Hellenism to be united with the motherland." This aim could only be won by the sword.

The presence of the General and rumours that he was organizing armed groups was naturally worrying to the Cyprus Government. Once again an attempt was made to strengthen the police. (The army, officered by mainland Greeks was useless in facing the Grivas threat.) Arms were imported by the Government from Czechoslovakia. On the eleventh of February 1972 the dictators' ambassador in Nicosia handed Makarios a communique. The communique demanded that the weapons which had been imported be handed over to the United Nations Force, since Makarios had refused two previous demands to hand them to the National Guard. A veiled threat of direct intervention was included. Athens, the note said, is the National Centre, but there is no intention to intervene at the moment. But the crux of the demands in the communique was the formation of a government of national unity.[65] In a press statement the ambassador made it clear that the demand did not mean the inclusion of the communists in the government (who had received a third of the votes at the 1970 elections), but rather of the supporters of General Grivas who had never stood for election.[66]

In his reply, Makarios implied that the arms issue was a pretext since the dictators knew about their importation beforehand. He reasonably pointed out that he could not see how a government, some of whose members are in favour of *enosis* and some in favour of independence, would function. He reserves the right of the Cypriots to resist in the case of a Greek intervention and accuses the Greek Ambassador in Cyprus and Greek army officers of scheming to overthrow him.[67]

The main achievement of the Greek Ambassador in fact was to rouse three of the Bishops of the Church of Cyprus to publicly oppose Makarios. Old men, of limited understanding, they were easily persuaded by the representative of the mother country that they were doing their patriotic duty. Especially since it was beyond their understanding or possible tolerance that a Church leader could cooperate with communists within Cyprus and internationally and do so in order to "betray" the aim of *enosis*.

Relations between Grivas and the Junta were not always those between master and servant. It seems that at some stage Grivas finally came to suspect the aims of the Junta. However, this in no way made him appreciate President Makarios' realism more. He tried to capitalize on the name of the first EOKA by calling his terrorist organization EOKA B, and proceeded to intimidate all who thought *enosis* to be impossible. A Minister of the Government was kidnapped and threatened with assassination. In February 1973 a plan for a coup received shape, intended to be used in July 1973.[68] The plan was later uncovered by government security forces and given full publicity at the trial of an EOKA B official. Curiously, the plan involved a takeover of government installations in all the districts of Cyprus other than Kyrenia.[69] Kyrenia had always been the epicentre of Turkish partitionary demands.

By the spring of 1973, police stations all over the island were being blown up. The aim was *enosis*. The Greek Ambassador legitimized the whole process. In a television speech in March 1973 he proclaimed:

> If belief, faith in Hellenic ideals and if pride in the unique past of the race recede, the Nation is in deadly danger ...
> ... if the unity of the Greeks is undercut by the erosion of the National Consciousness, the blood of the heroes will run in vain.

The aim is clear. The terrorism of Grivas and the Government measures to contain it are equally "threats to unity". In fact the cause is not the terrorism, but the "erosion of the National Consciousness", which in the *enosists'* code is a reference to President Makarios' pro-independence policy.

Through all this, the Greek dictatorship maintained its verbal attachment to the intercommunal talks. When in April 1973 the Greek Cypriot negotiator expressed an intention to resign, as he could not see himself signing an agreement with the Turkish Cypriots with such a degree of violence going on among the Greeks,[70] the Greek dictators reasserted their support for the talks[71] which their agents and supporters in Cyprus were subverting with armed attacks.

The historically based analysis which precedes explains the

135

paradoxical stances of the main political forces within Cyprus. To understand may indeed mean to forgive. But the vulnerabilities of the Republic were no less dangerous for being explainable. As the full-fledged attack of the Junta on Cyprus developed, the vulnerabilities became very evident.

As the war on Cyprus became open, the pro-Makarios front weakened largely due to the defection of the bourgeoisie. Because they had undertaken the liberation struggle, faced by the opposition of Britain and the U.S. they could later accept the alliance with AKEL through Makarios.[72] But when faced with the choice between the Greek dictatorship and Makarios they wavered. This was for two reasons. One was that they were hardly a genuine bourgeoisie, but rather an intermediary merchant group, recently developed and with too short a space of time to develop a national liberal ideology. But the second reason lay in the fact that the Junta's attack on Makarios was partly couched in terms of anti-communism. It was previously pointed out that the merchants of Cyprus in the "bonanza" situation in which they had found themselves for most of the independence period could find any limitation on their profits a matter for the most intense form of protest. The strength of the cooperative movement, and some limitations on bank lending could, with the encouragement of the Junta, be taken as indications that Cyprus was on the road to socialism, for example.[73] The two parties of the right defected in different ways. When the Junta presented its demand for the effective dissolution of the Cyprus Government in 1972 the largest right wing party took a position of neutrality between the Cyprus Government and the Junta. The smaller party effectively dissolved and one of its leaders, Nikos Sampson, would later become the figure-head "President" during the coup.

As far as security was concerned, matters were very difficult. Cyprus was a state faced with armed subversion, but unable to use its military forces to establish order. A special police force had to be established to attempt this. But it was never possible to establish a popular militia to face the threat of a coup since this would have involved arming the supporters of AKEL as well as right wing supporters of the Government. This might have produced definitive justification for the "free world", led by the Greek dictators, to act against Cyprus.

The fact that AKEL supported the Government, meant that effective opposition on internal issues was left to the *enosists*. Politically unsophisticated individuals dissatisfied with any internal government policy might then gravitate to the *enosist* opposition.

Finally the ideological weakness of the Government was evident in the stepping up of the *enosist* statements when under attack from EOKA B. This could create the illusion among the naive that the only difference between the Government and the *enosists* was that the *enosists* were sincere. This had its saddest consequences among the schoolchildren of Cyprus some of whom were seduced to the *enosist* fold.

When the coup finally came, it is significant that apart from sections of the police force, the main armed resistance came from the small socialist party of Cyprus, EDEK. This party was the only group of civilians ideologically and materially prepared for resistance. But it is also significant that there had to be a coup, for in spite of weaknesses, Cyprus had not fallen to gradual subversion.

# CHAPTER VII

## *The problems converge: the role of the imperial powers*

The first chapter, which examined the strategic interests of the imperial powers in the Eastern Mediterranean, concluded to the effect that Cyprus would have continued to be non-aligned and independent were it not for the fact that Turkey attempted to reopen the "Eastern Question", and for the further fact that a military Junta came to power in Greece. Many of the actions of the Greek military junta and of Turkey in Cyprus have already been mentioned in previous chapters. This chapter is necessary for two reasons. One is, in order to explicitly try and answer the question of why the partition of Cyprus, attempted in various ways since 1964, was finally achieved, albeit in a messy and unstable way in 1974. The second reason, which is connected with the first one, is to answer the question of how the interests of the imperial powers in the area articulated with the forces leading to the dismemberment of the Republic of Cyprus.

Three general trends will be examined. The first is the improvement in relations between Turkey and the Soviet Union. Detente played a significant role in this, though the earlier phase of the Cyprus problem itself also contributed. This fact had two implications. It partially removed the disincentive of Soviet disapproval against a NATO country invading a non-aligned one. It also made the rival imperial power, the U.S. anxious to satisfy its ally's wishes. The second trend to be examined in this chapter is that of relations between the United States and Greece. For the kind of forces which the U.S. encouraged in Greece contributed decisively, though indirectly, to the Junta's assault on Cyprus. Finally the evolving U.S. policy on Cyprus itself is examined in the light of its general interests in the area; the increasing significance of the area in view of the oil problem and the burgeoning Middle East crisis, the need to reconcile the NATO allies, Greece and Turkey, or at least to avoid the worst outcome—the neutralization of both as reliable bases. The chosen policy in relation to Cyprus had two implications. It weakened post-colonial nationalist forces on the island itself and supported both Greek and Turkish nationalist ones and opened the way to military intervention both from the Greek Junta and from Turkey.

The changing set of relations between the Soviet Union and the United States which has come to be known as detente had a considerable influence on the complex of forces surrounding Cyprus. From this point of view the main implication of detente seems to be that in the place of confrontation of two rigidly organized blocs in psychological and military preparedness to go to total war, the United States and the Soviet Union have substituted diplomatic manoeuvring for strategic advantage, including occasional support for "proxy" wars. The maintenance of the Warsaw Pact and NATO as monolithic blocs has decreased in relative importance since a total confrontation in Europe appears to be a less probable event than it did during, say, the late 1940's and early 1950's.

This has meant that individual countries in both blocs have felt a greater latitude to experiment both in relations with the dominant power of their own bloc, and with countries of the opposed bloc. France used these changed conditions to leave the military wing of NATO and establish trade and more agreeable diplomatic relations with the Soviet Union. The Federal Republic of Germany used it to develop its *Ostpolitik*. It is not being argued that either detente or these trends in loosening rigid lines of confrontation are irreversible, merely that they have been significant trends in international relations in the last fifteen years. In this international atmosphere, Greece and Turkey attempted to use this kind of leverage within the NATO alliance, both for internal and international reasons and also due to the specific stimulations emanating from the Cyprus problem itself. In Greece the trend was accompanied by internal political transformations which, given its specific history and U.S. involvement in Greek politics, resulted in the backlash of military dictatorship. The dictatorship incidentally itself had a tendency to "play the game" with the assurance that its dictatorial clamp-down assured that it would not be accompanied by internal transformations. Turkey, on the other hand did not have to such a degree as Greece the in-built breaks to a tendency to change its international orientation.

There are basically two reasons for the greater international flexibility and tolerance to variations in foreign policy in Turkey as compared to Greece. One was the intensely nationalist Kemalist influence on its officer corps, in contrast to Greek customary malleability to the wishes of the protecting power of the day. (This is not a difference due to "national character" as is sometimes implied, but rather due to the historical fact that Greece has, ever since it became an independent country, been within the ambit of great power rivalries connected with the Balkans and the Eastern Mediterranean.) Secondly, a fact which may be regarded as a subcategory of the first, Turkey had not, as Greece had done, experienced a civil war in the process of which the ruling political right had defined themselves as being attacked from the communist northern neighbours, so that in national ideology anything other than support for the social *status quo* and of a pro-U.S. orientation could be interpreted by the dominant belief system as national betrayal. Because they had not experienced a civil war in the recent past, the Turkish officer corps, though equally NATO trained, are unlikely to have experienced the same "counter-insurgency" indoctrination as the Greek one. The Turkish military did not until 1971, when after a CIA supported coup[1] they received their first purge since their Kemalist institution, normally act as a break to a leftward veer in Turkish politics. In fact in 1963 they acted effectively as a break to a rightward one. So detente, and the internal power structure of Turkey until 1971, enabled it to move toward closer relations with the Soviet Union. If one looks at the sequence of events, the implications for Soviet and Turkish positions in relation to Cyprus are fairly evident.

The reference to the Eastern Question is merely a shorthand way of referring to the competition by rival powers either to dominate or befriend Turkey (in the nineteenth century, the Ottoman Empire) in order to deny the use, to the opposed power, of the strategic area of Turkey. In the second half of the nineteenth century, Russia was classically the protector of the Christian populations of the Ottoman Empire, while Britain was the supporter of "the sick man of the Bosphorus". This corresponded with their opposed strategic interests. For Russia to control the straits in such a way was to give Russian ships free access to the Mediterranean and prevent enemy ships from entering the Black Sea. The British were determined to prevent the Russians from coming out of the Black Sea into the Mediterranean, so important for access to their Indian colonies.

In 1907 Anglo-Russian entente removed Britain as a protector of the Ottoman Empire and allowed the German penetration into the Empire. When war broke out in 1914, Turkey was courted both by the Entente and the Central Powers. Because of fear of participation in an alliance in which Russia was important, Turkey chose the side of the Central Powers and in 1917, by closing the straits, contributed to the military collapse of Russia. But with the Soviet Revolution Kemalist Turkey and the Soviet Union established good relations, a fact that, together with the World War positions, contributed to the British decision to back the Greek Asia Minor expedition.[2]

Between the mid 1930's and the end of the Second World War Soviet-Turkish relations deteriorated culminating, in 1946, in a Soviet demand for a revision of the Straits agreement and Georgian and Armenian territorial demands in the north-east of Turkey. This resulted in strenuous efforts on the part of Turkey, including participation in the Korean war, to be allowed to enter NATO.[3] Turkey was allowed in in 1952. In fact, as early as 1953 the Soviet Union gave signs of seeking a re-establishment of amicable relations with Turkey by renouncing the 1946 demands.[4]

By 1964, when the Cyprus crisis erupted, various contacts on a governmental or parliamentary level were either planned or had taken place. Various experiences had led Turkish governments to mild experimentation in foreign policy. The general precondition was of course detente. As Soviet parity in long-range missiles became evident, the NATO policy of "massive retaliation" was replaced by the principle of "flexible response". This, and the question it raised about the role of countries on the flank of NATO in case of war, became a political issue in Turkey.[5] (This was the most important issue on which de Gaulle led France out of NATO.)

Anti-westernism was to some extent also fuelled by internal problems—particularly the failure of economic development and resentment against entrepreneurial groups, those that is who had particularly close ties with the West.[6] There were also specific events and situations which fuelled anti-Americanism in the Turkish press. These incidents included the use of a Turkish base to transfer U.S. troops to the Lebanon in 1958, the revelation in 1960 that U.S. planes were spying on the Soviet Union from Turkish bases without the Turkish Government's knowledge as well as the existence of extraterritorial rights for U.S. citizens in Turkey.[7]

The course of events in Cyprus during 1964 has been previously outlined in Chapter I. What was clear was the strong support of the Soviet Government for the position of the Government of Cyprus. In fact Soviet support was so strong that a planned visit by Turkish Foreign Minister Feridun Erkin to Moscow in March was postponed.[8] In January 1964 a Soviet official statement condemned the London Conference called by the NATO guarantor powers on Cyprus. It warned the West not to interfere in the internal affairs of Cyprus and pointed out that safeguarding the independence of Cyprus was the responsibility of the U.N. Security Council[9]—a position identical to that of the Cyprus Government. By August the Soviet Union was announcing that it was ready to help Cyprus in case of a Turkish invasion. A Soviet statement said "If a foreign armed intervention takes place in Cyprus the Soviet Union will help Cyprus to defend its freedom and independence ... and is willing immediately to start negotiations on this matter."[10] The next month supplies of conventional arms, fighters, torpedo boats and anti-aircraft artillery were promised (and delivered to the extent of 70 million dollars worth by October 1965).[11]

Turkey was being left out in the cold. Not only was the Soviet Union giving strong support to Cyprus against the Turkish threat but also the U.S. was, in the Turkish Government's judgement, favouring Greece over Turkey. The Acheson Plan provided for partitioning the Republic of Cyprus in a manner that the Turks considered to favour Greece. They believed that the transfer of Greek troops to Cyprus was tolerated by the U.S. as a means of minimizing the trend of the Cypriots to rely on Soviet aid, and of course there was the Johnson letter of June 1964, warning Turkey against coming into confrontation with the Soviet Union over Cyprus.[12]

The "real thaw" in Turko-Soviet relations started with the visit of Turkish Foreign Minister Feridun Erkin, now rescheduled in the autumn of 1964. Before the visit the London *Times* reported a *volte-face* on the Cyprus problem on the part of Turkey. Turkey which

> ... for some time appeared inclined to accept the principle of *enosis* at a price (as Greek ownership of the island seemed the best answer both to national security and the safeguarding of the Turkish minority),

now would rather see the island independent. This, the *Times* thought, might have been a manoeuvre in connection with the forthcoming visit of Mr Erkin to Moscow.[13] Another favourable hint to Moscow was given by Turkey in January 1965, when the government declined to participate in the NATO multilateral force. The creation of this force was something the Soviet Union was strongly opposed to as it would have associated West Germany with the use of nuclear weapons.[14] A whole series of visits of Soviet officials to Turkey and Turkish Government officials to the Soviet Union followed. Cultural agreements and increased trade also followed.[15] This normalization of relations with Turkey appears to have qualified Soviet support for Cyprus.

The first stage was a statement by Soviet Foreign Minister A. Gromyko on the 20th January 1965. The statement, according to long-standing Soviet policy, reiterated that the Soviet Union supported a solution on the basis of independence, territorial integrity and non-alignment for Cyprus, demilitarization and intercommunal agreement arrived at by the Cypriots themselves. But the statement also added that

> They (the Cypriots) may choose the federal form. And this assumes the existence of a single central government, a single defence organization, and a single administrative and judicial mechanism.[16]

During the year, prime minister Kosygin sent a message through Metin Toker, (Inonüs son-in-law), expressing Soviet interest in a Treaty of Friendship and non-aggression with Turkey.[17] In December 1965, when the Cyprus problem was debated in the General Assembly, the world body came up with the strongest resolution so far in favour of the independence and sovereignty of Cyprus and of opposition to any external intervention in the island's affairs. But the resolution was passed with 54 abstentions. The Soviet Union was among them.[18] In December 1966, when Premier Kosygin was in Turkey, he was reported to have joined the Turkish Government in condemning the purchase by the Cyprus Government of arms from Czechoslovakia with which to strengthen the police force.[19]

The Soviet position was of course not "pro-Greek" or "pro-Turkish" at any stage, but rather defended the independence and non-alignment of Cyprus. Encroachment by either of these countries on Cyprus would be encroachment by NATO. Soviet policy turned against whichever of the two countries appeared to be a threat to such a status for the island. With the coup in Greece in 1967, the Soviet interpretation seems to increasingly have become that such a threat came primarily from Greece. In July 1967, four months after the coup, a Soviet statement implied that the U.S. had colluded with the Junta's seizure of power and explicitly charged that the new Greek regime would be used as a tool of the NATO leaders to establish a pro-western dictatorship in Cyprus.[20] During the crisis of 1967, Soviet reaction was primarily against Greece. A Tass communique spoke of the Greek military government "and their agents in Cyprus" ... "struggling to turn Cyprus into a NATO war base, and to eliminate the democratic forces in Cyprus with the same criminal and terrorist methods which they use within Greece".[21] But through their ambassadors, the Soviet Union also warned Ankara, London, Athens and Washington that they opposed a NATO base in Cyprus.[22]

During the early part of 1971, the Soviet Union on several occasions expressed concern about or issued warnings against interference in the internal affairs of Cyprus,[23] and in April, when President Podgorny visited Ankara, a joint communique on Cyprus said that "the two sides expressed worry on the recent developments". They affirmed their position as

> ... opposition to *enosis* in any form, for the safeguarding of the independence, sovereignty and territorial integrity of the Republic of Cyprus with respect to the legal rights and interests of the two communities in Cyprus—the Greek and the Turkish ...

and

> supported the continuation of the intercommunal talks which must be conducted on a basis of full equality ...[24]

During the same visit a Common Statement on Principles of good neighbourhood was issued "on the basis of the tradition of peace, friendship and good neighbourhood as they were adopted by V. I. Lenin and K. Ataturk".[25]

Turkish willingness to normalize relations with the Soviet Union had been particularly stimulated by the 1965 vote in the U.N. General Assembly. A large number of countries had abstained from voting against Turkey, but only five had voted in her favour.[26] In addition to the diplomatic exchanges that were noted above, between 1965 and 1970 trade between Turkey and the Soviet Union increased fourfold.[27] Turkish policy on the Middle East was also turning in favour of the Arabs after 1971. By the time of the Middle East war in October 1973 in fact, the Turkish Government refused to allow U.S. planes to overfly or use Turkish facilities on their way to Israel, but on the other hand permitted Soviet planes to overfly Turkey in order to bring arms to Syria and Egypt.[28] A Turkish political scientist has concluded that

> ... the rapprochement to the Soviet Union has consolidated the Turkish position on Cyprus and has permitted her to break out from isolation and improve her relations with her Balkan neighbours and the Third World in general.[29]

All this does not of course mean that Turkey was about to leave NATO. In a country of great internal instability it would be very unlikely that a right-wing government and army would make such a move. It would be to risk encouraging considerable internal changes. And in fact rapprochement with the Soviet Union was only one line which Turkish Governments have followed since discovering their isolation on the Cyprus issue in 1965. They have also attempted to move out of this isolation in all other conceivable directions. Moves have been made to find friends on the basis of Islamic nationalism. Within the NATO alliance Turkey has tried to project the view that it is more strategically important to the alliance than Greece is, and on Cyprus specifically that the largest Greek Cypriot party is communist and that within Cyprus the Turkish Cypriot community should be supported to counter its influence.[30] As will be seen later in this chapter, these lines had at least as much success as its rapprochement to the Soviet Union.

As far as the Soviet Union is concerned, improved relations with Turkey did not result in a lessening of the Soviet wish for an independent, non-aligned Cyprus. But it did perhaps result in a different interpretation of the problem from the Soviet viewpoint—that the independence and non-alignment of Cyprus could be made compatible with the satisfaction of some Turkish claims. There were serious reasons for this tendency. Besides the fact that, as any Soviet diplomat will point out, Turkey is a neighbour with which the Soviet Union would like to improve relations, and the importance of the Straits, which become increasingly significant as the Soviet Union develops a presence in Africa and the Indian Ocean, there are other considerations. They are connected with the increasing significance of the Middle East for the United States. This will be discussed subsequently in relation to U.S. policy on Cyprus. But as far as the Soviet Union was concerned one can consider the following likelihood. Its interest in the Cyprus problem can generally be conceived as a dual one. On the one hand there is "anti-imperialism", that is maintaining the independence of Cyprus from NATO powers, and keeping it non-aligned. But secondly, the Cyprus problem also provided an opportunity to encourage the disruption of the south-eastern flank of NATO. With detente and the increasing significance of the Middle East to the U.S., the former aim became more dangerous and the latter one more possible because of the manoeuvres of Turkish governments. The prospect of detaching Turkey even slightly from NATO must have seemed as important for the Soviet Union as maintaining Cyprus non-aligned.

Besides, no matter how non-aligned the Cyprus government was diplomatically and in the United Nations, the British bases and the U.S. radar installations on Cypriot soil were aimed at the Soviet Union and no degree of non-alignment on the part of the Cyprus Government appeared to be capable of changing these facts.

The Soviet Union never ceased giving full diplomatic support to the cause of independence and non-alignment for Cyprus. The Gromyko statement of 1965 was never repeated.[31] In fact when President Makarios visited the Soviet Union in June 1971 the joint statement expressed a wish for the success of the intercommunal talks based on "the absolute sovereignty and unity of the state".[32] But in the changed situation of the 1970's such support was unlikely to express itself in the dynamic manner of the 1960's. One reason is that it became more unlikely that the Soviet Union would take dynamic action against Turkey. The other was that due to its special involvement with the Greek Cypriots, the Greek dictatorship, the other main threat to Cyprus, could act in ways which confused and defied international opposition.

One must turn to the Junta and its international connections to see more of the doom converging on Cyprus. Before explicitly turning to U.S. policy on the Cyprus problem, it is important to examine the nature of the relationship between Greece and the United States. As will be shown later, much of U.S. policy on Cyprus was conducted through Greece, and it is just as well to bear in mind the degree to which U.S. interventions shaped the nature of the polity in Greece when evaluating subsequent claims of U.S. government officials that the tragic events on Cyprus were the responsibility of irrational Greek dictators.

U.S. involvement in Greek politics has a long history.[33] But the

145

general situation in the years since the permanent establishment of right-wing governments in Greece after the civil war has been summarized in this way by a conservative Greek political scientist:

> U.S. Ambassador Puerifoy's efforts were thus rewarded with a crushing majority for the Papagos rally in the elections and new and closer association with the United States. Membership in NATO was quickly followed in October 1953 with a Greek-American military agreement. Moreover since that time it had become clear that all Greek Governments, especially their prime ministers, had to be acceptable to Washington.[34]

During this time,

> Anyone who questioned Greece's membership in NATO was automatically labelled a communist and thus antinationalist.[35]

The extent of U.S. involvement in the Greek power structure is indicated by the fact that when A. Papandreou was Minister of Coordination in his father's Government, his attempt to bring the Greek Central Intelligence Agency under the Prime Minister's control rather than the U.S. CIA was unsuccessful.

The history and direction of U.S. interventions had, by 1965, made it clear to the King that if he responded to his Prime Minister's attempt to bring the armed forces under civilian (rather than Royal) control by dismissing him, he would have the support of U.S. agencies.[36] A U.S. Congressional mission has been explicit on the direction which U.S. intervention took during this time:

> The United States despite an official policy of neutrality and non-intervention in Greece's domestic affairs, appears to have sided, throughout 1965-7, with King Constantine (and the conservative forces which had coalesced around him) and against George Papandreou. Apparently the conservatives were expected to take a more moderate (i.e. pro-NATO) line *vis-à-vis* Turkey on the subject of Cyprus.[37]

In fact, another Congressional study mission[38] wrote that

> As the elections of May 1967 approached, predictions of another massive victory for the liberal Center Union Party brought ultra-conservative forces, supported implicitly by the U.S. to the brink of panic.

Such was the panic, that in 1967 at the strong urging of the CIA station chief and some members of the embassy staff, U.S. Ambassador Phillips Talbot recommended that the White House authorize the expenditure of one hundred thousand dollars in "black" funds to finance opposition to Papandreou.[39] (One should remind the reader that Papandreou had on the whole supported the line of President Makarios on maintaining the independence of Cyprus, and of seeking a U.N. rather than a NATO solution to the problem.)

The coup, when it took place, was led by a triumvirate of colonels who forestalled a Royalist intervention. Papadopoulos, who later became the dominant one among them, was the liaison officer between the Greek Central Intelligence Agency and the U.S. CIA.[40] And the success of the coup partly depended on the fact that many of the participants who were not in the central cabal thought that they were actually taking part in a coup approved by the King and the U.S.[41] In practice the U.S. embassy reportedly advised the King not to resist the coup.[42]

Given these circumstances, there was of course no reason for the U.S. to bring pressure on the dictators to restore democracy. As a Congressional study mission puts it again:

> It is possible that in the period after the 1967 coup Papadopoulos was waiting for signs from the United States and other NATO countries of the limits of the alliance's toleration of his government. When the alliance leaders failed to press vigorously for an early return to democracy, Papadopoulos' interest in the subject diminished rapidly.[43]

In fact there was more than toleration. It would be no exaggeration to say that the Junta was not a government based on the Greek people, but on the approval of the U.S. Government. Only some of the evidence need be mentioned. In February 1971 the Senate Foreign Relations committee reported that the U.S. embassy in Athens fully supported the Junta and its ideology.[44] In the summer of 1971, the secretary of commerce, M. Stans, visited Athens and told the colonels,

> We in the United States Government, particularly American business, greatly appreciate Greece's attitude toward American investment, and we appreciate the welcome that is given here to American companies and the sense of security that the government of Greece is imparting to them.[45]

Later when,

> ... the dictator Papadopoulos ruthlessly suppressed student and worker demonstrations and scores of young men and women were killed in November 1973 with tanks and machine guns (supplied by the United States), there was not a word of protest from Washington.[46]

U.S. Government officials pointed to military considerations

147

necessitating support for the Junta when questioned either by European allied countries or by U.S. congressmen.[47] The idea of bringing Karamanlis back, as a means to a conservative transition to democracy was often suggested in international conclaves. On these occasions, U.S. officials claimed that they had no influence on the internal affairs of Greece.[48]

Of course the basis of U.S. thinking must have been short-term and narrow-sighted strategic considerations. The colonels were safe and controllable since they were obsessionally anticommunist and materially dependent on U.S. aid, and were probably thought of as being the safest way of keeping U.S. air and naval bases in Greece secure and in operation.

The policy was short-sighted from the point of view of U.S. interests because the internal rot which the dictatorship spread in Greece made even the narrow strategic requirements of the U.S. seem untenable. By the beginning of 1974 it was clear to everyone that the Greek economy was toppling and that in the process of successive purges the dictators had weakened the army and even reduced its loyalty to NATO. It seemed that Ioannides was about to reduce Greece to chaos, threatening the U.S. presence.[49] "Our principal conclusion", the U.S. Congressional study mission reported at the beginning of 1974

> ... on the situation in Greece, is that the present government cannot long endure. Marked by inexperience, its members appear without the requisite talents or skills for extricating the country from its political and economic chaos. The important question is by whom and how this extrication will take place.[50]

As the next chapter will show, the extrication took place by an exercise which can only be termed political judo. The dictator was allowed to overreach himself in grabbing Cyprus. The predictable Turkish reaction followed.

"But how did officers of the Greek army sink to such moral degradation?" asked the prosecutor in an Athens court-martial after the restoration of democracy in Greece. The accused were officers of the Greek army accused of torturing other officers, students, and royalist civilians. The impeccable right-wing prosecutor felt impelled to supply the answer that "There is no doubt that those morally responsible are outside this court." Those morally responsible, he went on, in his summing up,

> ... are they who inculcated in the accused false judgements about the national interest. It is they who for long years taught them how to combat communism without sacrificing a single hour to teaching them

how to defend democracy. They who surfeited them with warnings about dangers from the East, without teaching them Western democracy. At one time a "nationalist" was whoever combatted communism. During the days when the accused flourished however, the meaning of nationalism changed according to the interests of those in power. Within a short time the term came to be applied to those who fully identified themselves with the dictatorial regime. Not only communists were now accused of being anarchists, but also Royalists, conservative democrats, and later the followers of the first dictator.[51]

If the U.S. encouraged such a government to solve the Cyprus problem above the heads of the democratically elected representatives of the Cypriots, one can neither absolve the U.S. from responsibility for the subsequent events in Cyprus, nor merely blame the U.S. for "inaction".

U.S. actions and attitudes on Cyprus have been so various and contradictory at various times that one would be tempted to conclude that there never has been a U.S. policy on Cyprus. But there are two points to remember. One is that the issues involved in Cyprus are so complicated and ambiguous from the point of view of a U.S. policymaker that it partly explains the lack of a constant observed course of action. This does not mean that there has been no policy, merely that the policy has been conditioned by many other considerations not directly concerned with Cyprus.

It is as well to start with an estimate of general U.S. aims in the Mediterranean and then point out the importance and the ambiguities surrounding Cyprus in terms of these aims. The aims can be summarized as:[52]

1. To maintain naval superiority over the Soviet Union in the Mediterranean.

2. To strengthen NATO militarily and politically, including the "border" allies, Greece and Turkey.

3. To encourage Yugoslavia's military and political independence from the Soviet Union.

4. To protect and strengthen Israel as a western outpost in the Middle East and to counter the Soviet presence in some Arab States.

5. To contain and reduce Soviet influence with states of the region.

"How does it happen", a prominent West German strategic analyst asked "that this economically meaningless and militarily non-existent small Cyprus with its 650,000 inhabitants has such an influence on the world scene?" He went on,

> The answer is simple. Geographically it is a securely anchored aircraft carrier at the intersection point of the lines of tension of the great nuclear powers.[53]

## CYPRUS

The basic ambiguities surrounding Cyprus have been created by the following basic facts:

1. The Government of Cyprus has basically followed a non-aligned policy designed to minimize the fetters on Cypriot independence. It has never considered that it could basically threaten the presence of the British bases on the island, but has maintained the treaty position that if the British left them they would revert to Cyprus and not to Britain's allies. A non-aligned policy naturally means maintaining good relations with the socialist bloc as well as the western one. Internally, it has also meant a government policy of cooperation with all parties including the communist one. This could not in any way have been directly threatening to the west, except for the long run consideration that "Moscow", in western estimates "was therefore tempted not to regard the position of the west in the Mediterranean as a given fact."[54]

2. Theoretically this problem from the point of view of the United States could be solved by subsuming Cyprus to one of its NATO allies: Greece or Turkey. Since neither would agree to the other totally controlling Cyprus, the resolution would appear to be some combination of both. This indeed would have been the Acheson Plan. (*Enosis* at the time when it was possible would also have filled the bill, but the boat was missed and was no longer possible after Turkey had established objections.) Indeed, Greece or Turkey could only secure Cyprus for the West if there could be agreement between them on the relative proportion of influence (or territory) of each.

3. The Greek Cypriot leaders (the Government of Cyprus) strongly objected to a Greco-Turkish agreement for the territorial division of Cyprus. More than that, the continuation of the problem at various times threatened conflict between the two NATO allies and resulted in anti-American reactions in Greek and Turkish public opinion. Moreover, the Soviet Union supported the position of the Cyprus Government for the independence and non-alignment of Cyprus, and overt Greek or Turkish interventions threatened wider complications.

As a result of their experiences of trying to reconcile their wider Mediterranean interests with the reduction of what they conceived of as communist influence in Cyprus and the satisfaction of their two NATO allies, U.S. policy makers apparently decided that it was best to let the problem be solved by Greece and Turkey without overt U.S. intervention.[55] For this reason very little has been made public about U.S. attitudes and actions in relation to Cyprus between 1964 and the time of the coup and invasion in 1974.

It has been argued that for the U.S. the "ideal solution" of the Cyprus problem since that time has been the partition of Cyprus between Greece and Turkey and it has further been implied that there is documentary evidence for this in the State Department Archives.[56] This was denied on the spot by a State Department representative, who proposed instead the theory that there has always been a dichotomy in U.S. policy on Cyprus. That is there have been people in the U.S. administration who have sought a solution to the Cyprus problem that would look mainly to the interests of NATO. That there were people who saw President Makarios as a threat to U.S. interests. But that there were others who looked for a solution based on the interests of the island and saw President Makarios as a freely elected leader who is the only long-term hope.[57] And finally, the idea was expressed that the dichotomy in policy which was observed and which could be located as being between the Top and Working Level of the Department of State might be one that "represented a formation that can be traced to a general design and pattern".[58]

Well, the definitive answer will have to wait the opening of the State Department Archives. Perhaps at this stage the theory of the "ideal solution" can be accepted as a hypothesis—and one that does indeed allow us to reconstruct the iceberg of U.S. policy on Cyprus from the tips that are in sight. There are two basic reasons for thinking that partition of the island between Greece and Turkey might have had some continuity in U.S. thinking as an ideal solution for the Cyprus problem.

One group of reasons is empirical and start with the fact that it was proposed by Dean Acheson in 1963. The fact that it has not been publicly offered again since then does not mean that policy makers no longer regarded it as a good "option", if it could come about without direct U.S. involvement. There is other empirical evidence that will unfold in the course of this and the subsequent chapter. It comes under two main categories. One is that at a time when the Greek Junta and extreme Greek and Turkish nationalists on Cyprus were behaving in ways that would directly lead to partition and implied that this was in the interests of Democracy and the West, no U.S. agency ever denied that this was in fact U.S. policy. Secondly there is the behaviour of U.S. agencies during the coup and the invasion.

The other basic reason is that a theoretical case can be made for partition being an "ideal" solution in terms of U.S. interests. (Of course only in terms of a certain kind of *Realpolitik* that we observed at work in Greece during the dictatorship. In fact its own crudeness guarantees the failure of such a policy. But there is no denying that such policies have been attempted in recent U.S. history in Cuba, Vietnam and Chile to mention a few well documented cases.) In this sense it could be regarded as being ideal because it solved both U.S. interests in Cyprus at one stroke. The cohesion of NATO would be assured by giving Cyprus in agreed proportions to Greece and Turkey. The same act would, by subsuming the troublesome island under NATO allies, dispel any strategic worries about the future of the British bases or conceivable Soviet hopes over Cyprus.

Now this policy could not be constantly followed for the simple reason that it could only be implemented at a very particular historical moment: one at which Greece and Turkey were agreed on the terms of the division. (And this varied from time to time and from government to government.) And secondly, that such a solution would have to be applied quickly enough so that the Cypriots would have no time to stall, protest, fight or appeal to anyone, particularly the Soviet Union which was constantly opposed to such a solution.

What has been said above does not even necessitate a presumption that such thinking was a permanent trend of U.S. policy. Merely that it had gone on once, was available on record or in memory, and was there to be seized on at the appropriate moment, not necessarily by *all* U.S. Government agencies, but, say, by the Secretary of State in cooperation with the CIA.

This way of thinking about U.S. policy on Cyprus makes sense of most of the occasions when U.S. actions were observable, their fluctuation in impact on Cyprus and the variations in actions and attitudes of different agencies and individuals in U.S. Government. In other words, the assumption may be that most of the time differences between Greece and Turkey, or the likelihood of an appeal by Cyprus to others to intervene, induced the U.S. to follow a "pragmatic" course of action designed to prevent either Greece or Turkey from intervening in Cyprus in such a way as to cause conflict between the two over Cyprus. Often this had the side effect of securing or even strengthening Cypriot independence. Yet avenues were being kept open for an application of the "ideal" solution.

When the U.S. offer to land troops on Cyprus as a peace keeping force, which would at the same time secure Cyprus for the West, failed, the U.S. turned to at least securing peace between Greece and Turkey.[59]

For the next few years it seems that U.S. efforts were limited to this objective.[60] So in February 1964 the U.S. gave material support to the U.N. peace-keeping force. Though it was controlled by the Security Council which gave a voice to the U.S.S.R., it tended to keep the peace in Cyprus and avert a Greco-Turkish war. But it is important to note that though the U.S. largely financed the U.N. force supporting the peace-keeping aim, it did not give support to the broader U.N. mediation effort. For example, the U.S. did not oppose the resignation of the U.N. mediator Gallo Plaza Lasso when his report was rejected by Turkey, nor did the U.S. seek the appointment of a new mediator.[61] In December 1965 the U.S. was, together with Turkey, Iran, Pakistan and Albania, the fifth state voting against the General Assembly resolution reaffirming the sovereignty of Cyprus and the illegality of external intervention.[62] In April 1967, during President Sunnay's visit to Washington, President Johnson officially supported the "two community" Turkish concept of Cyprus[63] tending to elevate the majority and minority to terms of equality.

During the 1967 crisis two things became evident. The first was that with a U.S.-dependent dictatorship in Greece it was easier for the U.S. to press Greece than Turkey. And in fact the Greek dictators acceded to all the Turkish demands.[64] The other was that President Makarios would not regard the Republic of Cyprus as being bound by an agreement between Greece and Turkey concerning the Republic. The only part of the Greco-Turkish agreement which was not implemented was that concerning the dissolution of the Cypriot National Guard.[65] The Archbishop has since admitted that this was a mistake on his part. (It is out of the question that he would have meant that the principle he stood on was mistaken. Rather the implication is that if he had agreed to the National Guard's dissolution, the Greek army officers would have lost their power base and *raison d'être* for being in Cyprus. An opportunity for this never reappeared when the full dangers inherent in their presence became evident.)

The basic thrust of U.S. policy on Cyprus becomes clear by examining the attitude of that government to the intercommunal talks and the various forces that tended to disrupt them. The U.S. official position was one of support for the intercommunal talks. As Chapter V indicates, the trend of the discussions were such that had they succeeded without outside intervention, they would have removed the last stumbling block to complete independence for Cyprus, with substantial guarantees for the Turkish Cypriot minority. But it seems that the U.S. attitude was not that the Cypriot interlocutors should come to a solution, but that the talks should legitimize an agreement on Cyprus reached by Greece and Turkey. The most substantial evidence on this comes from a legal expert who has had access to the archives of the intercommunal talks, has served as a constitutional advisor to the Government at the time when Mr Clerides was Acting President and who by no reach of the imagination could be described as being anti-American.

The main thrust of U.S. policy was to accommodate Greece and Turkey. Direct contacts between these two countries, with assistance from NATO and the U.S., were therefore the best way to reach a solution in the U.S. view. In this view Archbishop Makarios was an obstacle to implementing NATO plans. These plans had been finalized at the NATO foreign ministers conference in Lisbon in 1971.[66] The basic aim was to resolve the Cyprus problem on the basis of independence but with very substantial regional/communal autonomy for the Turkish Cypriots. The aim was that the monolithic

Turkish Cypriot community, lacking an organized Left, would provide an avenue for NATO and U.S. influence in Cyprus. This would be further reinforced by a strong Turkish military presence.[67] The trend of such a constitutional settlement was clear—partition. An eventual "removal of Archbishop Makarios from power", which was also visualized[68], would facilitate this trend.

Late in 1969 Greece and Turkey had resumed secret talks on Cyprus at the same time as the National Front started its subversion in Cyprus. As mentioned previously substantial agreement was reached at Lisbon at the beginning of June 1971. The Greco-Turkish contacts took place with U.S. encouragement and assistance.[69]

Independent information[70], though without citing a source, tells us that during the same month, June 1971, State Department analysts had concluded that Greece and Turkey were favourably disposed to "double *enosis*". It was proposed that the U.S. should restrain Greece and Turkey from "premature" moves in this direction. The same officials concluded that Makarios would accept "double *enosis*" if confronted with something worse as an alternative. A consensus was reached that "the Makarios problem must be left to Greece". Presumably this meant that if the Makarios problem were left to Greece, "cold war" complications could be avoided since Greece had the capacity to act "internally" in Cyprus through the presence of the Greek army officers and the small *enosist* opposition group.

The Greek dictators acted, though even at this stage there is an indication of western "prompting". In November 1973 during Cyprus security forces operations against EOKA B, some documents were found. Among them was a letter from a Cypriot to George Grivas in Athens. In it, the man (named in the published letter but who will here be referred to as X), says that a man called Fletcher from the British High Commission Intelligence Service visited him in July 1970. They discussed the communist danger in Cyprus and the worry about the "increasing popularity" of the communist and socialist parties in Cyprus. Fletcher wanted X to find out from Grivas whether he would accept a form of the Acheson Plan in the future. X told Fletcher that in the event that the Greek and Turkish Governments and Grivas agree on a plan, they should not worry about Makarios for all that had to be done would be to send Grivas to Cyprus. The newspaper that published the letter stated that a Cyprus Government spokesman had confirmed that it was found during a search by security forces in the house of an EOKA B suspect.[71] The actual letter was dated 29th July 1971, a little under two months after the Lisbon meeting. A month later Grivas, who had been under house arrest in Athens, turned up in Cyprus. Before the Lisbon NATO Foreign Ministers' conference was over, President Makarios was in Moscow (between the 2nd and 9th June). He said to the Soviet press:

I have informed the Soviet leadership of a danger of a worsening of the situation ...

We will resist any attempt to enforce a solution which will lead to political or geographic partition of our island. Nor will we suffer a limitation on the independence and sovereignty of Cyprus.[72]

Perhaps this is what the NATO secretary general Mr Luns had in mind when a year later in an interview with the Greek programme of the BBC he criticized the Cypriot president for "flirting" with Moscow. At the same time he described the three Bishops who, with Athens and EOKA B support, were seeking to force Makarios to resign from the presidency as "safeguards" against his dangerous policy. He also stressed the contribution of the Athenian colonels to the Free World.[73] Of course this kind of statement gave legitimacy to the EOKA B terrorists' claim that they were acting in the interests of democracy, Greece and the Free World.

In fact State Department officials are very likely to have been in the game of crushing the independence of Cyprus between Ankara and the Turkish Cypriot leadership it controlled, the Athens Colonels and EOKA B. Ankara and the Turkish Cypriot leadership were of course not a problem, for a "wide measure of regional autonomy" was something that probably few Turkish Cypriots after ten years of lack of political discussion would have the perspicacity to object to. Whether they did or not was in any event irrelevant since the Turkish Cypriots were monolithically controlled by their leadership and the leadership by Ankara.

The Greek dictators were not a problem either. They had ample psychological, ideological and economic reasons to satisfy U.S. aims, especially since the ultimate result of the kind of settlement for an independent Cyprus that the U.S. appeared to favour was very likely to result in partition. This was likely in view of the *methods* used to subvert the Cyprus Government. The only side to disagree with the whole process was the Government of Cyprus.

It is in this way that sense can be made of the apparent support of "everyone" for the intercommunal talks. Their existence would provide legitimacy for a "solution" of the Cyprus problem. But the real determinants of the solution would be the facts of *enosist* subversion by the Greek Junta and EOKA B, the separatist demands of the Turkish Cypriot leadership and their correspondence to what some U.S. policy makers regarded as their country's interest. This explains three apparently incomprehensible facts:

1. That the Greek Junta was at the same time pressing the Cyprus Government to make concessions to the Turkish Cypriot leadership's separatist demands at the intercommunal talks in order to reach an

intercommunal accommodation and, at the same time, encouraging pro-*enosis* subversion within the Republic.

> Could he control the nationalist movement of Cyprus so that it would merely weaken Archbishop Makarios without attempting to overthrow him or plunge Greece into dangerous adventures with Turkey? And what if in spite of all the pressures, Makarios refused to bow to Papadopoulos stratagem and sought help from elsewhere? In that case, the Greek Government had already decided, he would be overthrown in a coup and the way would then be paved for complete resolution of the Cyprus problem ...
>
> This decision was communicated to the American Government.[74]

Of course such a policy, especially one which the U.S. tolerated through its lack of private pressure on the Junta or public condemnation, presupposed an agreement with Turkey.

2. That the Turkish Cypriot leader, Mr Denktas, was, by 1972, arguing for a greater role in Cyprus not only for Turkey, but also for Greece. There is a surprising similarity between the statements of Denktas and Colonel Papadopoulos:

Papadopoulos:

> First of all we must persuade out respective communities that we are not prepared to spoil our good relations and that we do not intend to quarrel on their behalf. Therefore they should arrange their differences and in fact in a way that is acceptable to us.

He added for good measure that

> developments lead to a federation between Greece and Turkey.[75]

Since this was the first time the world had heard of any such conception in relation to Greece and Turkey, it was surely intended as an admonition to the Cypriots.

Denktas:

> I feel that nothing short of geographical separation will save this community from future harassment. If we are not to have geographical separation then Turkey and Greece should take more active and physically visible responsibility in Cyprus in maintaining law and order.[76]

and,

> How can it be said that attempts to settle the problem with the active help of Greece and Turkey is "outside the interference in the affairs of Cyprus" ... Turkey and Greece can settle this problem in 24 hours and it is high time they did so, once and for all.[77]

The similarity is of course due to the fact that there was basic agreement between Turkey and the Turkish Cypriot leadership, the

Greek Junta and the United States on what a desirable solution should be.

This method of arriving at a solution would doubtless in the long run result in the partition of Cyprus between Greece and Turkey—not merely because it would provide for wide regional autonomy for the Turkish Cypriots, but because in addition it would provide for a Turkish military presence inducing the Greek Cypriots to seek a Greek military presence. And finally, because the method of pressing the Cyprus Government to accept such a solution was to incite an attack against the government on the most fanatical and extremist grounds of Hellenic nationalism.

3. Since this accorded with the "ideal" solution for at least some State Department analysts it explains why, whereas the official U.S. position supported the intercommunal talks, appeals from the U.S. ambassador in Cyprus and others for the U.S. to take a stand against the subversion of the Republic failed.

If such indeed was the U.S. preference for Cyprus, why was this policy not more energetically and immediately pursued, and, more importantly, why did the U.S. in early 1972 dissuade the Greek dictators from engaging in a coup against the Government of Cyprus?

The Czechoslovak arms crisis and the Papadopoulos ultimatum to Makarios in early 1972 were described in Chapter VI. At this time the U.S. moved through its Athens ambassador to "cool off" the Colonels.[78] There are several factors that are likely to have contributed to this. Firstly, Grivas at this time refused to move against Makarios. The Junta-controlled National Guard would have had to move for a coup without the kinds of disturbances that would have justified its claim that it was "averting civil war". It would also have looked too much like direct intervention by Greece. (Of course neither of these two considerations were sufficient to stop Ioannides in 1974.) In 1972, however, the Junta's ultimatum was followed by a massive popular demonstration in Nicosia at which something like a third of all Greek Cypriot men must have been present. This show of mass determination might have made it appear that a coup might at this time be a protracted and messy affair with unforeseen complications. There is little doubt that even the keenest devotees of the "ideal" solution would prefer it to come about by attrition of the integrity of the republic, rather than by a reduction of the island to chaos. The scenario would in general have gone much better with Makarios capitulating to Athens after having his wings clipped by the Athenian *enosist* campaign, signing a "federal" solution in the intercommunal talks, with strong presence of Greece and Turkey on the island, which in itself would resolve many problems from the U.S. point of view or would in time result in more definitive partition.

Finally, the existence of the dissenting view within the State

157

Department may have at times constrained the *élan* with which the advocates of the "ideal solution" could proceed.

Why did not similar forces prevent the events of the summer of 1974? No definitive answer can of course be given, but there are various factors that might account for the fact that, in combination with past preferences, the United States decision makers might have shifted to accepting a "high risk" outcome of the struggle over Cyprus in 1974.

The first group of factors probably has to do with an increased urgency to secure the British bases for use by NATO in general, but more specifically, by the United States. Perhaps a review of the nature and strategic significance of the British bases would be useful here. This 2.9% of Cypriot territory which was kept as sovereign British territory in 1960, plus the numerous other privileges which the British retain for the military use of Cypriot airspace, transport and land, have had an increasing significance to the U.S. for a variety of reasons.

The significance of the bases may be summarized in this way:

(a) Akrotiri is the Royal Air Force's largest base anywhere. Until recently its most important function was to survey and defend NATO's southern flank and it also contributed strategically to CENTO, the alliance of Britain, Turkey, Iran and Pakistan.[79] Warplanes leaving bases on Cyprus could reach deep into South Russian airspace and of course in a nuclear war no treaty could prevent other NATO countries from using the bases as well as Britain.[80]

(b) Cyprus has a network of communication and surveillance centres of enormous value both in terms of global and regional strategy. "What is possibly the best radar in the World" is located on Mount Olympus and run by the British.[81] It is not quite clear whether this is the same as the "over the horizon radar installations for the detection of intercontinental ballistic missile launches in the Soviet Union".[82] Based on the information from the radar facilities British planes intercept any unidentified aircraft in the Eastern corner of the Mediterranean.[83] Since a few years a few hundred CIA men are reported to be on the British bases to use the strategic reconnaissance equipment.[84] Unlike a conventional aircraft carrier, planes can leave from the aircraft carrier Cyprus to survey the Soviet Mediterranean fleet under any weather conditions.[85]

> The potential value of such a base to NATO bang in the middle of the Soviet Union's Mediterranean anchorage can hardly be exaggerated.[86]

(c) Finally, Cyprus is potentially important as a regional base in case of limited wars in the Eastern Mediterranean. Since the early

1960's strategists in Washington have laid increasing stress on preparing for limited wars. Part of this preparation involves the use of staging points necessary for transferring men and supplies and for "forward stockpiling". Such provision is of course also important for supporting allies.[87]

The treaty provisions involved in the establishment of the Republic of Cyprus preclude the use of the British bases by any other country and also provide that in the event of the British abandoning the bases they should revert to the Republic of Cyprus. Of course come a nuclear war there could hardly be a way for the Cyprus Government to prevent the bases being used by any NATO ally (assuming that it had the inclination to do so at the time). But the situation is rather different as far as the regional use of the bases is concerned. The Cyprus Government has naturally often stated opposition to the bases being used against its Arab neighbours. By 1974 two things had happened which may have made the Cyprus Government's attitude tiresome in U.S. eyes.

A British defence review was announced on the 21st March 1974, involving considerable cuts in military spending overseas. In Cyprus they involved the withdrawal of the British Vulcan nuclear bombers stationed there and the virtual closing down of one of the bases, Dhekelia.[88] The next month some American Marines were landed at one of the British bases. There were protests from Cypriot political parties and it was clarified that the marines had arrived with the knowledge of the Cyprus Government to assist in clearing the Suez Canal. This has been interpreted as an attempt by the Americans "to test their political chances of becoming an accepted successor of British military rights in the island ...".[89]

The significance of the British bases, the need by the U.S. to control them, particularly in view of British withdrawal, through ensuring a long-run compliant Cyprus rather than a conceivably recalcitrant non-aligned or leftist one, were facts which were reinforced by what may be termed "the Mediterranean crisis"[90] of the last few years.

This is not the place for a history of the geopolitics of the Eastern Mediterranean and the Middle East, nor is this author competent to write one. So I shall proceed by indexing a few facts indicating an increasing need by the U.S. of a strategic bulwark such as increasingly only Cyprus could offer.

The first relevant fact is the vastly increased Soviet naval presence in the Eastern Mediterranean in the last twenty years. Between 1960 and 1966 Soviet naval power in the Mediterranean increased ten-fold,[91] whereas more recently Britain has reduced its own to virtually nothing and France, while maintaining a naval force, does not submit it to NATO command.[92]

In the Middle East, after the 1967 war, Egypt, Syria and Iraq turned to the Soviet Union for support. In 1969 the U.S. lost its Libyan air base, while developments in Italy and in Portugal during 1974 indicated that these countries might be slipping out of the Western Alliance or be rendered useless allies.

The aftermath of the 1973 war was the oil crisis. This highlighted the significance of the oil producing areas and virtually made their control a *casus belli*. But more than that, the 1973 war showed something which might have been particularly significant for intentions over Cyprus. As mentioned previously in this chapter, one aim of U.S. policy in the area was to protect and strengthen Israel. The NATO allies however do not share this concern. The European countries tend to see the Middle East problem from the point of view of how it immediately affects their economic rather than military or political interests. The United States as a global power confronting another such power, and, for the present, being more self-sufficient in oil, regards long-term and global strategic considerations as being much more important. This divergence resulted in an important difference between the United States and its NATO allies during the 1973 Middle East War. None except for the Federal German Republic and the then dictatorial Portugal allowed the United States to use their territory as a staging post for resupplying Israel during the war.[93] In fact in November 1973 the nine EEC states were so fearful of loosing their oil supplies that they issued a statement leaning further to the Arab point of view on the conflict with Israel than ever before.[94] As mentioned earlier, Turkey, in the process of her new-found understanding with the Arab countries and the Soviet Union, allowed Soviet planes to fly over her territory to supply Syria, while denying the U.S. the right to use her territory to supply Israel. By 1974 Portugal was in a state where it would certainly have denied the U.S. similar facilities in a future Middle Eastern war. And Germany of course could in the future follow the general EEC trend. That only leaves the British bases in Cyprus. A fact that earns a mention to an article appearing in an Israeli journal in April 1974, reporting that the rumours that Israel was at that time "lending substantial support to Grivas forces", were too strong to be ignored.[95] The government of Archbishop Makarios would have protested very strongly had U.S. planes used the British bases to supply Israel against the countries which had given such strong support to Cyprus since independence.

One other trend should be mentioned. At least three times previously the U.S. had secured the independence of Cyprus as a by-product of attempting to settle Greek-Turkish relations. But during 1974 the Greek dictator Ioannides and Turkey seemed to be developing a source of conflict totally independent of Cyprus: Aegean oil. By June and July 1974 both Ioannides and the Turkish

Government believed that the other was preparing for possible war over the Aegean.[96] In fact a press release by the Turkish embassy in Athens in early July 1974 said that attempts to set up a negotiating procedure when the government heads had met in Brussels in June had failed due to the "new Junta" (Ioannides) who

> seeks a position of strength before entering into direct negotiations and wants to complete its military build up.[97]

If the U.S. saw signs of rupture between the two allies in any event, it would be more willing to risk such a rupture over Cyprus.

Finally we must recall Turkey's signs of infidelity with the Soviet Union raising the question of attracting Turkey back through an opportunity to "solve" the Cyprus problem in its favour.

It is perhaps odd to end a chapter with someone else's words. But in working out the details of such international madness, you sometimes come to feel that you are becoming paranoic yourself and need the reassurance of someone else who has come to a similar conclusion, a West German strategic expert writing on the day before the Turkish invasion of Cyprus:

> (How the results of the current explosion can be dammed up is not yet predictable. With tricks and half measures NATO can no longer make do.) Somehow the main demands of the Turks must be met by those who want to be present politically and militarily in Cyprus, openly or secretly. Turkey wants to set up its own credible protection for the Turkish minority. But the Turks are also convinced that in the Atomic age a strategic base in Cyprus is necessary for the security of the Turkish motherland. In exchange the Greeks and Greek Cypriots could be allowed union with the motherland. The division of the population groups and the dissolution of the existing state of Cyprus would be the price. One needed to be sure a Kissinger in high form to realize such a project.[98]

# CHAPTER VIII

## *The problems converge: the coup and the invasion*

U.S. policy as it has been outlined was certainly not conducive to the strengthening of the independent Republic of Cyprus. But the main consequence would have been to "cut Makarios down to size", that is to weaken him in relation to the Greek Government. After all the organisers of subversion against the Republic took a great deal of trouble to make it appear an internal dissident movement. The overthrow of the legal government by the National Guard, which was widely known to be controlled by the Greek Junta, was a last resort. In a sense what precipitated the last resort was the success of the Cyprus Government in withstanding the pressures that came from the Junta-organized insurrection.

The Cyprus Government had withstood all pressures for immoderate concessions in the intercommunal talks. In late 1973 and in the summer of 1974 the process of discussion had made it clear that the Cyprus Government would only accept a constitutional settlement that would leave the independence and non-alignment of Cyprus intact and the Greek Cypriot community clearly in the position of a majority, not in the fictive position of an "equal partner". EOKA B, though it had succeeded in creating destruction, terror and a good deal of ideological confusion, was by early summer of 1974 dislocated. Its deputy commander and many of its leaders were in jail, many of its arms caches had been located and confiscated and, as if that were not enough, it was split by internal dissention. Makarios had outlived the dictator Papadopoulos. He had been overthrown by the commander of the Military Police, Ioannides, in November 1973. This meant that the provisions of the Greco-Turkish agreement of 1971 would likely suffer a similar fate.

We do not know in detail what the reactions of the U.S. State Department were to these developments. It is likely that they were not regarded with a great deal of pleasure. In the last chapter it was noted that in 1971 the first dictator of Greece had communicated to the U.S. Government his intention of proceeding with a coup if his "brink-manship" with Grivas and EOKA B did not bring about Makarios' capitulation.[1] We do not know what the direct response of the State Department was. But later in this chapter we will show that it resisted all requests from its staff to condemn the dictator's subversion in Cyprus. We have already seen what the U.S. attitude was to the intercommunal talks. It is therefore a fair interference that the Secretary of State would have thought that in the summer of 1974 things were not developing in the best way from the point of view of U.S. interests.

A brief sketch of the chronological sequence of events in the spring and summer of 1974 is necessary before going into them in more detail. George Grivas the commander of EOKA B died on the 28th January 1974. Shortly before his death he had complained that the Greek dictatorship had sent three officers to Cyprus to assassinate him, but there is no evidence that he died violently. Even before his death there had been rumours that EOKA B would desist from violence and become a political party. Perhaps in order to encourage this the Cyprus Government had ordered an amnesty. Grivas' designated successor, Karousos, announced a cessation of EOKA B activities. Karousos in fact very shortly afterwards left, or was forced to leave Cyprus. From then on EOKA B was directly commanded from Athens and run by agents of the Greek dictatorship, though there may have been elements which resisted this which would account for the dissension within the organization.

In April and June 1974 the Cyprus Government spokesman made it clear that EOKA B was directed from Athens and financed at the rate of a million Cyprus pounds a year. (Almost two and a half million dollars.) It was only this vast amount of money that prevented EOKA B from dissolving completely in view of its factionalization and the blows it received from the Cyprus security forces.[2] On the 20th June 1974, Colonel Ioannides informed a CIA officer in Athens that he was planning a coup against President Makarios, and asked what the United States would think about this.[3]

In Cyprus, subversion by the Junta intensified. The Greek military authorities refused a Cyprus Government decision disallowing the military authorities' choice of Cypriot cadets for officer training. There was an incident at the presidential palace itself when a Greek officer tried to enter its grounds with a photograph of George Grivas on the windscreen of his vehicle. There were rumours in Nicosia that the Greek army officers were practising handling armoured vehicles, presumably in order to dispense with the services of Cypriot conscripts.

On the 2nd July, President Makarios wrote a letter to President Gizikis of Greece, accusing the Greek army officers of subversion and demanding that they be removed from Cyprus. On the 6th July, the President of Cyprus gave an interview on the letter (which had been given to the press). The Greek dictatorship, he said, is financing and directing EOKA B with the aim of dissolving the Cypriot State. If they give the appearance of controlling the National Guard, "it would give ground for exploitation to the enemies of Cyprus". This was a last appeal to the dictators not to bring the Turkish army into Cyprus. But asked whether he expected a reply from Gizikis, his reply was: "Yes either in words or actions."

Makarios' letter to Gizikis, is, at first, a puzzle. It was not in line with the caution that had led to his (and Cyprus') survival through 13 Greek governments, including one dictatorship. It is conceivable that he had read the signs to mean that a coup would be attempted by Ioannides, no matter how cautious he was in his dealing with him.

The events which followed are well known. On the 15th July the Greek army officers struck. The resistance which the Cypriot police and socialists put up was sufficient to enable Makarios to escape from Cyprus but not sufficient to prevent the establishment of a dictatorship on the island, with Nikos Sampson as the puppet president. Turkish Prime Minister Bulent Ecevit flew to London to persuade the British Government to intervene jointly in Cyprus, as guarantors. The British Government refused, and on the 20th July the Turkish army attempted to land in the north of Cyprus. Faced with the resistance of bands of boys and reservists armed with First World War rifles, they failed to partition Cyprus by the time the U.N. Security Council had moved to call for a cease-fire. But they had gained a foothold. They continued to land troops and heavy equipment and to edge forward across successive cease-fire lines for almost a month, driving the Greek Cypriot civilian population before it.

On the 22nd July the Junta collapsed, both in Athens and in Nicosia, followed by a civilian government with Mr Karamanlis and Mr Clerides at their heads respectively.

Between the 25th and 30th of July the Foreign Ministers of the guarantor powers met in Geneva, agreeing to the implementation of the cease-fire and for a return to constitutional normality in Cyprus, as well as to the implementation of Security Council Resolution 353 which called for the withdrawal of all foreign troops from the island.

When the guarantors met again, on the 9th of August, none of these agreements had been implemented. The Acting President of Cyprus expressed readiness to return to the 1960 constitution, the Turkish Vice President taking up his functions, while negotiations continued from where the intercommunal talks had left off. Mr Günes, the Turkish Foreign Minister insisted on a form of federation putting over a third of Cyprus under Turkish control. When the Cypriot Acting President asked for 36 hours to consider the proposals, the Turkish army, on the 14th of August, went from the nibbling tactics to a full scale offensive, which at last completed the occupation of an area of Cyprus virtually identical with the area demanded in 1965.[4] All pretext that Turkey was aiming at the restoration of the constitutional order, overthrown by Colonel Ioannides' coup had disappeared. Turkey was at last in military control of 40% of the territory of the Republic of Cyprus. No mention was ever again made of restoring constitutional order. Rather there were veiled threats of further fighting if the legal president, Archbishop Makarios, returned to the island.

What did these events mean? And who was to benefit from them? In much of the international press they were reported as if in the nature of a natural catastrophe. Yet already there was a report that,

> ... the Cyprus crisis in July produced such happy results that the State Department Cyprus task force was dissolved, after congratulations all round in the belief that the problem had disappeared along with the Greek military dictatorship.

In fact the immediate crisis was not yet over, and the Cyprus task force was reassembled in mid-August in view of the second Turkish offensive. Even after it,

> In fact the end result is not so far from what the U.S. has been seeking: a viable separate Turkish community on Cyprus. War between Greece and Turkey was averted.[5]

It was this congruence of U.S. interests with the course of events which created initial suspicions that the United States might have favoured the course of events on Cyprus in the summer of 1974. However, two theories dominated the views of both establishment and dissenting political commentators on the events.[6] The theory of the State Department itself implied that the United States had neither the right nor the possibility of checking the coup or the invasion and that in any event the piecemeal nature of U.S. foreign policy formulation means that it is impossible to hold anyone responsible for a complex course of events such as that in Cyprus. Critics of the Secretary of State, on the other hand, point out the distraction created by the Watergate scandal and say the incidental inaction of Washington damaged the interests of NATO.

Let us start with the assertion of the Secretary of State himself. The implication is that he was caught unawares by such an irrational action as that of Ioannides. He could not predict and therefore could not forestall it. "The information was not exactly lying around on the streets."[7] In fact, information about operations against the Makarios government had been lying around on the streets for at least the past four years, both in Cyprus itself, where a U.S. Embassy and information collecting agencies are maintained, and in Washington, where there is a Cypriot Embassy and a Cyprus Desk at the State Department.

Previous moves against Makarios had been much more easily concealed because they did not involve a move of the National Guard for a coup, but rather a conspiratorially organized assassination attempt against the life of the President. Yet the State Department had been fully informed on them, and in line with preventing things from moving to the stage of chaos in Cyprus, had acted to forestall them.

In late January 1970 the Cypriot President had been warned by the American ambassador in Nicosia of a planned assassination attempt against him. Mr Popper had erred by only two days on the date of the attempt.[8]

In 1972, after the president of the Cypriot National Assembly warned Ambassador Popper in Nicosia that the Junta was planning a coup and bloodshed in Cyprus, the U.S. Ambassador in Athens, Mr Tasca warned the Junta against such a course.

Coming to the events of 1974, as early as March of 1974 the Cypriot Ambassador to Washington visited the State Department where he told the Assistant Secretary of State for Near Eastern Affairs, Rodger Davies, and the man in charge of the Cyprus Desk, Tom Boyatt, that a serious effort would be made to assassinate the President of Cyprus before Easter and that a coup in Cyprus would mean that the Turks would move in and a crisis with an unforeseeable outcome would develop.[9] As already mentioned, the message from Ioannides himself was transmitted on the 20th June. On the 3rd July Makarios' letter to Gizikis was published in full in the Cypriot newspapers and given coverage in the world press. On the 5th July, the Cypriot newspaper *Apogevmatini* wrote that there would be a coup in a few days, with the aim of assassinating the President and that Turkey already has plans to move in and partition the island. The next day, the *Times* of London correspondent transmitted the same information from Athens.[10] President Makarios himself has implied that the U.S. Ambassador in Nicosia hinted to him two days before the coup that he knew what was being prepared.[11]

In view of these, which are only a few of the known facts about access to information, the implication that the U.S. State Department was "caught napping" can be denied outright. But there is stronger evidence than this which however indicates actual acquiescence to the assault on Cyprus. It is however difficult to determine to what extent this acquiescence was merely designed to "cut the Cypriot President's wings", and make him toe the Junta line, and to what extent the acquiescence actually favoured a coup and Turkish invasion all along. The likeliest explanation is it was in line with the Junta's plan to proceed with a coup, if Makarios refused to have his wings clipped.

We know that some State Department officials, particularly from the U.S. Embassy in Nicosia and from the Cyprus Desk in Washington, had appealed to the higher officials in the Department to express themselves against the assassination attempts against Makarios inspired by the Greek Junta. These appeals were ignored by the Secretary of State.[12]

As early as April 1974, "working level" officers at the State Department tried to persuade Secretary of State Kissinger to act so as to prevent Greek moves against Makarios.[13] Obviously these officers believed that it was both within the ability and rights of the State Department to bring influence to bear on the heavily U.S.-dependent regime. Yet it was "weeks" before Kissinger was persuaded to instruct Ambassador Tasca to warn Ioannides not to create a *fait accompli* in Cyprus which would move the Turkish Government to invade.[14] Though messages were sent to Tasca to restrain Ioannides after his 20th June message, neither Kissinger nor Under-secretary of State Sisco warned the Junta's ambassador in Washington against the coup.[15] Tasca, who had in fact been kept in the dark by the CIA about the 20th June message from Ioannides,[16] did not regard the situation as critical. Tasca also maintained that Under-secretary of State Sisco did not tell him that the situation was urgent.[17] Nor was the 20th June message widely disseminated in Washington[18]; under the circumstances Tasca confined himself to sending a middle-grade CIA officer to see Ioannides.[19] "The implication" according to Ambassador Belcher of the mild and low level warning to Ioannides "was obvious". This situation was in marked contrast to 1972, when Tasca effectively dissuaded Papadopoulos from proceeding with a coup. If, Tasca later said to a congressional investigator, he had had the full information about the situation, "he would have turned the place upside down to prevent a coup this time".[20]

It appears in fact that U.S. foreign policy in Greece was not conducted by the normal channels of the State Department and the Embassy at all, but by the CIA. The relationship between Ioannides and Tasca was always mediated by the CIA.[21] Before the coup, a high ranking American diplomat had confided to the *Washington Post* journalist Laurence Stern that, as far as the CIA in Greece was concerned, "Most of us don't know what they are doing. I hope the Ambassador does." It turns out that the Ambassador did not know either Who did?

If a "conspiracy" theory is to be dismissed, we have to believe instead that the world's most powerful intelligence agency is capable of a tremendous and coincidental series of blunders and omissions. But the series is far from complete at this stage.

Soon after 20th June message from Ioannides, several Foreign Ministry Officials in Greece resigned, purportedly for personal reasons, but in fact because they were in strong disagreement with the dictators' intended course of action.[22] At this time, the CIA passed on a message to Washington from a "new and untested source" that Ioannides had decided not to move against Makarios. According to a Congressional investigator[23] "the intelligence community chose to ignore the mountain of evidence" that there would be a coup and preferred the new and untried source. In fact reports from now on, "including one on the day of the coup consistently provided reassurances and these were widely disseminated".[24] The mountain of evidence included the fact that the Turks were preparing for an invasion. Representative Murphy in a Congressional investigation later summed it up like this:

> Then our State Department was told that the coup was not going to take place: And yet the Turks continued their preparations. So one can only assume that their intelligence was better than ours. The Turks knew the coup was imminent. They were preparing for the coup. We were led astray on the matter.[25]

Surely, the inaction indicates that somewhere there was acquiescence to the coup. Certainly the atmosphere among some diplomats was favourable to it. Eric Rouleau of *Le Monde* reports that when he was in Nicosia, thirty six hours before the coup, he heard "from Anglo-American sources" that Makarios had become a tool of the socialists; that EOKA B was a popular movement; that Makarios was flirting excessively with Russia; that he would never agree to solve the Cyprus problem; and that his removal from power was in western interests.[26] Unless the eminent journalist is lying, he observed the kinds of attitudes that motivated the EOKA B terrorists to think that they were serving the free world, but also the kind of attitudes which are congruent with tolerating or even encouraging Ioannides' coup against Makarios.

This is in fact enough evidence to attribute responsibility. If a regime, heavily indebted to U.S. policy for being in power at all, moves against a small, independent country, and the U.S. in full knowledge of the moves does nothing whatsoever to stop it, one could deduce that someone in the U.S. administration was in fact in favour of this course of events.

One could stop here. But it is worth also mentioning some of the more sinister evidence, which actually points to the possibility of active involvement of the CIA.

One has to start with CIA links in Greece. Apart from the general information on the effect of U.S. policy on Greek society and politics contained in the previous chapter, one can point to more specific evidence that the groups involved in both the dictatorial Greek Government and in the coup in Cyprus were no strangers to the American secret services. The first dictator, Papadopoulos, was liaison

168

officer with the American CIA for the organization the CIA had created in Greece, KYP, which is the Greek acronym for CIA.[27] Ioannides was also known to cooperate closely with the CIA.[28] Greek KYP officers were not only trained by the CIA, but in some cases directly paid from Washington.[29] There is evidence that it was the Greek KYP which took over EOKA B after the ousting of Grivas' nominated successor.[30]

Coincidences just continue to pile on coincidences. In early 1974 the Cypriot secret services observed a contact between the attempted dictator of Cyprus, Nikos Sampson and an ex-CIA station chief in Cyprus, Eric Neff. The meeting took place in Athens. This was not reported by leftists. Mr Clerides went to the U.S. Embassy in Nicosia and related this, saying that the meeting had taken place in the second week of February. Initially, the Americans told Clerides that Neff had not been in Athens at that time. The Cyprus Government supplied more information and specific dates. It was then admitted that Neff had been in Athens, but had not met with Sampson. It is a further interesting coincidence that Neff had been the CIA's station chief in Nicosia between 1969 and 1971, the years when anti-independence terrorism had started in Cyprus. A former European Ambassador to Nicosia remembered Neff. "He would say openly in the diplomatic community that it was necessary to get rid of Makarios." Neff had also had contacts with the man convicted for conspiring to organize the assassination attempt against the Archbishop in 1970. Finally, the Cypriot president asked for the agent to be recalled.[31]

Closer to the time of the coup, security forces in Cyprus had captured EOKA B documents which indicated that money was coming from Athens at the rate of 6,000 dollars a day. Yet again a link turns up. The man who sent the money "had influential connections in the CIA station in Athens".[32] Makarios after the coup spoke of a cheque for 33,000 dollars issued in the U.S. for a leading member of EOKA B who could give no explanation for this transfer of money.[33]

This is the kind of evidence that led responsible people in Cyprus to think it unlikely that the CIA had not been involved in the attempt to destabilize the Cypriot Government. There is no high government official in Cyprus who by any stretch of the imagination belongs to the Left. Yet when Ambassador Belcher visited Cyprus in May and June of 1974, "very senior officials" in the Cyprus Government told him that there was considerable involvement of the U.S. in trying to overthrow Makarios. These officials said that they had documentary evidence that the CIA was financing EOKA B via Ioannides and the National Guard officers.[34]

After the coup, Archbishop Makarios repeatedly said that he never expected a unilateral Greek coup. What he expected was an attempt to assassinate him or an intervention in an *agreed* way with Turkey to establish "double *enosis*". Ioannides, the Archbishop said, acted stupidly. As an example of his stupidity he related how in 1964 when Ioannides was posted in Cyprus he visited him, together with Sampson, and suggested the elimination of all Turkish Cypriots as a solution to the problem.[35] Makarios chased both out of his office.

Ioannides' stupidity may have been an essential ingredient. But it is not sufficient as an explanation for his actions. It takes very little to work out that a coup by Greece in Cyprus would result in a Turkish invasion, that militarily Greece would have been in an inferior position and therefore the terms of the final result would be dictated by Turkey. There is one report[36] that Ioannides received assurances from Turkish military officials that they would not react against the objective of operation Aphrodite (the coup), that is getting rid of Makarios. But in view of the deteriorating relations between the two countries over the Aegean, it is doubtful whether this is enough. There is no firm evidence for this, but it makes much more sense to hypothesize that Ioannides received assurances from the CIA that the Turks would not intervene before proceeding with the coup. Reports to this effect did appear in the Greek press after the fall of the dictatorship.[37] Certainly after the coup, CIA and State Department behaviour was such as to prevent the restoration of the constitutional government, a change which might have removed the Turkish pretext for invading.

Both the chiefs of the Greek navy and the air force were, after the coup, told by Ioannides that he had assurances from the Americans that there would be no Turkish intervention in Cyprus. The chief of the air force in a confidential report to the Prime Minister soon after the restoration of democracy in Greece said that when, he, Papanicolaou, questioned Ioannides, on the 16th July about whether he had made a suitable estimation of the consequences of the coup, Ioannides replied that "neither the Americans nor the Turks wanted Makarios".[38] The Chief of the Navy, Arapakis, said in an interview, that a little before the invasion Ioannides was saying that "he had assurances from the Americans that there would be no Turkish intervention in Cyprus".[39] The Junta's man in the London Embassy did warn Ioannides that a Turkish invasion looked likely, but "Ioannides preferred the view of the CIA men in Athens that it was all a show."[40] There is even a report that Under-secretary Sisco himself assured Ioannides that the Turks would not invade.[41]

Again a dichotomy in behaviour appears between the diplomats and the CIA. In Cyprus, the U.S. Ambassador told Glavkos Clerides that if Sampson did not resign and the Greek officers withdraw, there would be an invasion. Clerides warned the "foreign minister" of Cyprus appointed by the Junta. He communicated with Athens and told Clerides: "What the ambassador told you does not worry us, because we have different assurances from Athens."[42]

The behaviour of the officers who had been engaged in the coup in Cyprus was mixed. It varied between certainty that there would be no Turkish intervention at all, a belief that there might be a "token" landing to force agreement on the Cypriots, and total confusion once it became apparent that the Turks were playing for real. The first landing came at five a.m. on the 20th July but it had seemed more than likely to the average newspaper reader for two to three days previously. The commander of the Cyprus navy recounted that he received no order for any move until an hour *after* the first Turkish landing. Mobilization was ordered in Cyprus more than two hours after the Turkish forces has landed, approximately the same time as the move of the National Guard Headquarters to wartime quarters.[43] On the other hand, a Cypriot lieutenant in the National Guard has related how his Greek commander told him on the day of the invasion: "The Turks will come and fuck all you Cypriot officers and I shall be looking on from afar and enjoying it."[44]

The assurances on the part of the U.S. secret services to the Greek dictators that there would be no Turkish intervention took the pressure off them for a restoration of the *status quo*. U.S. diplomats at the time said that the reason for this was that if the Greek officers in Cyprus were removed, it would create a power vacuum, into which the Cypriot communists would step.[45] In other words, the threat of the Cypriot communists stepping in was to be met by making no move to inhibit a Turkish army of occupation from moving in. At this time, U.S. diplomacy gave every sign of preparing to accept the Junta's coup, even publicly. This took the form for example of denying that there had been Greek intervention in Cyprus. It has been claimed that this was so that a Turkish pretext for invasion would be removed. But for this to have been so, it should have been combined with urgent secret warnings to Ioannides about Turkish preparations, and urgings to "undo" the coup. As noted above, the opposite was true.

On the day after the coup a State Department spokesman in Washington refused to comment on whether the State Department recognized the Makarios government and expressed the view that there had been no external intervention.[46] The day before the invasion, U.S. Ambassador Scali in the U.N., said that it would be a serious error to rush judgement on whether there had been foreign intervention in Cyprus.[47]

Nor was there any U.S. support for the Turkish prime minister's compromise demand for the resignation of Sampson and the establishment of a federation in Cyprus to be negotiated immediately by the Greek and Turkish Cypriot interlocutors in the intercommunal talks.[48] The U.S. seemed intent on doing nothing which, however

171

indirectly, might inhibit the possibility of a Turkish invasion in Cyprus.

The U.S. intelligence agencies themselves and the State Department were acting in an odd way. In the "post mortem" that the State Department conducted on the adequacy of the intelligence services, it states that "intelligence provided an explicit warning, including date on the invasion": "The State Department takes little if any preventive action; claims it did not get the message." The staff director for the Congressional committee of inquiry into the intelligence services stated though that the prediction by the CIA of the invasion came on the day of the invasion and was not disseminated. The CIA's warning never went beyond the National Intelligence offices.[49] The behaviour of both the CIA and the State Department is very odd, for the invasion was widely predicted in newspapers two to three days before and this included reports of Turkish ships moving to Cyprus.[50]

Naturally under the circumstances, Turkish higher officials reported that only "minimal" pressures were exercised on them by U.S. officials not to invade.[51]

Immediately after the Turkish attacks on Cyprus, U.S. policy extended its efforts in three directions. One was to preventing Greece from going to the help of the Cypriots. As the intelligence post-mortem puts it:

> CIA with Embassy concurrence passes reassuring intelligence to Greeks which helps cool the ardour.[52]

This time not only the CIA but also the Embassy was in on the act of passing misleading information, assuring the Greek military chiefs that the U.S. would do all it could to stop the Turkish advances.[53] Ioannides feeling at last that the U.S. had been leading him up several garden paths, decided on the 21st to go to war with Turkey.[54] In some way the three service chiefs of Greece, who had for over a year obeyed his orders, were roused to opposition, refused to go to war and demanded the return of a civilian government. In fact, Kissinger had been promoting the overthrow of Ioannides soon after the coup against Makarios, since he had decided that the dictator was a bad investment,

> ... incapable of maintaining the kind of safeguards that the U.S. seeks for its bases in Greece, and for the southern flank of NATO. From that moment of truth, the General's fate was virtually sealed.[55]

There has also been an assertion that the "German Ambassador" (presumably of the Federal Republic), in Athens collaborated with the Americans in promoting inactivity in Greece. He reportedly told the chief of the Greek navy that an attack on Greece "from the North" was to be expected.[56]

Kissinger's non-interventionist qualms seemed to have disappeared about this time, for he promoted a cease-fire agreement on the 22nd by promising Turkey that Glavkos Clerides would be president in Cyprus, "pending new elections to take over the Cyprus presidency".[57] The fact that Cyprus already had a constitutionally elected President was overlooked. In fact U.S. diplomacy was busy trying to compensate for the failure of the Greek officers during the coup. Makarios had got away. Shortly after the return of democratic government in Greece (on the 22nd) in the vacuum created by the collapse of the Junta, Arthur Hartman, Assistant Secretary of State for European Affairs, came to Athens to inform the new Greek Government that "it is important in the interests of the future settlement of Cyprus that Archbishop Makarios not return to Cyprus".[58] In Cyprus itself, Mr Clerides who had agreed to assume the presidency when Nikos Sampson stepped down, presumably as a condition for a cease-fire arrangement mediated by Kissinger, said that he wanted to hold elections for the House of Representatives and for the presidency.[59] (President Makarios' term had at least three years to run.)

A knowledgeable German writer on strategic affairs had written on the day before the invasion:

> How the results of the current explosion can be dammed up is not yet predictable. With tricks and half measures NATO can no longer make do. Somehow the main demand of the Turks must be met by those who want to be present politically and militarily in Cyprus, openly or secretly. Turkey wants to set up its own credible protection for the Turkish minority. But the Turks are also convinced that in the atomic age a strategic base in Cyprus is necessary for the security of the Turkish motherland. In exchange the Greeks and Greek Cypriots could be allowed union with the motherland. The division of the population groups and the dissolution of the existing state of Cyprus would be the price. One needed to be sure a Kissinger in high form to realize such a project.[60]

It was indeed a high-risk course of action for the American Foreign Secretary, one which officials in his own department would not believe that he would engage in. Ambassador Belcher for example said later:

> I do not subscribe to the theory that I have heard expressed that there was a conscious effort on our part to bring about the downfall of Makarios. Perhaps my reasons for this are based too much on logic, but I can't see how anybody could propose such a solution to the Cyprus

problem and not see clearly what it implied with regard to Turkish reaction.[61]

Most knowledgeable people agree about this. But it seems that the evidence lends itself not to making U.S. support for the coup unlikely, but rather leads to the direction of thought that the U.S., at least as represented by the Foreign Secretary and the CIA, fully endorsed the coup *and* the inevitably succeeding invasion.

We have already shown why, U.S. foreign policy under Kissinger might have oriented itself to sacrificing Greece at the expense of Turkey in the context of Eastern Mediterranean strategy in the 1970's. In fact in November 1973 a very high level political-academic gathering of individuals connected with the Cyprus problem, including the current Greek Foreign Minister, an ex-U.S. Ambassador to Greece and Cyrus Vance, was told, presumably by the Americans present that,

> there is no guarantee that the United States would once again find it possible or desirable to exert itself in order to prevent hostilities between Greece and Turkey: The NATO alliance is today in disarray and the character and assumptions of the policy of the United States toward Europe and the Eastern Mediterranean may be profoundly changed.[63]

In any event, the successful prosecution of any kind of war by Greece was in considerable doubt. It was widely known that the effectiveness of the Greek armed forces had been reduced by the forced retirement of hundreds of senior officers in favour of Junta appointees. In September 1974 it was reported that the U.S. Auditor General was investigating the possibility that Greek army weapons had been sold for cash, "a fact which may help explain the inaction of the Greek Junta during the Cyprus invasion".[64] There was even a report that the U.S. had delivered warplanes to the Greek air force without bomb and rocket attachments.[65] Finally, there were the deceptive assurances by the U.S. secret services to Ioannides, the attempt to "cool his ardour". So there was a risk, but it was not as great as would appear at first sight, and in any event, what was being risked, the cohesion of NATO, had partly disappeared on its own accord.

Given the Turkish Government's views and policies on Cyprus, it is not necessary to go very deeply into Turkish thinking on the invasion. Militarily, Turkey in 1974 was fully equipped for a landing. This was in contrast to the 1963 and 1967 Cyprus crises when the Turkish forces had no landing craft at their disposal.[66] The preparation of landing craft after 1967, at a time when there was no intercommunal incident whatsoever in Cyprus, is a good indication of the fact that the prime motivation of Turkish policy on Cyprus is strategic rather than the normally propounded covering ideology which is the purported protection of the Turkish minority. The fact that the Turks were preparing for an invasion[67] before the Greek dictator's coup probably indicates no more than a fairly adequate Turkish intelligence network, since without the Greek takeover attempt a Turkish invasion would have been unthinkable. As it was, the invasion exposed severe Turkish military inadequacies, but was a triumph for Turkish foreign policy. An opportunity had appeared to be on the way since the Junta came to power in Greece. (The time when the Turkish landing craft began to be constructed.) The readiness was rewarded not only by U.S. support, but also, in the first stage when the Junta was in power in Greece and Cyprus, by Soviet support. Ecevit managed to align Turkish nationalism and Turkish strategic needs with "anti-imperialism".

In October 1973 elections in Turkey Ecevit, leading the Republican People's party, won 185 out of 450 seats in the National Assembly. It is an irony of history that it is the party that is the successor of Ataturk that has attempted to acquire a colony in mid-twentieth century. But this may be partly explained by the internal political problems which Ecevit faced. He only succeeded in forming a government after three months by allying his party with Erbakan's Islamic-oriented National Salvation Party. The coalition was an odd one since Ecevit had won the elections on Kemalist principles and Erbakan was a right-wing Islamic reactionary. Ecevit's proposed internal reforms were in jeopardy. Like George Papandreou when he came to power in Greece, he tried to liberalize Turkish political life. He proposed an amnesty of political prisoners of the 1971-3 period of military rule. He was opposed on this by Demirel's Justice Party, the second largest with 149 seats in the House of Representatives. And on this issue, Demirel could easily carry some of the M.P.s of Ecevit's coalition partner, the National Salvation Party. Furthermore the military had just handed over power to the politicians and their reaction to such reforms was uncertain. One of the main results of the 1971 coup was that the army purged itself of most of its Kemalist and left-wing officers.

Under the circumstances the invasion of Cyprus provided an opportunity for Ecevit to become a second Ataturk, combining nationalist ardour with reform and of course securing his government at the same time. In fact what he unleashed in Turkey was a resurgence of Turkish nationalism, including Islamic fervour which may well vitiate any reformist attempts in the future. As early as the 23rd July it was reported that the Atlantic Alliance was worried that the population in Turkey was so "enthusiastic" about the Ecevit government's action that it might have led to a policy of "final reckoning" with Greece.[68]

Even after the landing, Ecevit faced criticism on the grounds that he had not done enough. Suleyman Demirel claimed that the government had safeguarded only *one* out of *seventy-three* Turkish enclaves on Cyprus.[69] The mighty Turkish army, navy and air forces had had very limited success against what should have been a "toy army", with no navy or air force and very limited and virtually entirely obsolete armour. It was indeed to be expected that on the 25th July "the mood in parliament was sombre in contrast to the jubilation when the invasion started".[70]

The experts' verdict was that there was a "disproportion between effort and success". When the Turkish invasion fleet arrived in Famagusta, the armed force controlled by the Turkish Cypriot leadership had already been overrun by the Greek Cypriot forces and no landing was attempted. So the Turkish invasion forces had captured no port and no airport. "The Turkish invasion forces did not achieve militarily what was claimed by them politically."[71] At the second Geneva meeting therefore, according to American specialists speaking "off the record":

> The Turks were in effect letting the clock run. They didn't get the territory they wanted by the end of the first cease-fire and they decided not to stop moving forward until they get it.[72]

When the Turkish army attacked in full force the second time, they had some two hundred tanks as well as forty thousand troops at their disposal.[73] These they had landed on Cyprus during a U.N. supervised cease-fire with no protest from any quarter other than the Cypriots.

In fact they still received full support from the U.S. Secretary of State. Kissinger was privately reported to be telling diplomats that he would not try to stop the Turks until they had reached their territorial objectives.[74] Turkish belligerence at the Geneva conference was in fact encouraged by U.S. Under-secretary A. Hartman, who made it clear to the Turks that the U.S. favoured a strong independent Turkish community on Cyprus. This of course was in private. The public attitude of the U.S. representatives was that the U.S. favoured a return to the pre-July constitution.[75] On 13th August when the British Foreign Secretary, who was also present at Geneva, declared the Turkish refusal of a thirty-six-hour time period requested by the Cyprus Government to consider the Turkish demands to be "arbitrary and unreasonable", the State Department was legitimizing the Turkish attack which was to materialize early the next morning. "We recognize" a State Department statement said the position of the Turkish community requires considerable improvement and protection. We have supported a greater degree of autonomy for them.[76]

Indeed such was the encouragement or deafening silence from all quarters as Turkey swallowed more and more of a small neighbouring country, that it is likely that the Turkish Government and military thought it worth going even further than their original plan, to acquire some geopolitical leeway for future "concessions" in their Aegean dispute with Greece. Turkey has since informed its allies that the second offensive was for "bargaining reasons".[77] On the 18th when, after a second cease-fire, the Turkish army was still edging forward and had among other gratuitous acts of conquest emptied of its 60,000 inhabitants the town of Famagusta, U.S. Secretary of Defense Schlesinger pointed out that,

... we've understood the desire of the Turks to protect the minority Turkish problem, but the Turkish moves at this point have gone beyond what any of its friends or sympathisers would have accepted ...[78]

In a situation where Cyprus was in the grips of the Greek dictators, the Soviet Union could naturally provide no disincentive to a Turkish invasion of what had been a non-aligned state. In fact, the Western Alliance was quite worried about the fact that the Soviet Union supported Turkey.[79] Ecevit himself said after the fighting was over,

... not only the United States, but the Soviet Union tried to be objective and constructive *vis-à-vis* the recent eruptions and we don't have anything to complain about regarding the attitude of the two countries.[80]

But Soviet inactivity was not just connected to the fact that Cyprus was in the hands of the dictatorship. It has to do with several of the factors mentioned in the previous chapter. Detente for the Soviet Union means the reduction of danger of global war. This is all important, given the faith that socialism will triumph so long as it is allowed to do so without being attacked from the West. Besides limitations on the arms race and the acceptance of existing borders and arrangements in Europe, it also means trade and credits from the West.

There is of course no stabilization comparable to that in Europe in the Mediterranean, the Middle East and the Balkans. But gains in these areas have to be weighed carefully against the risks they involve of endangering detente in Europe. This is paricularly so since there are fairly strong voices inside the U.S. claiming that detente favours the Soviet Union and that it should be made clear to the Soviet Union that even peaceful "moves to upset the existing balance can bring detente to an abrupt end and greatly increase the chances of war".[81]

These considerations become particularly important in the Eastern Mediterranean and the Middle East, an area crucial for the United States and for most of the NATO countries, at least economically. In any event, on a scale of priorities, maintaining the non-alignment of Cyprus cannot come all that high since the British bases are sovereign, and are firmly placed on the *island* of Cyprus, though the *Republic* of Cyprus is non-aligned.[82] This must not be misconstrued. Cypriot non-alignment *is* important to the Soviet Union, if only because it is conducive to preventing the British bases from being turned into American or NATO bases. But the *degree* of interest and commitment could not be anywhere near as great as if the whole island was demilitarized.

But perhaps the most weighty element has been the development of good relations with Turkey. For reasons connected with the structure of power within Turkey it is very unlikely that Turkey would actually detach itself from NATO. But these are the days of bilateral strategies and degrees of commitment in military alliances. And every little bit, with a country as strategically placed as Turkey, counts. There have been reports that the Soviet Union considers that Turkey is at least amenable to promising that no NATO base will be established on the part of Cyprus which it controls.[83]

After the coup, the Soviet Union clearly called for the restoration of the pre-coup situation and of President Makarios. But the call was, one may say, platonic in the sense that no real pressure was exerted in that direction. The Turkish intervention, when it came, purported to be in the cause of restoring legality. The Soviet Union let it be known that it supported it.[84] In fact it seems that the Soviet Union might have contributed to a delay in the Security Council resolution calling for a cease-fire immediately after the invasion.[85]

There was no conflict with the U.S. over what was happening in Cyprus. In fact there are reports that the Soviet Union asked the U.S. to remove some of its citizens from Cyprus during the fighting.[86] On the 4th August, when the Greek Foreign Minister, George Mavros, pointed out to the Soviet Ambassador in Athens that if the Soviet Union made a clear declaration that all forces, Greek and Turkish, should leave Cyprus the Turks would withdraw, the Ambassador asked whether the Americans were willing to make a common declaration with the Soviet Union.[87]

Even on the 10th August, when it seemed very likely that the Geneva conference would collapse under the weight of Turkish intransigence, the Soviet Union continued to be "correct and unbelligerent", and strongly denied reports that any of their forces were put on the alert.[88] The Soviet leaders presumably remembered that during the Middle East war the previous year the U.S. responded to a statement favouring joint Soviet and American intervention by bringing their missiles to an advanced state of readiness.

In general the Soviet Union said all the correct things but practically did little to further them. Even criticism when it came was directed vaguely towards "NATO" rather than the immediate perpetrators.

The consequences of the invasion were unspeakable for the Cypriots. In an island with a total population of 650,000, 3,000 Greek Cypriots and 500 Turkish Cypriots were killed within a month. A third of the population were refugees. (The figure was yet to increase after August 1974.) The Turkish army had occupied and rendered virtually useless almost 60% of the productive resources of Cyprus which were in the northern 40% of the area. All but about 30,000 Greek Cypriots were forced to flee from the North and concentrate, initially, in the open air, in the South. Three of the four main roads out of Nicosia, the capital, were cut off.

The likeliest consequence of this would have been that the Cypriots would collapse and sign anything that the Turkish Government handed them. But this did not happen.

In fact, the Cyprus problem is in a more explosive situation than it has ever been. The possibility of Turkey declaring a puppet Turkish Cypriot State in the North, the Greek Cypriots' willingness to find allies anywhere, and their increasing feeling that they have nothing to lose will be indefinite ingredients for instability in the Eastern Mediterranean.

# CHAPTER IX
## *Conclusions*

A detailed history of the events in Cyprus during the last twenty years cannot yet be written. It was in any event not the intention of this book. What was attempted here is an interpretation of how a small island in the Eastern Mediterranean has come to periodically occupy the first pages of the world's press in most unpleasant ways. An involved observer with some training in detachment cannot wait for the statesmen and politicians to open their archives before attempting to interpret the maiming of a minor but important society. An interpretation of the shape of events can be based on those that have come to be publicly available to date. Enough of the facts are available to construct a story which must have implications extending further than the limited area of Cyprus, or even the Eastern Mediterranean. They present evidence of the dangers to humanity, particularly to that part of it that lives in small and defenceless states and of the arrogantly destructive consequences of the ways in which the dominant or "imperial" states of the world pursue what their leaders define as their interests. In the process, it was necessary to grapple with the problem of how people living in a country with a potential of satisfying all their real human needs come to behave in most self-destructive ways, caught up in world power games which they only now begin to understand.

The two facets of events in Cyprus—the international power struggles surrounding it and the behaviour of the Cypriots who did not always have a clear vision of the consequences of their actions—are highly interdependent. Greek and Turkish nationalism in Cyprus, it is true, resulted in local squabbles. But their adjudication by self-interested outside powers more than influenced their course. In the perspective of world power struggles these squabbles appeared as instruments, albeit frequently recalcitrant ones. This process has been facilitated by the fact that the world political scene is a social system where the powerful exercise power in such ways that it is often possible to even deny that the power exists. And the arrogance with which it is used on occasion is only matched by the smugness of refusing to use it when trends seem satisfying.

In fact, imperial powers, including Britain, have repeatedly been involved in the development of nationalist movements in Cyprus. They did this directly as rulers of the island and through diplomatic and other interventions. They also had indirect effects because of their determining influences on the intercommunal system of power. The involvements of the imperial powers have not aimed primarily at the reconciliation of inter-Cypriot ethnic or any other kind of conflict. They have aimed at various times to preserve strategic bases, to maintain the coherence of the NATO alliance or to frustrate the development of a leftward trend in Cyprus. If a "basic" cause of the explosion of 1974 were to be sought, it would have to be sought in the corridors of Whitehall, where decisions were taken not to allow Cypriots self-determination during the seventy-two years they were demanding it. During this time inter-ethnic conflict, to the degree that it existed in Cyprus, was not a significant factor affecting international politics.

Greek nationalism developed into a political movement in Cyprus as a reaction to the transition from Ottoman to British rule. It took the "normal" European form of seeking incorporation with a state entity with which historical and linguistic unity was felt. Greece itself could not effectively support this movement due to its dependence on Britain, the same imperial power from which the Cypriots were trying to escape.

The nationalist movement was led by the Church in Cyprus, and conflicted later with a developing communist movement. Though the latter also claimed union with Greece as the ultimate aim of the struggle, it had the characteristics of an "anti-colonial" rather than a "European nationalist" movement. It is partly because of this internal conflict that the "Cyprus Problem" first erupted on the international scene, during the 1950's. It came however at a time when Cyprus was of crucial importance for British strategic interests. In the process of effectively blocking the movement, British policy makers used methods which showed complete indifference to inter-ethnic harmony in Cyprus, and even to the harmony of the NATO alliance. The cultural separation of Greek and Turkish Cypriots—with its unfortunate overtones of traditional national enmity—was aggravated by its use as a bargaining counter in diplomatic wrangles. Mainland Turkish interest was solicited. A problem which had, in international terms, been a relatively simple one of "decolonization" began to appear as a complex international issue, to be settled by covert mediations.

Britain was mainly interested in safeguarding its own oil resources, but its senior partner, the United States, had more global interests. For a long time, in the Eastern Mediterranean as elsewhere, they consisted in "containing communism". This was pursued through the creation of anti-communist alliance of nations and also by attempting to prevent internal political changes which looked as if they would result in governments with a non-western orientation. Once Turkey was involved with Cyprus, a further problem was added from the point of view of the Western Alliance. Previously, the preservation of such internal conditions and international control over Cyprus such as would not endanger the western military presence were the two main ones. The third problem was that the coherence of the Alliance itself was threatened by the conflicting claims on Cyprus of two of its members, Greece and Turkey.

U.S. pressures on Britain to consider the interests of the West more globally and the high cost to Britain itself of militarily occupying Cyprus against guerilla warfare created the preconditions for a kind of decolonization in Cyprus. The fact of conflicting intra-alliance aims made this solution "independence" rather than the union with Greece. The "communist danger" within Cyprus could have been contained by various arrangements, one of which could have been making membership of NATO a condition of independence. But two NATO powers, Greece and Turkey already had nationalist claims on the island. Part of their recompense for abandoning their territorial claims on Cyprus was being made the guarantors for NATO. At the same time they would be acting as guarantors for the security of the respective ethnic communities on Cyprus. The need to use the rights of a guarantor power was of course more likely to arise in the case of Turkey, since the Turks were a minority in Cyprus. It is not likely that such intervention was visualized by the framers of the arrangements.

It would have been reasonable to believe that the common interest of Greece and Turkey in the cohesion of NATO would transmit itself to their respective ethnically linked groups in Cyprus. Intervention, if the occasion arose, would be joint and aimed at preventing "internal subversion" in Cyprus.

Internationally, this set of arrangements was neat. Internally, it assumed astonishing powers of rationality, maturity and self-denial on the part of groups of people who had been reared with emotions of heated nationalist fervour. Greek Cypriot political leaders could appeal to the frustration of Hellenic nationalist aims. They could also appeal to "anti-imperialism", given the omnipresent British military. They could all unite against the Turkish Cypriots who had served as the "trojan horse" to frustrate *enosis,* but also, after an independence they had not fought for, been given a share in the power structure of Cyprus which seemed disproportionate. In spite of cooler voices among the Greeks, these were the dominant notes heard by the Turkish Cypriots. Their leaders could appeal to the need to preserve the gains of the Turkish Cypriot struggle against Greek nationalism. The situation was unstable because the external power balance created an internal power imbalance. In their attempt to rectify the internal power balance, the Greek Cypriot leaders created international imbalances of such magnitude as could only surround a small island due to the complicated involvements of imperial powers.

# Conclusions

During the intercommunal fighting of 1963-4 and the periodic minor recurrences which lasted until 1967, the Cyprus problem appeared to become transformed. While the sectarian conflicts of the 1960-3 period had reheated Greek and Turkish nationalism in Cyprus, the events of 1963-7 led to the internal dominance of the Greek Cypriots. Gradually this very dominance in an independent state defused the power of Hellenic nationalism. But at the same time it pushed the Turkish Cypriots to complete economic and political dependence on Turkey. The Greek Cypriots developed a strong "regionalist" consciousness in relation to Greece due to economic development and divergence in cold-war alignments, which even made them conscious of cultural particularities. The Turkish Cypriots increasingly identified with Turkish nationalism, Turkish state power and the ideologies of communist phobia. This meant that the Greek Cypriots felt the need of military support from Greece, to fend off the ever-present threat of "liberation" of the Turkish Cypriots by Turkey. In the last six years the military representatives of Greece turned a political movement within Cyprus, whose leaders under different circumstances would have been harmless cranks or eccentrics, into the representatives of a most intense and violent Greek nationalism. This with at the very least the toleration of the U.S. on the basis of a narrow interpretation of strategic interests. Thus, in a Greek Cypriot dominated island, with strong trends towards consciousness of distinctive identity and statehood, non-alignment and lack of "anti-communism"—in other words all the preconditions for the development of a post-colonial nationalism—a paradox developed. A small, intense movement irrationally advocated Hellenic nationalism against the most fantastic international odds and internal interests. Since nationalisms feed on and are justified by each other, this movement was one of the main means by which Turkey achieved the long-sought partition of Cyprus.

The imperial powers aggravated the problem of incorporating the Turkish Cypriots into the kind of "post-colonial nationalist state" that was developing in Cyprus as a by-product of the pursuit of their interests.

The United States supported the Greek dictators and did not in anyway dispel the impression which was dominant in Greece and among Greek Cypriot nationalists, that it was in favour of some kind of partition of Cyprus between Greece and Turkey, on the basis of "proportional" allocation of the territory of the Republic of Cyprus. It is in any event quite clear that this would have neutralized the "communist danger" within Cyprus which the unchecked development of a fully independent post-colonial nationalist state might have involved. Partition could also, in this theory, re-establish the cohesion of NATO which had seen the possibility of war between two of its members in 1964 and 1967. Some Greek governments and Hellenic nationalists in Cyprus took the line that the Cyprus Government was not only frustrating a passable form of *enosis,* but was also encouraging Greek Cypriots to develop their own consciousness of being a national entity. Among other terrors this would lead to a communist-dominated Cyprus. "Anti-communism", by an odd process, came to unite NATO, the Greek dictators, Turkey and the Turkish Cypriot leaders against the Republic of Cyprus.

The Soviet Union, on the other hand, contributed to the impression that ethnic tensions in Cyprus were only due to "imperialist interventions" and that these tensions would disappear as soon as the British bases were closed down. In a sense, as an ideology, this was less damaging. At least it provided diplomatic, and for a while, military support enabling Cyprus to disentangle itself from the State Department's carving designs. But it also contributed to the Greek Cypriots' "sectarianist" insensitivity to the need to reintegrate the Turkish Cypriots politically and economically.

The Greek Cypriot dominated Government of Cyprus took increasing steps after 1964 towards non-alignment and reliance on Soviet support against Turkish and later Greek military intervention. This moved the problem to a much bigger league. In this game Cyprus became a dispensable pawn. The relative success of Cypriot tactics in 1964 and 1965 in appealing to non-alignment and Soviet support had important implications. One of them was to contribute to the strengthening of a feeling of statehood among the Greek Cypriots and a feeling of separateness from American-dominated Greece. But another implication was that the use of these tactics was adopted by Turkey. If one wanted to find a second basic cause for the events of 1974 in Cyprus it would be this: Turkey was able to mount a "peace-keeping" operation in Cyprus seven years after the last intercommunal incident because during those seven years it had reopened the "Eastern Question" in a Cold War form. The Soviet Union and the United States came to be competing suitors.

This leaves the role of the Greek dictatorship. Its existence reinforced the position of the two great imperial powers. Turkey gained support from the Soviet Union because of friendly diplomatic initiatives. But this support was strengthened as the Greek dictatorship became an increasingly dangerous threat to Cypriot independence and non-alignment. For the United States, Turkey's inconstancy reinforced the need for strategic Greek facilities. Fear of being deprived of them led to tolerance of explosively nationalist acts in Cyprus on behalf of its protégés, the Greek Colonels. At the same time the United States sought means of attracting Turkey back to the secure haven of its pre-1965 relation to the NATO alliance. One can almost hear State Department policy makers think: we almost lost both Greece and Turkey in 1964-7 in trying to prevent a war between the two. If we let them both have their heads, and support the stronger, we might loose the weaker (but this is unlikely with a communistophobic dictatorship ruling Greece). One way or another Greece and Turkey between them will have solved the "Makarios problem". (The "Makarios problem" being presumably the way in which some American policy makers thought of the dangers of an independent, non-aligned Cyprus.)

This crude and amoral policy, based purely on strategic considerations, has by 1979 been proved to be a clear failure, even defined in terms of narrow strategic interests themselves. But after the Turkish invasion of Cyprus, it manifested itself even more clearly. A U.S. Congressional mission visiting Cyprus a few months after the invasion summarized U.S. policy in this way:

> Given the omissions in our country's diplomacy and our apparent approval of the Turkish invasion, it is inevitable, perhaps, that the United States would give its tacit recognition to Turkey's *fait accompli* on Cyprus, and clearly associate itself with a bi-regional settlement on the island—or geographical separation of the Greek and Turkish communities.

Their report cited statements of the U.S. Secretary of State for Foreign Affairs implying that the U.S. accepted a demarcation line across the island, with Turkey (a very different implication from "the Turkish Cypriots") showing "flexibility" in terms of the size of the territory it occupies and in terms of the size of the military forces it maintains on the island.[1]

The same Congressional mission reported that conversations with U.S. officials indicated to them that the purpose of U.S. humanitarian aid to Cypriot refugees was to counterbalance the favour shown to the political and military aims of Turkey on Cyprus, "... to keep the refugees contained, so as to buy time to assist Ankara in consolidating its position on the island", and "to help refurbish Turkey's international image, thereby strengthening its bargaining position in pursuing its bi-regional objectives on Cyprus".[2]

U.S. Government statements tended to support the Turkish position on Cyprus and the use of U.S. arms in the operation, by arguing that the invasion was necessary to protect the suffering Turkish minority on Cyprus and that Greeks and Greek Cypriots should be happy because the invasion brought democracy to Greece.[3]

For a while at the end of 1974, it seemed as if the "final solution" of the Cyprus problem might be within sight. A package deal seemed to be there for the wrapping, with the independence of Cyprus maintained as a public relations concept, the northern part being integrated with Turkey, and the remaining "half a Greek loaf allied to Athens in a loose federation".[4] What had been achieved was this:

> The island has been effectively partitioned though the proportions may be varied in a cosmetic way. The U-2 planes continue to take-off from British bases to overfly the Middle East. The possibility of a communist takeover internally or externally has been aborted by the simple fact that there are nearly as many NATO soldiers on the island as there are left wingers.[5]

The initial, personal intentions of Bulent Ecevit are opaque. His stated intention was to maintain an independent, non-aligned Cyprus with the kind of local autonomy for the Turkish Cypriots which would not result in partition.[6] But this seems at best naive, given his knowledge of the strategic aims of the Turkish army and the weakness of his government. In fact, his government fell in March 1975. Mr Demirel succeeded him as Prime Minister, and his coalition government includes the neo-fascist National Action Party, whose policy is the takeover of the whole of Cyprus. In Parliament the party is insignificant, but the same cannot be said of Necmettin Erbakan's National Salvation Party which holds 48 seats and the fate of Mr Demirel's government in the balance. Erbakan is opposed to any Turkish "concession" on Cyprus.

But apart from Turkes and Erbakan, the intentions of Turkey in Cyprus are evident from the past history of her claims, from proposals for a settlement, and from the actions it has engaged in the occupied part of Cyprus.

The main aim of Turkey in Cyprus continues to be the maintenance of a foothold in Cyprus in order to

> ... effectively influence the future military status and international alignment of Cyprus as a whole.[7]

The key points are the fact that Turkey's dominant concern is strategic (this being compatible with a fair amount of suffering on the part of the Turkish Cypriots), and secondly, that this strategic concern extends to the whole of Cyprus. This is why now that the Turkish presence in Cyprus is a fact, Turkish policy is against outright partition between Greece and Turkey which would result in a Greek presence in the South. "Federation" between a Turkish protectorate in the North, and an independent Greek Cypriot state in the South would preserve a legal basis for Turkish involvement in the whole of Cyprus.[8].

In practice these aims have been pursued in the following way: the occupied part of Cyprus is being integrated economically, politically and socially with Turkey, while Turkish proposals for a solution provide for a partitioned Cyprus with two states. One would be a Turkish protectorate in the North, the other, a Greek Cypriot state in the South. The two states would be linked by a joint foreign policy, in which Turkey and the Greek Cypriots would have an equal say.

On the 13th February 1975 the occupied part of Cyprus was declared to be a "Turkish Cypriot Federated State". In August 1975 the 45,000 Turkish Cypriots who still lived in the Cyprus Government controlled area were transferred by the U.N. force to the occupied area after threats that the Turkish forces would come and liberate them and promises that if this happened, the remaining Greek Cypriots in the North (30,000) would be allowed to stay. By the beginning of 1977, all but the inhabitants of one village (about 2,000) were also expelled, completing the elimination of a centuries old mixed settlement pattern, making it possible to assert that a "purely Turkish" and a "purely Greek" state exist on Cyprus.

Accounts of occupied Cyprus are that it is being fully "Turkified".[9] All the instruments of a separate state have been set up. To bolster claims that there are two "equal communities" on Cyprus, there are plans to increase the population of the North from 110,000 to 200,000 by importing and settling mainland Turks. The "Turkish Federated State" is totally dependent on Turkish economic aid. (In 1975 fiscal year a half of the budget was covered by grants from Turkey.)

The figure for the settlers do not include the 40,000 mainland troops who were given the "right" to acquire Cypriot citizenship after the invasion. By March 1976 the Cyprus Government was estimating that apart from these troops, 44,000 Anatolian settlers had been imported to colonize the occupied area.[10]

Additional indications of Turkish intentions are provided by the introduction of Turkish currency to the occupied area, linking it to the Turkish television network, making the postal address of northern Cyprus "Mersin, Turkey", and building a large military air base on the north coast.

In spite of the accomplished facts, however, the Cyprus problem is far from solved from anyone's point of view, with the possible exception of Turkey. The Government of Cyprus, which now only controls 60% of the area of the island, has not, by the mere fact of occupation, lost international recognition. The United Nations General Assembly and Security Council have repeatedly called for the withdrawal of all foreign troops, the return of the refugees to their homes and respect' for the sovereignty and territorial integrity of Cyprus, clearly separating the issue of foreign occupation from that of constitutional negotiations between Greek and Turkish Cypriots over the future constitutional arrangements of Cyprus. There have also been significant reactions against U.S. policy on Cyprus, most importantly by the U.S. Congress. Contrary to what has generally been reported, voting patterns in Congress have not depended on mindless ethnic pressure, but rather on a reaction against a trend of U.S. Government policy widely discrepant from the professed ideals of U.S. Governments.[11]

The invasion has clearly not solved any of the *Realpolitik* objectives of U.S. policy. After the return of President Makarios to Cyprus, and the re-establishment of agreement between virtually all political forces in Cyprus, there is a continuing refusal on the part of the Cypriots to acknowledging the existing situation through a signature. The worry has been expressed that in a partitioned Cyprus, the South, with more than a third of its inhabitants refugees, would have all the more reason to go to the left.[12]

The development of the Aegean dispute, as well as the Cyprus Government's refusal to put its signature under the facts of occupation and dismemberment, has meant that there can be no Greco-Turkish accommodation either. In fact the relations of the U.S. to both is worse than it was before the invasion. Greece has partially withdrawn from military participation in NATO[13] as a result of U.S. approval of the second attack of Turkey on Cyprus. Turkey in July 1975 closed down all intelligence facilities used for monitoring the Soviet Union which were functioning under bilateral agreements with the U.S.[14]

Lastly in terms of U.S. aims, though Turkey was allowed to realize the invasion of Cyprus, it has in no way desisted from her rapprochement with the Soviet Union. By the end of 1975 agreement had been reached between the two countries to sign a document on Friendly Relations and Co-operation,[15] at the end of 1976 it was reported that a non-aggression agreement was being considered,[16] and in March 1977 during the Turkish Foreign Minister's visit to Moscow it was expected that a ten-year economic agreement would be signed providing for 1,230 million dollars in credits for Turkey.[17]

These facts mean that the aims of U.S. policy have not been satisfied, though from the point of view of the Cypriots it hardly brings a solution closer. The irony is that internally, forces are at work in both Greek and Turkish Cypriot communities which probably make them more conscious of the interests they share in an integral, independent Cyprus than ever.

Among Greek Cypriots there is more consciousness than there ever was of the fact that their interests are distinct from those of Greece—with one important exception: both countries are faced, one

## Conclusions

in the Aegean and the other on its own territory with Turkish aggressiveness. And Greece is the only country that might be expected to provide military assistance for Cyprus in case of a third Turkish offensive.

As for the Turkish Cypriots, reports indicate that they cannot be too satisfied with their "liberation". It has not been possible to make the occupied area function economically and living standards are lower for many Turkish Cypriots than before they were "liberated". There is a housing shortage and food supply problems, and health problems have developed, with the danger of malaria spreading over the island.[18] Greek Cypriots who have recently been expelled from the occupied areas report widespread dissatisfaction on the part of the Turkish Cypriots with the Turkish colonization programme, particularly since many of the colonists come from the most under-developed parts of Turkey. And foreign correspondents have been reporting that "... the behaviour of the Turkish military ... has been that of a conquering army".[19] In fact, a U.S. Senate study mission reported in January, 1976 that "the Cypriot Turks in the occupied northern part of the island seem to have joined their compatriots in the South as victims of Turkish aggression and occupation".[20]

But though among both Greek and Turkish Cypriots there is a growing sense of "Cypriotness"[21] everyone is more aware than ever of how much of the fate of Cyprus is outside Cypriot hands and never have the "intercommunal talks" been more international.

If the full impact of imperial powers on other societies is to be understood it seems important to bear in mind that they can, in many ways, influence not only "international behaviour", but also the internal social structure. This is obvious in the colonial situation, but not limited to that situation alone. It has long been recognized, particularly by U.S. scholars as far as the Soviet Union is concerned, that its existence can encourage internal movements in various societies, even apart from the case of what in political usage would be called "intervention". In many countries there are communist parties that have an invariable tendency to identify their country's interests with those of the Soviet Union. More than that, assisted by the behaviour of U.S. foreign policy makers, the Soviet Union has broad latitude in defining the aims of the "world anti-imperialist struggle" in which much wider groups sometimes participate.

But a similar fact has not so often been recognized in relation to the United States. Yet in areas such as Greece, Cyprus and Turkey in which U.S. influence is paramount the impact of the U.S. on internal politics is frequently decisive, so that internal and international politics are not easily separable.

It is true that in recent years much has come to light about the "destabilization activities" of U.S. agencies. But it is rather odd that so many critics of the position of the U.S. in world politics place so much emphasis on the activities of the CIA. For such activities are a very small part of U.S. foreign policy and the part which, by definition, is least accessible to study. Surely what is much more important is the influence which the United States has in building political and military institutions through its economic and military dominance, and the ideologies it disseminates through training schemes and embassies in countries which frequently have severe limitations due to their small size or underdevelopment, on access to independent information, and for whom these ideologies can easily become accepted fact. Such U.S. institutions create individuals who have certain expectations about what kinds of activities will be conducive to a continuation of U.S. aid to their countries and by extension will maintain their own positions in the local power structure.

Since 1947 U.S. military aid programmes have had the tendency to reinforce those social and political forces which tend towards conservatism and established vested interests.[22] The anti-communism which provides a link between such groups and U.S. policy is not limited to preparing for the eventuality of external aggression. It is quite capable of developing into an instrument for maintaining the power position of an increasingly marginal group of officers. This had happened in Greece by 1974 with no opposition on the part of the U.S.

In current international conditions of military and ideological confrontation, it is impossible to set strict boundaries between internal and international politics, or even clearly distinguish what is endogenous from what is exogenous. Internal politics, particularly in weak countries, are influenced by perceptions of what outside powers, particularly the two great imperial ones, are trying to achieve. Communism and anti-communism are frequently strong internalized and emotionally held links between the interests of the imperial powers and native politicians. The activities of native politicians are also influenced by what the imperial powers are likely or unlikely to tolerate, and what they are likely to give support to once it is accomplished. The signals are there. The U.S. Secretary of State for Foreign Affairs was quoted in September 1974 in the *Washington Post* as having said in a meeting on the 27th June 1970.

> I don't see why we need to stand by and watch a country go communist because of the irresponsibility of its people.[23]

Dr Kissinger was reported not to remember having said this, but has often reiterated that the United States had to do everything short of military intervention to prevent the establishment of a communist regime in the western hemisphere,[24] and the history of U.S. policy towards Greece is ample evidence of such activities.

## Conclusions

The question of whether a country like the U.S. can coordinate all its governmental agencies and inveigle its legislative institutions and its public opinion to a conspiratorial course of action contrary to its overt, stated objectives in the world is a different question and a much more complicated one. Part of the answer is contained in the labelling process described above. A scare of a communist takeover or the dangers of Soviet expansion, whether real or imaginary, can make otherwise unacceptable actions appear necessary.

It does seem likely though that both of the imperial powers are constrained by their ideologies to some extent, at least verbally, and though there can be an enormous distance between the statements and actions of their representatives it does ultimately create problems for them. In the case of the United States there also seems to be a genuine lack of consistency in actions by different agencies, the same agencies over time, and even different levels of the same bureaucracy. Of course much of such discrepancies can be explained by differences in views, changes in objective conditions and differences between maximal and minimal aims. But at least one serious observer has expressed the suspicion that such discrepancies are projected in a purposeful way.[25] It is not possible to resolve the problem here. But its implications are clear. The fact that messages from the imperial powers are spoken with a "forked tongue" has the consequence of keeping local allies guessing and enemies off their guard, but it also has the function of enabling local allies to adapt to being "let down" by attributing a failure of support on the part of the relevant power to a faulty reading of the message, or insufficient devotion on their own part.

The final point on the relation between the international power structure and internal power processes has to do with the pervasiveness of the power of the imperial powers and changeability in its objectives in relation to one small country, since the aims are global. Sihanouk of Cambodia is now deposed and Makarios of Cyprus dead, but together these two Heads of State have been accurately described as "survival acrobats struggling to maintain national sovereignty in the shadows of the great power triangle".[26] If their act is thought of as being tight rope walking, it is tight rope walking with the added danger that one of the ends of the rope may, at any time, be released while the safety net is still down. The rather long-drawn metaphor may indicate the complex interdependence of imperial and small powers in a situation where an imperial power may have overwhelming consequences for a small one merely by desisting from acting as it has habitually acted in the past. These broad comments set some of the kinds of interrelations between indigenous and international political relations in a development process in which from the viewpoint of relatively powerless countries "internal contradictions are used by the external ones, and external contradictions are in turn used by the internal ones".[27]

# NOTES

## INTRODUCTION

[1] Gellner, Ernest. *Thought and Change*, London, Weidenfeld and Nicholson, 1964.

[2] Kedourie, E. *Nationalism*, London, Hutchinson University Library, 1966.

[3] ibid.

[4] *op. cit.*

[5] Lewis, B. *The Emergence of Modern Turkey*, Oxford University Press, 1968, pp. 352-3.

[6] Stephens, R. *Cyprus: A Place of Arms*, London, Pall Mall Press, 1966.

[7] Kedourie, *op. cit.*, p. 73.

[8] For example, Stephens, *op. cit.* Chapters 2-6.

[9] Worseley, P. *The Third World*, London, Weidenfeld and Nicholson, 1967.

[10] ibid.

[11] The introductory essay in J. H. Kautsky, ed., *Political Change in Underdeveloped Countries: Nationalism and Communism*, New York, John Wiley, 1967.

[12] This definition of regionalism comes from P. Schneider *et al.* "Modernization and Development: The Role of Regional Elites and Non-corporate Groups in the European Mediterranean", *Comparative Studies in Society and History*, 14: pp. 328-50, 1972.

[13] *The Economist*, 18 October 1975.

## CHAPTER I

[1] Heinritz, Gunter. "Der grieschisch-türkische Konflikt in Zypern", *Geographische Rundschau*, 27: 93-99, March 1975.

[2] Storrs, Ronald. *Orientations*, London, Nicholson & Watson, 1945, p. 463.

[3] ibid., p. 461.

[4] ibid., p. 462.

[5] The following account of relations between Turkey, Russia and the West is based on Gunter Gillesen "Hundert Jahre türkischer Erbfolgkrieg". *Frankfurter Allgemeine Zeitung*, 27 July, 1974.

[6] Storrs, *op. cit.*, p. 463.

[7] Linardatos, S. I Kypros os tin Anexartisia, in A. G. Xydi *et. al. O Makarios kai oi Symmachi tou*, Athens, Gutenberg, n.d. Linardatos mentions some of the occasions on which Greek Prime Ministers emphasized the importance of friendship with Britain as a barrier to a militant pursuit of the aim of incorporating Cyprus.

[8] Rodinson, Maxime. *Israel and the Arabs*, Penguin, 1968.

[9] Tsolaki, A. L. *Politiki Istoria tis Neoteras Kyprou*, Vol. A, 1950-4, Famagusta, 1972, p. 21.

[10] Kyrou A. *Elliniki Exoteriki Politiki,* Athens, 1955, p. 405.

[11] Rodinson, *op. cit.*, p. 59.

[12] Coufoudakis, V. "United States Foreign Policy and the Cyprus Question: A Case Study in Cold War Diplomacy", in Theodore A. Couloumbis and Sallie M. Hicks, eds., *U.S. Foreign Policy Towards Greece and Cyprus: The Clash of Principle and Pragmatism.* Washington, D.C. The Center for Mediterranean Studies & The American Hellenic Institute, 1975.

[13] Great Britain. *Parliamentary Debates* (1955-56), Vol. 550, pp. 403-19. Quoted in S. Kyriakides, *Cyprus: Constitutionalism and Crisis Government,* Philadelphia, University of Pennsylvania Press, 1968. Cyprus bases were used twice by the British during the period 1955-9. In 1956 they were used during the "Suez expedition", and in 1958 in support of King Hussein of Jordan.

[14] *The Economist,* 13 October 1955, quoted in Kyriakides, *op. cit.*

[15] Erlich, T. *International Crises and the Rule of Law: Cyprus 1958-1967,* Oxford University Press, 1974, p. 23.

[16] Kyrou, *op. cit.*, p. 289.

[17] ibid., p. 416.

[18] Quoted in S. G. Xydis, "Toward 'Toil and Moil' in Cyprus", *Middle East Journal,* Winter 1966.

[19] The following account of the birth of the idea of partitioning Cyprus between Greece and Turkey is based on Erlich, *op. cit.*, pp. 15-28.

[20] ibid.

[21] Bahcheli, Tozun S. *Communal Discord and the Stake of Interested Governments in Cyprus, 1955-1970,* Doctoral Dissertation, London School of Economics and Political Science, University of London, 1972.

[22] Xydis, 1966, *op. cit.*

[23] Salih, H. Ibrahim. *Cyprus: An Analysis of Political Discord,* Brooklyn, Theo Gaus Sons, 1968, p. 51.

[24] Foley, C. *Legacy of Strife. Cyprus from Rebellion to Civil War,* Penguins, 1964, p. 35.

[25] Eden, A. *The Memoirs of Anthony Eden: Full Circle,* Cambridge, The Riverside Press, 1960, p. 400.

[26] Kyriakides, *op. cit.*, p. 41.

[27] Erlich, *op. cit.*, p. 19 and Foley, *op. cit.*, p. 89.

[28] Bahcheli, *op. cit.*, p. 53.

[29] Erlich, *op. cit.*, p. 25.

[30] Foley, *op. cit.*, p. 61.

[31] Quoted in Kyrou, *op. cit.*, p. 417.

[32] Xydis, 1966, *op. cit.*

[33] Goldbloom, M. "United States Policy in Post-War Greece", in R. Clogg and S. Yiannopoulos, eds., *Greece Under Military Rule,* London, Secker and Warburg, 1972.

[34] Kyrou, *op. cit.*

[35] Xydis, 1966, *op. cit.*

[36] Sulzburger, C. L. "Strength of Communists Poses Problems in Cyprus". *The New York Times,* 17 May 1949.

## Notes

[37] Athens newspapers, 5 May 1955. Quoted in Kyrou, *op. cit.*

[38] Rodinson, *op. cit.*, pp. 60-1.

[39] M. Delarue, *The Guardian Weekly*, 19 July 1975.

[40] Grivas-Dhigenis, Georghios. *Apomnimonevmata Agonos EOKA; 1955-9*, Athens, 1961, p. 200.

[41] Stephens, *op. cit.*, p. 158.

[42] Erlich, *op. cit.*, p. 20.

[43] ibid.

[44] Foley, *op. cit.*, p. 147.

[45] Windsor, P. *Nato and the Cyprus Crisis*, London, The Institute of Strategic Studies, Adelphi Papers No. 14, 1964, p. 3.

[46] Grivas-Dhigenis, *op. cit.*, p. 377 and p. 384. In fact S. Xydis in *Cyprus: Reluctant Republic*, The Hague, Mouton, 1973, p. 519, mentions a "gentlemen's agreement" between the Greek and Turkish Prime Minister to this effect.

[47] Weinstein Adalbert. "Zypern ist nicht Kuba", *Frankfurter Allgemeine Zeitung*, 16 July 1974.

[48] Quoted in Linardatos, *op. cit.*, p. 329.

[49] Adams, T. W. and A. J. Cottrell, *Cyprus Between East and West*, Baltimore, The Johns Hopkins Press, 1968. The first author is a former political specialist in NASA's Office of Policy Analysis, and the second, a former professor at the National War College, Washington, D.C. For an outline of British strategic and political thinking on Cyprus just before independence see, Field-Marshal The Lord Harding of Petherton, "The Cyprus Problem in Relation to the Middle East", *International Affairs*, 34(3): 291-6, 1958.

[50] *New York Times*, 17 May 1949.

[51] *The Observer*, 11 August 1974, quoting *Aviation Weekly*. Also reported in *Paris Match* as being one of a set of three in the world, the other two being in Okinawa and Suffolk. Quoted in *Akropolis*, 6 February 1975.

[52] Weinstein, 16 July 1974, *op. cit.*

[53] Windsor, *op. cit.*

[54] Weinstein, 16 July 1974, *op. cit.*

[55] ibid.

[56] Adams and Cottrell, *op. cit.*, pp. 58-60.

[57] Foley, *op. cit.*, p. 164.

[58] Salih, *op. cit.*, p. 63.

[59] Adams and Cottrell, *op. cit.*, p. 33.

[60] ibid., p. 34.

[61] Vanezis, P. N. *Makarios: Pragmatism versus Idealism*, London, Äbelard-Schuman, 1974, p. 141.

[62] Adams and Cottrell, *op. cit.*, p. 24.

[63] Bahcheli, *op. cit.*, comments that they all became "suspicious of Makarios".

[64] This account of the changing nature of the Cold War is based on Rodinson, *op. cit.*, p. 140.

[65] Weinstein, Adalbert. "Zyperns Strategische Bedeutung", *Frankfurter Allgemeine Zeitung*, 19 July 1974.

[66] Windsor, *op. cit.*

[67] ibid.

[68] Glavkos Clerides in a B.B.C. interview reported in *The Washington Post*, 31 January 1964.

[69] Vanezis, *op. cit.*, p. 130.

[70] Adams and Cottrell, *op. cit.*, pp. 35-7.

[71] ibid., pp. 34-40.

[72] Vanezis, *op. cit.*, p. 128, Adams and Cottrell, *op. cit.*, p. 35, *The New York Times*, 25 August 1964.

[73] Garoufalias, Petros, "Apomnimonevmata", *Akropolis*, 26 September 1974.

[74] *The Economist*, 4 July 1964.

[75] Garoufalias, 26 September 1974, *op. cit.*

[76] Windsor, *op. cit.*

[77] Salih, *op. cit.*, p. 122.

[78] The various aims of U.S. policy in Cyprus at this time as listed in Coufoudakis, *op. cit.*, Windsor, *op. cit.*, and Adams and Cottrell, *op. cit.*, can be reduced to these two broad problems.

[79] cf. Smith Hempstone from Athens, *Chicago Daily News*, 21 February 1964; *Baltimore Sun*, 31 March 1964; *The Washington Post*, 12 March 1964; Tad Szulc reported in the *New York Times* on 21 June 1964 as follows: "That Cyprus has ceased to be viable as a sovereign state is a fact of political life that by now has been tacitly accepted in Washington and in virtually every major foreign office in the world."

[80] Coufoudakis, *op. cit.*

[81] cf. Windsor, *op. cit.*, Bahcheli, *op. cit.*, Adams and Cottrell, *op. cit.*, and Coufoudakis, *op. cit.*

[82] Bahcheli, *op. cit.*

[83] *The Washington Post*, 24 August 1964.

[84] *The New York Times*, 25 August 1964.

[85] The two letters (Acheson's dated 20 August 1964 and Papandreou's, dated 22 August 1964) are reproduced in Greek without reference to source in K. Hatziargyri, "Sta Plokamia mias Lerneas", in A. G. Xydi *et al.* eds., *op. cit.*

[86] *The Washington Post*, 5 September 1964.

[87] *The Washington Post,* 27 August 1964, reported a statement by Makarios that he would welcome the "unconditional" union of Cyprus with Greece.

[88] Windsor, *op. cit.*

[89] B. Nossiter reporting from Athens in *The Washington Post*, 11 November 1964.

CHAPTER II

[1] See for example C. Spyridakis, *A Brief History of Cyprus*, Nicosia, Greek Communal Chamber, 1964.

[2] See Adamantia Pollis, "Intergroup Conflict and British Colonial Policy: The Case of Cyprus", *Comparative Politics*, 5 July 1973.

# Notes

[3] Storrs, *op. cit.*, p. 470.

[4] Georgallides, G. S., "Churchill's 1907 Visit to Cyprus: A political Analysis", *Epetiris Kentrou Epistimonikon Erevnon*, Nicosia, 3: 167-220, 1970.

[5] Linardatos, *op. cit.*, p. 251.

[6] Kyrou, *op. cit.*, p. 366.

[7] 30, Sept. 1954, quoted in Kyrou, *op. cit.*, p. 370.

[8] Hill, G. *A History of Cyprus*, Volume IV. Cambridge, The University Press, 1952.

[9] ibid., p. 421.

[10] ibid., p. 426.

[11] Storrs, *op. cit.*, pp. 474-6. A detailed account of British colonial policy and Cypriot grievances until the First World War is given in C. W. J. Orr, *Cyprus Under British Rule*, London, Zeno, 1972. First published in 1918.

[12] Storrs, *op. cit.*

[13] Katalanos, N. *Kypriakon Lefkoma*, Nicosia, Zeno, 1914.

[14] For a detailed account of the issue of representation see Hill, *op. cit.*

[15] Gavriilidis, A. Ch., *Ta Ethnarchika Dikaiomata kai to Enotikon Demopsephesma*, Nicosia, 1972 (first published in 1950), pp. 72-7.

[16] For other important accounts of the development of Greek Nationalism in Cyprus see, P. Loizos, "The Progress of Greek Nationalism in Cyprus, 1878-1970", in J. Davis, ed. *Choice and Change: Essays in Honour of Lucy Mair*, London, Athlone, 1974. Also, K. Markides, "Social Change and the Rise and Decline of Social Movements: The Case of Cyprus", *American Ethnologist*, 1975.

[17] Georgallides, G. "British Policy on Cyprus During 1931", in Th. Papadopoulos and M. Christodoulou, eds., *Praktika tou Protou Kyprologikou Synedriou*, Vol. III, Nicosia, 1973, p. 96 and M. Attalides, "Forms of Peasant Incorporation in Cyprus during the Last Century", in E. Gellner and J. Waterbury eds., *Patrons and Clients*, London, Duckworth, 1977.

[18] Contemporary account by a French National, quoted in J. Koumoulides, *Cyprus and the Greek War of Independence 1821-1829*, London, Zeno Publishers, 1974.

[19] Terlexis, P. *Diplomatia kai Politiki tou Kypriakou*, Athens, 1971, p. 52.

[20] The information in this paragraph is derived from K. P. Kyrrhes, *Istoria tis Mesis Ekpaidevseos Ammochostou, 1191-1955*, Nicosia, 1967.

[21] Newham, Rev. F. D. *The System of Education in Cyprus*, Board of Education Special Reports, No. 12, 1905.

[22] At the foundation of the Greek State, only 750,000 Greeks were within it, and two to three million were outside it. Vatikiotis, *op. cit.*, p. 7.

[23] Newham, *op. cit.*

[24] Gavriilides, *op. cit.*

[25] Gavriilides, *op. cit.*, pp. 42-3.

[26] Storrs, *op. cit.*

[27] Gavriilides, *op. cit.*

[28] ibid.

[29] Kyrrhes, *op. cit.*

[30] ibid.

[31] This account emerges from Storrs, *op. cit.*, and Georgallides, 1973, *op. cit.*

[32] Hill, *op. cit.* gives a detailed account of such opposition activities.

[33] Katalanos, *op. cit.* pp. 74-6.

[34] ibid., p. 222.

[35] ibid., p. 309.

[36] Hill, *op. cit.*, p. 424.

[37] If one relies on Worseley, *op. cit.*, in his account of anti-colonial movements in the Third World.

[38] Vatikiotis, *op. cit.*

[39] Georghiadis, Kl., *I Katagogi ton Kyprion*, Nicosia, 1936. Author's translation of the quotation.

[40] ibid.

[41] Gavriilides, *op. cit.*, p. 65. Author's translation of the quotation.

[42] Royal Institute of International Affairs. *Cyprus: The Dispute and the Settlement*, Oxford University Press, 1959, p. 11.

[43] Hatziargyri, *op. cit.*, p. 272.

## CHAPTER III

[1] Lewis, *op. cit.*, p. 345.

[2] Quoted ibid., p. 338.

[3] ibid., pp. 350-1.

[4] ibid., pp. 352-4.

[5] ibid.

[6] Loizos, P. "Aspects of Pluralism in Cyprus", *New Community* (Journal of the U.K. Community Relations Commission), Summer, 1972.

[7] cf. some of the incidents described by L. P. Di Cesnola, *Cyprus: Its Ancient Cities, Tombs and Temples,* London, John Murray, 1877.

[8] Hill, *op. cit.*, p. 261.

[9] ibid., p. 183.

[10] ibid., p. 211.

[11] ibid., p. 261.

[12] ibid., pp. 105-10. On the power of the Church during the Ottoman period see the accounts of visitors to Cyprus between the seventeenth and nineteenth centuries collected in C. D. Cobham. *Excerpta Cypria: Materials for a History of Cyprus,* Cambridge University Press, 1908. Also H. Luke. *Cyprus Under the Turks 1571-1878,* Oxford University Press, 1921.

[13] Hill, *op. cit.*, pp. 70-110.

[14] ibid., p. 158.

[15] ibid., pp. 162-5.

[16] ibid., p. 203.

[17] ibid., pp. 199-203.

## Notes

[18] Jenness, D. *The Economics of Cyprus: A Survey to 1914*, McGill University Press, 1962, p. 58. Also Hill, *op. cit.*, p. 211 and p. 266.

[19] Loizos, 1972, *op. cit.*

[20] Storrs, *op. cit.*, pp. 471-2 and Hill, *op. cit.*, p. 420.

[21] Loizos, 1972, *op. cit.*

[22] Storrs, *op. cit.*, p. 472 and p. 501.

[23] Hill, *op. cit.*, p. 531.

[24] Beckingham, C. V. "Islam and Turkish Nationalism in Cyprus", *Die Welt des Islam*, 5: 65-83, 1957.

[25] ibid.

[26] Suha, Ali, "Turkish Education in Cyprus", in Th. Papadopoulos and M. Christodoulou, eds., *Praktika tou Protou Diethnous Kyprologikou Synedriou.* Nicosia, 1973, Vol. III.

[27] ibid.

[28] ibid.

[29] ibid.

[30] ibid.

[31] Beckingham, *op. cit.*

[32] ibid.

[33] Hill, *op. cit.*, p. 498.

[34] ibid., p. 510.

[35] ibid., p. 518.

[36] ibid., p. 519.

[37] ibid., p. 530.

[38] The facts in this paragraph are deived from Beckingham, *op. cit.*, and Georgallides G. "Turkish and British reactions to the emigration of the Cypriot Turks to Anatolia, 1924, 1927", *Institute of Balkan Studies Journal*, Forthcoming. Forthcoming.

[39] Storrs, *op. cit.*

[40] Kyrou, *op. cit.*, p. 390.

[41] Salih, *op. cit.*, p. 41.

[42] The following account is based on Beckingham, *op. cit.*

[43] ibid.

[44] Kyriakides, *op. cit.*, p. 45.

[45] Republic of Cyprus, *Brief Biographies of the President, The Vice President and the Ministers of the Republic of Cyprus*, Public Information Office, 1963.

[46] Terlexis, *op. cit.*, p. 64.

[47] Patrick, R. A. "A General System Theory Approach to Geopolitical Aspects of Conflict between Communities with particular Reference to Cyprus since 1960". *Doctoral Dissertation*. London School of Economics and Political Science, 1972, p. 2, 3.

[48] Grivas-Dhigenis, *op. cit.*, pp. 51-2.

[49] Following account is derived from Foley, *op. cit.*

[50] ibid., p. 30.

[51] ibid., p. 89, pp. 119-29.

[52] ibid., p. 121.

[53] ibid., p. 122.

[54] ibid., pp. 124-9. The relationship between the economic problems of the Turkish government at this time and the organization of nationalist riots is described by F. Tachau, "The Face of Turkish Nationalism as Reflected in the Cyprus Dispute", *Middle East Journal*, 13: 262-72, 1959.

[55] Salih, *op. cit.*, p. 63.

[56] Aziz, Ibrahim H. and N. M. Seferoglu, *Victims of fascist Terrorism*, Nicosia, 1975.

[57] Republic of Cyprus, Ministry of Labour and Social Insurance, *Annual Report*, 1968.

[58] Grivas-Dhigenis, *op. cit.*, p. 371.

[59] Bahcheli, *op. cit.*

[60] See Kyriakides, *op. cit.*, Erlich, *op. cit.*, Salih, *op. cit.*

[61] Adams and Cottrell, *op. cit.*, p. 10.

[62] ibid.

[62] Denktas, Rauf. *The Problem of Cyprus: Constitutional and Political Aspects*, Nicosia, 1974.

[64] ibid.

[65] Salih, *op. cit.*, p. 63.

[66] Vanezis, *op. cit.*, p. 112.

[67] Enloe, C. H. *Ethnic Conflict and Political Development*, Boston, Little Brown, 1973.

[68] The best accounts are in Stephens, *op. cit.*, and Kyriakides, *op. cit.*

[69] The information in the preceding paragraph is from Kyriakides, *op. cit.*

[70] Stephens, *op. cit.*, p. 173.

[71] For the main features of the Treaties and Constitution see Kyriakides, *op. cit.*, pp. 53-71.

[72] Bahcheli, *op. cit.*

[73] Stephens, *op. cit.*, p. 174.

[74] Bahcheli, *op. cit.*

[75] Interview in *Cyprus Mail*, 25 May 1975.

[76] Denktas, *op. cit.*, p. 14.

[77] Salih, *op. cit.*, p. 109.

[78] *Washington Post*, 26 February 1964.

[79] This point is made by Stavrinides, Z. *The Cyprus Conflict, National Identity and Statehood*, Nicosia, 1975. It was also made in relation to the nationalist consequences of the Communal Chambers at the time when they were functioning. See N. C. Lanitis *Our Destiny*. A series of articles reprinted from *Cyprus Mail*, 3-7 March 1963.

[80] Salih, *op. cit.*, p. 125.

[81] Suha, *op. cit.*

# Notes

[82] Garoufalias, P. "Apomnimonevmata," *Akropolis*, 25 September 1974.

[83] ibid.

[84] ibid.

## CHAPTER IV

[1] Xydis, S. G. *Greece and the Great Powers 1944-7*, Thessaloniki, 1963. Also D. Eudes. *The Kapetanios*, London, Basic Books, 1972.

[2] See for example, P. Williams, *Athens Under the Spartans*, Fabian Social Research Pamphlet No. 264, London, 1967.

[3] Anthem, Th. *Enosis*, London, St. Clement's Press, 1954.

[4] Greek Parliamentary Record, 18 November 1931. Quoted in Linardatos, *op. cit.*

[5] ibid.

[6] S. Xydis, 1966, *op. cit.*

[7] ibid.

[8] Servas, P. *I Kypriaki Tragodia*, Athens, 1975, p. 44.

[9] S. Xydis, 1966, *op. cit.*

[10] Kyrou, *op. cit.*, p. 273.

[11] Xydis, 1966, *op. cit.*

[12] Servas, *op. cit.*, p. 44.

[13] Linardatos, *op. cit.*

[14] ibid., pp. 271-2.

[15] Xydis, 1966, *op. cit.*

[16] Quoted in Servas, *op. cit.*

[17] Grivas-Dhigenis, *op. cit.*, p. 53.

[18] ibid., p. 134.

[19] ibid., p. 285.

[20] ibid., p. 287.

[21] ibid., p. 287-8.

[22] T. Papadopoulos in a letter reproduced in Grivas, *op. cit.*

[23] ibid., p. 379.

[24] Turkish Information Centre, *The Cyprus Problem in the Light of Truth*, Nicosia, 1967.

[25] Barston, R. P. "The Foreign Policy of Cyprus", in *The Other Powers*, George Allen and Unwin, 1973.

[26] Windsor, *op. cit.*

[27] *To Vema*, 24 January 1964. Quoted in Hatziargyri, *op. cit.*, p. 61.

[28] ibid.

[29] *Washington Post*, 6 March 1964. Quoted in Hatziargyri, *op. cit.* p. 79.

[30] Hatziargyri, *op. cit.*, p. 91.

[31] ibid.

32 *The New York Times*, 25 August 1964.

33 ibid.

34 ibid.

35 B. Nossiter reporting from Athens, *The Washington Post*, 11 November 1964.

36 Garoufalias, P. "Apomnimonevmata", *Akropolis*. 6 October 1974.

37 *The New York Times*, 9 May 1965. Reported in Salih, *op. cit.*, p. 133.

38 Adams and Cottrell, *op. cit.*, p. 43.

39 Garoufalias, 6 October 1974.

40 Hatziargyri, *op. cit.*

41 *The Washington Post*, 24 August 1964.

42 *The Washington Post*, 27 August 1964.

43 *The New York Times*, 25 August 1964.

44 ibid.

45 *The Washington Post*, 27 August 1964.

46 Hatziargyri, *op. cit.*, p. 95.

47 ibid.

48 Salih, *op. cit.*, p. 127.

49 *The Washington Post*, 27 August 1964.

50 Garoufalias, P. "Apomnimonevmata", *Akropolis*, 6 October 1974.

51 Vanezis, *op. cit.*, p. 166.

52 *The Washington Post*, 11 November 1964.

53 Salih, *op. cit.*, p. 131, citing the Greek Cypriot centrist newspaper *Kypros*.

54 Salih, *op. cit.*, citing *The New York Times*, 22 November 1964.

55 Salih, *op. cit.*, p. 131.

56 Hatziargyri, *op. cit.*

57 Salih, *op. cit.*, p. 131.

58 Hatziargyri, *op. cit.*, p. 112.

59 Coufoudakis, *op. cit.*

60 ibid., citing Weintal and Bartlett, *Facing the Brink*.

61 ibid.

62 Garoufalias, P. "Apomnimonevmata", *Akropolis*, 4 October 1974.

63 Coufoudakis, *op. cit.*

64 S. Gregoriadis. *Akropolis*, 23 February 1975.

65 Garoufalias, P. "Apomnimonevmata", *Akropolis*, 8 October 1974.

66 ibid.

67 ibid.

68 Garoufalias, 11 October 1974.

69 See A. Papandreou. *Democracy at Gunpoint*, Penguin Books, 1968.

70 Garoufalias, 8 October 1974.

71 Hatziargyri, *op. cit.*, p. 112.

[72] ibid., p. 148.

[73] Papadopoulos, Th. *I Krisis tis Kypriakis Synidiseos*, Nicosia, 1964.

[74] ibid.

[75] ibid.

[76] Evdokas, T. *To Aitima tis Enoseos: Psychika Empodia kai Planes*, Nicosia, Epitropi Kypriakou Agonos, 1965.

[77] Lanitis, *op. cit.*

[78] Press Conference of the Director General of the Ministry of Agriculture, *Eleftheria*, March, 1969.

[79] Solomides, R. *Analysis Katamerismou Varous tis Ektaktou Forologias Eisodimatos*, Nicosia, 1975.

[80] Hald, M. *A Study of the Cyprus Economy*, Nicosia, 1968.

[81] Solomides, *op. cit.* The increase in standards of living is slightly exaggerated since the figures are not at constant prices. However due to the relative monetary stability in Cyprus, a Cypriot pound had an exchange value in 1974 of about 17% more than a pound sterling.

[82] *The Times*, 26 October 1964.

[83] ibid., and Evdokas, *op. cit.*

[84] *The Times*, 26 October 1964.

[85] Lanitis, *op. cit.*

[86] ibid.

## CHAPTER V

[1] Papadopoulos, Th. *Social and Historical Data on Population, 1570-1881*, Nicosia, 1965.

[2] ibid.

[3] Beckingham, *op. cit.*

[4] Plaza, G. *Report of the United Nations Mediator on Cyprus to the Secretary General*, 1965.

[5] Harbottle, M. *The Impartial Soldier*, Oxford University Press, 1970, p. 163.

[6] ibid., pp. 116-20.

[7] Harbottle, M. *"Why Cyprus is Doomed to Become a Political Volcano"*, *The Times*, 17 October 1974.

[8] Stephens, *op. cit.*, pp. 116-7.

[9] MacHenry, J. A. "Prelude to Confrontation: An Historical Sketch of Cyprus Between 1923 and 1945". *Dis Politika*, Vol. 4, Nos. 2 and 3, 1974.

[10] *Bozkurt.* Reprinted in translation in *Phileleftheros*, 11 November 1975.

[11] See the statements of Prime Minister Menderes during the 1950's in Salih *op. cit.*

[12] Xydis, *op. cit.*, Kyriakides, *op. cit.*, p. 41.

[13] Salih, *op. cit.*, p. 126.

[14] Clerides, L. *The Demands of the Turkish Cypriot Community Since 1955*, Nicosia, 1974.

[15] *The Times*, 26 October 1964.

[16] Vanezis, *op. cit.*, Hadziargyri, *op. cit.*, p. 126.

[17] Keskin, H. "Die Haltung Der Ecevit Regierung" in Y. Pazarkaya *et al. Zypern*, Berlin, 1974.

[18] Clerides, *op. cit.*

[19] *The Times*, 26 October 1964.

[20] Patrick, *op. cit.*

[21] Jeness, *op. cit.*, pp. 58-61.

[22] ibid., p. 61.

[23] Hutchinson, J. T. and C.D. Cobham, *A Handbook of Cyprus*, London, 1901. The figures are derived by attributing the practitioners listed by name to ethnic group.

[24] Figures from Panagides, S. S. "Communal Conflict and Economic Considerations: The Case of Cyprus", *Journal of Peace Research*, 1968.

[25] Patrick, *op. cit.*

[26] Panagides, *op. cit.*

[27] Notel, R. "Economic Integration on Cyprus". Paper presented to seminar on the Cyprus Problem, *American Universities Field Staff*, Rome, 1973.

[28] Panagides, *op. cit.*

[29] Economides, Chr. "I Exelixi tou Ellinikou kai Tourkikou Plithismou tis Kyprou epi Tourkokratias", *Kypriaka Chronika,* Vol. 53, July 1966.

[30] Censuses, 1881, 1960.

[31] Patrick, *op. cit.*

[32] Beckingham, *op. cit.*, and Georgallides, *op. cit.*

[33] Stegenga, J. A. *The United Nations Force in Cyprus*, Ohio, State University Press, 1968, p. 155.

[34] Patrick, *op. cit.*

[35] Stegenga, *op. cit.*, p. 146.

[36] Patrick, *op. cit.*, p. 3.36.

[37] U.S. Senate, Subcommittee to Investigate Problems Connected with Refugees and Escapees, *Crisis on Cyprus: 1975*, Washington, 1975.

[38] Report by the United Nations Secretary General, 12th December 1964. Quoted in Republic of Cyprus, Public Information Office, *The Attila Peacemakers*, Nicosia, 1974.

[39] ibid., p. 24.

[40] quoted ibid.

[41] Kardianou, Dionysiou. (Pseudonym for S. Papageorgiou, who participated in the Sampson administration.) *O Attilas Plitti tin Kypro*, Athens, 1976, p. 106.

[42] According to a statement by the president of a Turkish Parliamentary Mission to occupied Cyprus, *Simerini*, 14 March 1976.

[43] Account of Turkish Cypriot political developments based on Patrick, *op. cit.*

[44] ibid.

[45] *Eleftheria*, 17 February 1971.

[46] Republic of Cyprus: Public Information Office, *Facilities Granted to Turkish Cypriots*. Nicosia, 19 February 1971.

# Notes

[47] U.S. Senate, 1975, *op. cit.*, p. 21.

[48] Notel, R., *op. cit.*

[49] Cyprus Turkish Information Centre, *The Clearing Up of Certain Misrepresentations*, Nicosia, 1969, and Denktas, R. *The Problem of Cyprus: Constitutional and Political Aspects*, Nicosia, 1974.

[50] Bahcheli, *op. cit.*

[51] Cyprus Turkish Information Centre, *op. cit.*

[52] Stegenga, *op. cit.*, p. 141.

[53] Denktas, *op. cit.*

[54] Patrick, *op. cit.*, p. 4.11.

[55] ibid.

[56] ibid., p. 4.13.

[57] Harbottle, *op. cit.*

[58] ibid. for a full consideration of the incident by the man who was Chief of Staff of the U.N. force at the time.

[59] Comment of "official circles" in the censored Greek press, 1 July 1967. Quoted in Hadziargyri *op. cit.*, pp. 129-20.

[60] Polyviou, P. *Cyprus in Search of a Constitution: Constitutional Negotiations and Proposals, 1960-75*, Nicosia, 1976.

[61] ibid., pp. 82-8.

[62] Kedourie, Elie. *The Cyprus Problem and its Solution. An International Seminar Report*, American Universities Field Staff, Rome, 1974.

[63] Polyviou, *op. cit.*

[64] ibid., p. 199.

[65] ibid.

[66] ibid., p. 190.

[67] ibid., p. 202.

[68] *Cyprus Mail*, 3 October 1973.

[69] *Eleftheria*, 20 June 1974. Interview given by Mr Denktas to the Turkish Cypriot News Agency.

[70] Denktas, Rauf R. *A Short Discourse on Cyprus*, 1972.

[71] *Cyprus Bulletin*, 14 March 1973.

[72] Interview published in *Kypros*, 24 September 1973.

[73] Interview published in *Agon*, 17 November 1973.

[74] Polyviou, *op. cit.*, p. 203.

[75] ibid., pp. 265-315, and Kedourie, *op. cit.*

[76] Kedourie, *op. cit.*, p. 15.

## CHAPTER VI

[1] This observation is derived from P. Loizos, "The Progress of Greek Nationalism in Cyprus, 1878-1970", in J. Davis, ed. *Essays in Honour of Lucy Mair*, London, Athlone Press, 1974.

# CYPRUS

[2] See "N.N.", "Traditionalism and Reaction in Greek Education", and R. Roufos, "Culture and the Military", in R. Clogg and G. Yiannopoulos, *Greece Under Military Rule*, London, Secker and Warburg, 1972.

[3] Adams, T. W., *AKEL: The Communist Party of Cyprus*, Stanford, Hoover Institution Press, 1971.

[4] Ioannou, N., "Cyprus", in Conference of the Communist Parties of the British Empire, 1947, *We Speak of Freedom*.

[5] Servas, 1975, *op. cit.*, p. 14.

[6] E. Papaioannou, "Cyprus Fights for Liberation", in the Report of the Second Conference of Communist and Workers' Parties of the Countries within the Sphere of British Imperialism, *Allies for Freedom*, London, The Communist Party of Great Britain, 1954.

[7] Adams, *op. cit.*, p. 43.

[8] Democritos, *I Akeliki Igesia kai o Enoplos Agon: Marxistiki Kritiki*, Nicosia, 1959.

[9] Adams, *op. cit.*, p. 45.

[10] ibid., p. 219.

[11] *Saranta Chronia tou KKE 1918-1958: Epilogi Ntokoumenton*, Athens, Politikes kai Logotechnikes Ekdoseis, 1958.

[12] Democritos, *op. cit.*

[13] ibid.

[14] Tenth Congress of AKEL, 1962. Cited in *Endekato Synedrio tou AKEL. Ekthesi Drasis tis K.E. kai tis K.E.E. tou AKEL*, 3-6 March 1966.

[15] Endekato Synedrio, *op. cit.*

[16] Tenth Congress, *op. cit.*

[17] Fantis, A., "Imperialist Intrigues Around Cyprus", *World Marxist Review*, 9 (2):48-9, February 1966.

[18] Endekato Synedrio, *op. cit.*

[19] Adams, *op. cit.*, p. 63.

[20] General Secretary's Address, *13 Synedrio tou AKEL: Ekthesi Drasis tis K.E. kai tis K.E.E. tou AKEL.*, 25-28 April 1974.

[21] Endekato Synedrio, *op. cit.*

[22] AKEL, *Deka Chronia Agones*, Nicosia, 1970.

[23] Quoted in Adams and Cottrell, *op. cit.*, p. 22.

[24] Sixteenth Congress of the Pancyprian Labour Federation, *Charavghi*, 19 November 1971.

[25] Papaioannou, E. "Die Einheit des Volkes Festigen". *Probleme des Friedens und des Sozialismus*, August 1974.

[26] Endekato Synedrio, *op. cit.*

[27] ibid.

[28] Grivas-Dhigenis, *op. cit.*, p. 171.

[29] ibid.

[30] Anthem, Th. *Enosis*, London, St. Clement's Press, n.d.

[31] Grivas-Dhigenis, *op. cit.*, p. 255.

[32] ibid., p. 365.

# Notes

[33] Mayes, Stanley. *Cyprus and Makarios*, London, Putnam, 1960.

[34] Speech by the Bishop of Kitium reported in *Ethniki*, 26 March 1973. Also interview in *Tachidromos*, 17 July 1975.

[35] Endekato Synedrio, *op. cit.*

[36] R. Estabrook in the *Washington Post*, 3 March 1964.

[37] Papandreou, Λ. *Democracy at Gunpoint*, Penguin Books, 1973, p. 141.

[38] Interview with Oriana Falaci reprinted in *Ethniki*, 22 November 1974.

[39] ibid.

[40] Loizos, *The Progress of Greek Nationalism, op. cit.*

[41] G. Vassiliades, at a press conference reported in *Ethniki*, 30 March 1973.

[42] General Grivas in interview by *To Vema* of Athens. Reprinted in *Kypros*, 24 September 1973.

[43] Public Information Office of the Turkish Cypriot Administration, *Cyprus: The Paradox of Enosis.*

[44] For example the fourth quotation on p. 8.

[45] *New York Times*, 9 May 1965, reported in Salih, *op. cit.*, p. 133.

[46] Weintal E. and Λ. Bartlett, *Facing the Brink: An Intimate Study of Crisis Diplomacy*, New York, 1967, p. 33.

[47] *Cyprus Mail*, 4 and 7 December 1966.

[48] Interview in *Ethnos*, Athens, 18 March 1970, reprinted in Hadziargyri, *op. cit.*

[49] Xydis, Λ. G., "The Military Regime's Foreign Policy", in Clogg and Yannopoulos, *op. cit.*

[50] *The Guardian*, 7 September 1967.

[51] Polyviou, 1975, *op. cit.*, pp. 89-92. The author had access to the Cyprus Government's archives on the intercommunal talks.

[52] Gregoriades, S. *Akropolis*, 6 February 1975.

[53] Article in *Der Spiegel* No 12, 1970, cited by Hadziargyri, *op. cit.* p. 162.

[54] S. Gregoriades, *Akropolis*, 16 February 1975.

[55] S. Gregoriades, *Akropolis*, 15 February 1975.

[56] Coufoudakis, *op. cit.*

[57] Stern, L., "Bitter Lessons: How we Failed in Cyprus", *Foreign Policy*, Summer 1975.

[58] S. Xydis in Clogg and Yiannopoulos, *op. cit.*

[59] *Milliyet*, 30 May 1971, cited ibid., p. 203.

[60] Cited in Hadziargyri, *op. cit.*, p. 157.

[61] Polyviou, *op. cit.*, p. 194.

[62] Xydis in Clogg and Yiannopoulos, *op. cit.*

[63] Interview by *Le Monde*, reprinted in translation in *Nea Ellada*, 18 September 1974.

[64] Polyviou, *op. cit.*, p. 197.

[65] Hadziargyri, *op. cit.*, pp. 188-91.

[66] ibid.

[67] ibid.

[68] *Agon*, 14 November 1973.

[69] S. Gregoriades, *Akropolis*, 21 February 1975.

[70] *Cyprus Mail*, 16 April 1973.

[71] *Cyprus Mail*, 21 April 1973.

[72] T. Hadjidemetriou, "Anatomy of the Right", *Ta Nea*, March 1973.

[73] See the Greek Ambassador's speech at the Annual Meeting of the Cyprus Chamber of Commerce and Industry. He said, "In every country of the Free World, the body of merchants and industrialists is the bulwark on which the anarcho-communist attack of economic sabotage is broken". (*Charavgi*, 1 July 1971.) On the same occasion, the President of the Chamber of Commerce and Industry complained of "discrimination and unequal competition with the commercial and industrial class" and asked whether the policy of the government was to change the existing regime to a socialist one! (*Eleftheria*, 1 July 1971.) In February 1971 the Employers' Association submitted a memorandum, also released to the press, to the President complaining about "the unfavourable treatment of private enterprise". They cited the continuously expanding activities of the cooperatives, the expansion of the activities of the Marketing Boards, Central Bank Measures against inflation, and the suggestion by AKEL that the foreign owned Cyprus Mines Corporation should be taxed more heavily. (*Eleftheria*, 9 February 1971.) In February 1974 a prominent businessman declared, in the House of Representatives, his pessimism because the government was moving in "leftist directions" and expressed his fears that private capital would be persecuted. (*Eleftheria*, 28 February 1974.)

## CHAPTER VII

[1] Interview given by the then Turkish Foreign Minister Mr Caglayangil to the former director of Turkish Radio and Television, *The Guardian*, 12 March 1976.

[2] Based on Günther Gillesen, "Hundert Jahre türkischer Erbfolgkrieg", *Frankfurter Allgemeine Zeitung*, 27 July 1974.

[3] Harris, G. S., "Turkey and the United States", in Kemal H. Karpat and contributors, *Social Change and Politics in Turkey: A Structural-Historical Analysis*, Leiden, E. J. Brill, 1976.

[4] Karpat, K. H., "Introduction", to Karpat and contributors, *op. cit.*

[5] Mehmet Gonlubol, "Nato, USA and Turkey", in Karpat and contributors, *op. cit.*

[6] Karpat, "Introduction", *op. cit.*

[7] Gonlubol, *op. cit.*

[8] Karpat, Kemal H., "Turkish-Soviet Relations", in Karpat and contributors, *op. cit.*

[9] Adams and Cottrell, *op. cit.*, p. 35.

[10] Hadziargyri, *op. cit.* p. 90.

[11] Adams and Cottrell, *op. cit.*, p. 44.

[12] Vanezis, *op. cit.*

[13] *The Times*, 26 October 1964.

[14] Gonlubol, *op. cit.*, p. 31.

[15] Karpat, "Turkish-Soviet Relations", *op. cit.*

[16] Hadziargyri, *op. cit.* pp. 97-8, citing *Isvestia*, 20 January 1965.

[17] Karpat, "Turkish-Soviet Relations", *op. cit.*

[18] Adams and Cottrell, *op. cit.*, p. 44.

[19] ibid., p. 47.

[20] ibid., p. 51.

[21] Hadziargyri, *op. cit.*, pp. 142-3.

[22] ibid., p. 143.

[23] ibid., pp. 205-6.

[24] ibid., pp. 209-10.

[25] ibid., p. 214.

[26] Gonlubol, *op. cit.*

[27] Karpat, "Turkish-Soviet Relations", *op. cit.*

[28] Oren, Stephen, "Turkey Moves Right—And East", *Contemporary Review*, July 1975.

[29] Karpat, "Turkish-Soviet Relations", *op. cit.*

[30] Patrick, *op. cit.*

[31] Bahcheli, *op. cit.* p. 205.

[32] Hadziargyri, *op. cit.*

[33] Goldbloom, *op. cit.*, gives a general account.

[34] Vatikiotis, P. J. *Greece: A Political Essay*, Washington, The Centre for Strategic and International Studies, 1974.

[35] ibid., p. 34.

[36] Goldbloom, *op. cit.*

[37] U.S. Congress, *Controlling the Damage: U.S. Policy Options for Greece*, Report of a Study Mission to Greece, January 18 to 21 1974, Washington, U.S. Government Printing Office, 1974.

[38] U.S. Congress, *Europe, South and East: Redefining the American Interest*: Report of a Study Mission to Portugal, Greece, Yugoslavia and Hungary from January 1-12 1975. Washington, U.S. Government Printing Office, 1975.

[39] Stern, *op. cit.*

[40] ibid.

[41] Goldbloom, *op. cit.*, p. 240.

[42] ibid.

[43] *Controlling the Damage, op. cit.*, p. 6.

[44] Goldbloom, *op. cit.*

[45] ibid.

[46] *Europe South and East, op. cit.*

[47] ibid., p. 14.

[48] Leslie Finer in the *Evening Standard*, 24 July 1974.

[49] *Controlling the Damage, op. cit.*

[50] ibid.

[51] *Kathimerini*, 9 August 1975.

# CYPRUS

[52] Cambell, *op. cit.*

[53] Weinstein, Adalbert, "Zyperns Stratigische Bedeutung", *Frankfurter Allgemeine Zeitung*, 19 July 1974.

[54] ibid. A similar worry is expressed by Adams and Cottrell, *op. cit.*

[55] Weinstein, 19 July, *op. cit.*, and Adams and Cottrell, *op. cit.*

[56] Van Coufoudakis in Panel Discussion, in Theodore A. Couloumbis and Sallie M. Hicks, eds., Conference Proceedings, *U.S. Foreign Policy Toward Greece and Cyprus: The Clash of Principle and Pragmatism*, Washington, The Center for Mediterranean Studies and the American Hellenic Institute, 1975.

[57] Tom Boyat in Panel Discussion, *op. cit.*

[58] Laurence Stern in Panel Discussion, *op. cit.*

[59] Weinstein, 19 July, *op. cit.* and Van Coufoudakis, "United States Foreign Policy and the Cyprus Question: A Case Study in Cold War Diplomacy", in Theodore Couloumbis and Sallie M. Hicks, *op. cit.*

[60] Weinstein, 19 July, *op. cit.*

[61] Coufoudakis, *op. cit.*

[62] ibid. and Adams and Cottrell, *op. cit.*

[63] Adams and Cottrell, *op. cit.*, p. 69.

[64] ibid., p. 72.

[65] ibid., p. 73.

[66] Polyviou, 1976, *op. cit.*, and Coufoudakis, *op. cit.*

[67] Polyviou, 1976, *op. cit.*, pp. 255-7.

[68] ibid., p. 256.

[69] ibid., p. 196, p. 256.

[70] Coufoudakis, *op. cit.*

[71] *Ta Nea*, Nicosia, 29 November 1973.

[72] Hadziargyri, *op. cit.*, p. 167.

[73] *Tagesspiegel*, Berlin, 16 August 1972.

[74] Polyviou, *op. cit.*, p. 197.

[75] Interview in *Milliet*, 30 May 1971, cited by Hadziargyri, *op. cit.*

[76] Press Conference, 22 February 1972.

[77] Denktas, Rauf, R., *A Short Discourse on Cyprus*, February 1972.

[78] Coufoudakis, *op. cit.*, and Tom Boyat in Panel Discussion, *op. cit.*

[79] David Fairhall in *The Guardian*, 29 May 1974.

[80] Weinstein, Adalbert, "Zypern ist nicht Kuba", *Frankfurter Allgemeine Zeitung*, 16 July 1974.

[81] David Fairhall, 29 May 1974, *op. cit.*

[82] *The Observer*, 11 August 1974.

[83] David Fairhall, 29 May, *op. cit.*

[84] Weinstein, 16 July, *op. cit.*

[85] ibid.

[86] Fairhall, 29 May, *op. cit.*

[87] C. L. Sulzberger in *The New York Times*, 23 April 1962.

[88] David Fairhall, *The Guardian*, 7 December 1975.

[89] Kadritzke, Nils, "Changes in Geopolitical Conditions Leading to the Last Stage of the Cyprus Conflict in 1974", in Cyprus Geographical Association, *International Symposium on Political Geography, Proceedings*, Nicosia, 1976.

[90] See Cambell, *op. cit.*, for an American point of view and Kadritzke, *op. cit.*, for one which regards the U.S. as an imperialist power.

[91] Adams and Cottrell, *op. cit.*

[92] Cambell, *op. cit.*

[93] Kadritzke, *op. cit.*

[94] Cambell, *op. cit.*

[95] Drooz, Daniel B., "The Quiet Civil War", *The Times of Israel*, April, 1974.

[96] *Tachidromos*, 25 September 1975, and Bulletin of the Turkish Embassy in Athens published in *Cyprus Mail*, 3 July 1974.

[97] ibid.

[98] Weinstein, Adalbert, 19 July, *op. cit.*

## CHAPTER VIII

[1] Polyviou, *op. cit.* p. 197.

[2] S. Gregoriades, *Akropolis*, 26 February 1975.

[3] A. Searle Field, Staff Director. *U.S. Intelligence Agencies and Activities*: Committee Hearings. Proceedings of the Select Committee on Intelligence, U.S. House of Representatives 94th Congress, 1st session. September 10, 29, October 1, November 4, 6, 13, 14 and 20, 1975. Part 4, p. 1301.

[4] Polyviou, P. G. *Cyprus: The Tragedy and the Challenge*, London John Swain, 1975.

[5] Jim Andersen reporting from Washington, *Observer*, 18 August 1974.

[6] Couloumbis, Th., "Five Theories on Kissinger's Policy on Cyprus", reprinted in Greek in *Agon*, 12 October 1975.

[7] L. Stern, "Bitter Lessons: How we failed in Cyprus", *Foreign Policy*, Summer 1975.

[8] ibid.

[9] ibid.

[10] ibid.

[11] Interview to *Le Monde*, Reprinted in translation in *Nea Ellas*, 18 September 1974.

[12] Stern, *op. cit.*

[13] Ambassador Taylor G. Belcher in evidence *U.S. Intelligence Agencies and Activities: Committee Hearings*. Proceedings of the Select Committee on Intelligence, U.S. House of Representatives 94th Congress, 1st session, September 11, 12, 18, 30, October 7, 30 and 31, 1975, Part 2.

[14] ibid.

[15] Stern, *op. cit.*

16 Evidence collected by Counsel John L. Boos from Ambassador Henry J. Tasca. *U.S. Intelligence Agencies and Activities*, Part 4, *op. cit.*, p. 1293.

17 ibid., p. 1294.

18 A. Searle Field in *U.S. Intelligence Agencies and Activities* Part 4, *op. cit.*, p. 1298.

19 Ambassador Belcher, *op. cit.*

20 Counsel John L. Boos in *U.S. Intelligence Agencies and Activities*, Part 4, *op. cit.*, p. 1293.

21 ibid.

22 *Epikaira*, 3-9 June 1976.

23 Counsel John L. Boos, *op. cit.*

24 A. Searle Field, *op. cit.*, p. 1299.

25 *U.S. Intelligence Agencies and Activities*, Part 4, *op. cit.* p. 1302.

26 Conference on Cyprus at the Panteios School of Political Science, Athens, 1975. Report by G. Georgallides, mimeo.

27 Stern, *op. cit.*

28 President Makarios in *Le Monde* Interview, *op. cit.* and also often repeated in testimonies in *U.S. Intelligence Agencies and Activities*, Part 4, *op. cit.*

29 Interview with ex Greek Minister, I. Zigdis by E. Rouleau in *The Guardian Weekly*, 24 August 1974.

30 Evidence presented at the trial of L. Papadopoulos in Nicosia, July 1977.

31 The information in this paragraph is from Stern, *op. cit.*

32 ibid.

33 President Makarios in *Le Monde* interview, *op. cit.*

34 Ambassador Belcher, *op. cit.*

35 Interview with Oriana Falaci reprinted in translation in *Phileleftheros*, 7 November 1974.

36 Stern, *op. cit.*

37 e.g. report from *Politika Themata,* reprinted in *Akropolis*, 22 February 1975.

38 *To Vema*, 22 June 1975.

39 *Ta Nea* (Athens), 30 December 1975.

40 *Sunday Times*, 20 October 1974.

41 ibid.

42 Glafkos Clerides in interview to *Tachidromos*, 17 July 1975.

43 Commander Papayiannis in *Epikaira*, 15-23 July 1975.

44 Lieutenant A. Photiades, *Phileleftheros*, 20 July 1975.

45 *Observer*, 28 July 1974.

46 Stern, *op. cit.*

47 United States Senate, Committee on the Judiciary, Ninety-Fourth Congress, First Session, *Crisis on Cyprus: 1975 One Year After the Invasion*, Washington, 1975, p. 20.

48 ibid.

49 A. Searle Field, *op. cit.*, p. 1299.

## Notes

[50] ibid.

[51] Stern, *op. cit.*

[52] *U.S. Intelligence Agencies and Activities*, Part 4, *op. cit.* p. 1291.

[53] Stern, *op. cit.*

[54] Interview with Ambassador Tasca, *Newsweek*, 7 September 1974.

[55] Hella Pick in *The Guardian Weekly*, 26 July 1974.

[56] Letter from Palainis, one of the accused in the conspiracy to overthrow Prime Minister Karamanlis in February 1975, *Akropolis*, 17 July 1975.

[57] Hella Pick, *op. cit.*

[58] Ambassador Tasca in interview to J. Boos. *U.S. Intelligence Agencies and Activities*, Part 4, *op. cit.*

[59] *Evening Standard*, 24 July 1974.

[60] Adalbert Weinstein, "Zyperns Strategische Bedeutung", *Frankfurter Allgemeine Zeitung*, 19 July 1974.

[61] Testimony, *U.S. Intelligence Agencies and Activities*, Part 2, *op. cit.*

[62] See for example the testimony of A. Searle Field, *op. cit.*, p. 1299.

[63] Kedourie, E., "The Cyprus Problem and its Solution: An International Seminar Report". The Center for Mediterranean Studies, American Universities Field Staff, Rome, January 1974, p. 15.

[64] Evans and Novak, *International Herald Tribune.*

[65] *Der Spiegel*, reported in *Ta Nea* (Athens), 22 September 1974.

[66] V. Vasiliou, ex minister to the Greek Prime Minister in talk to the Foreign Press Association, Athens, September 1974.

[67] Ambassador Tasca, interview to J. Boos, *op. cit.*

[68] Adalbert Weinstein, "In Zypern behält Clausewitz recht", *Frankfurter Allgemeine Zeitung*, 23 July 1974.

[69] *The Guardian Weekly*, 26 July 1974.

[70] ibid.

[71] Adalbert Weinstein, "Das Atlantishes Bündnis hat den Krieg verhindert", *Frankfurter Allgemeine Zeitung*, 26 July 1974.

[72] Stern, *op. cit.*

[73] The International Institute for Strategic Studies, *Strategic Survey, 1974*, p. 79.

[74] Stern, *op. cit.*

[75] Jim Andersen reporting from Washington, *The Observer*, 18 August 1974.

[76] U.S. Senate, 1975, *op. cit.*, p. 21.

[77] North Atlantic Assembly, Report on the Activities of the Subcommittee on the Southern Flank, September 1975.

[78] U.S. Senate, 1975, *op. cit.*, p. 44.

[79] A. Weinstein, "In Zypern ...", 23 July 1974.

[80] Interview in *The Middle East*, No. 3, Sept.-Oct., 1974.

[81] Campbell, J. C., "The Mediterranean Crisis", *Foreign Affairs* 53(4): 605-624, July 1975.

[82] For an estimate of Soviet strategic interests in the Eastern Mediterranean and in Cyprus see editorial in *The Guardian*, 10 August 1974.

[83] Dev Murka in *The Observer*, 18 August 1974, and E. Rouleau at Conference on Cyprus at the Panteios School of Political Science, *op. cit.*

[84] "Gemeinsamkeiten und Unterschiede in der Haltung Moskaus und Pekings zum Zypern-Konflikt", *Frankfurter Allgemeine Zeitung*, 24 July 1974.

[85] ibid.

[86] Jan Reifenberg in *Frankfurter Allgemeine Zeitung*, 24 July 1974, and R. Held in *Frankfurter Allgemeine Zeitung*, 26 July 1974.

[87] S. Psycharis, *70 Krisimes Meres*, Athens, Papazisi, 1976, extract in *Ta Nea* (Athens), 8 January 1976.

[88] *The Guardian*, 10 August 1974.

## CHAPTER IX

[1] U.S. Senate, 1975, *op. cit.*, p. 45.

[2] ibid., p. 46 for the aims of U.S. humanitarian relief to Cyprus. See also State Department memo cited in *International Herald Tribune*, 16 October 1974.

[3] See for example statement by Vice-President Rockefeller, *To Vema*, 17 April 1975.

[4] *The Guardian*, editorial, 21 October 1974.

[5] Hitchens, Christopher, "Talking Geography over Cyprus", *New Statesman*, 5 September 1975.

[6] Interview in *The Middle East*, No. 3, September/October 1974.

[7] Robert Stephens, *The Observer*, 18 August 1974.

[8] See account of Turkish policy in Kemal Karpat, "War on Cyprus: The Tragedy of Enosis", in Karpat and contributors, *op. cit.*

[9] Following account based on Metin Munir, "A State in all but Name", *Financial Times*, 30 September 1975.

[10] Republic of Cyprus, Public Information Office, *Colonization of Cyprus: Facts and Figures*, Nicosia, May 1976.

[11] Couloumbis, Theodore A. and Sallie M. Hicks, "The Impact of Greek Americans Upon United States Foreign Policy: Illusion or Reality?" in M. Attalides ed., *Cyprus Reviewed*, Nicosia, The Jus Cypri Association, 1977.

[12] Tremayne, Penelope, "Ringed with a Lake of Fire: Cyprus 1976", *The Army Quarterly and Defence Journal*, 106(1): 101-107, January 1976.

[13] North Atlantic Assembly, *Report on the Activities of the Sub-Committee on the Southern Flank* International Secretariat, September 1975.

[14] ibid.

[15] *Financial Times*, 30 December 1975.

[16] U.P.I. despatch in *Phileleftheros*, 5 November 1976.

[17] *Cyprus Mail*, 15 March 1977.

[18] U.S. Senate, Subcommittee to Investigate Problems Connected with Refugees and Escapees, A Staff Report, *Crisis on Cyprus 1976: Crucial Year for Peace* Washington: U.S. Government Printing Office, 1976, pp. 16-17.

[19] D. Doder, *International Herald Tribune*, 14/15 December 1974.

# Notes

[20] U.S. Senate, 1976, *op. cit.*

[21] ibid.

[22] The effects of U.S. policy in this respect in Greece are documented by, among others, Vatikiotis, *op. cit.*, pp. 20, 32-3, 55-9.

[23] *The Sunday Times*, 22 September 1974.

[24] ibid.

[25] Stern in Panel Discussion, Couloumbis and Hicks, eds., *op. cit.*

[26] Stern, Bitter Lessons, *op. cit.*

[27] Moskof, K., *I Ethniki kai Koinoniki Sineidisi stin Ellada 1830-1909,* Athens, 1974.

215

# BIBLIOGRAPHY

Adams, T. W. and Alvin J. Cottrell, "The Cyprus Conflict", *Orbis*, Vol. 8, 1964.

Adams, T. W., *Cyprus between East and West*, Baltimore, The Johns Hopkins Press, 1938.

*Akel: The Communist Party of Cyprus*, Stanford, Hoover Institution Press, 1971.

AKEL, Fifth Congress, *Gia mia Levteri kai Evtychismeni Zoi*, Nicosia, 1947.

—, *O Dromos pros tin Levteria*, Nicosia, 1952.

—, Eleventh Congress, *Anendoti Pali tou Kypriakou Laou gia Adesmevti Anexartisia-Avtodiathesi*, Nicosia, 1966.

—, *Deka Chronia Agones*, Nicosia, 1970.

—, Thirteenth Congress, *Ekthesi Drasis*, Nicosia, 1974.

Anthem, Th., *Enosis* London, St. Clement's Press, 1954.

Attalides, Michael, ed., *Cyprus Reviewed*, Nicosia, The Jus Cypri Association, 1977.

Bahcheli, Tozun S., *Communal Discord and the Stake of Interested Governments in Cyprus 1955-70*, Dissertation, London School of Economics and Political Science, London University, 1972.

Barker, D., *Grivas, Portrait of a Terrorist*, London, The Cresset Press, 1959.

Barston, R. P., "The Foreign Policy of Cyprus", in R. P. Barston, ed., *The Other Powers*, London, George Allen and Unwin, 1973.

Beckingham, C. F., "Islam and Turkish Nationalism in Cyprus", *Die Welt des Islam*, 5:65-83, 1957.

—, "The Turks of Cyprus", *Journal of the Royal Anthropological Institute of Great Britain and Ireland*, 87:165-174, 1957.

Bitsios, Dimitris, *Krisimes Ores*, Athens, Estia, n.d.

"Briefing on Cyprus", *International Socialism*, 71:9-12, 1974.

Byford-Jones, W., *Grivas and the Story of EOKA*, London, Robert Hale, 1959.

Campbell, John C., "The Mediterranean Crisis", *Foreign Affairs*, 53:605-624, July 1975.

Di Censola, L. P., *Cyprus: Its Ancient Cities, Tombs and Temples*, London, John Murray, 1877.

Clerides Lefkos, *The Demands of the Turkish Cypriot Community Since 1955*, Nicosia, 1974.

216

# Bibliography

Clogg, R. and G. Yannopoulos, *Greece Under Military Rule*, London, Secker and Warburg, 1972.

Cobham, Claude Delaval, *Excerpta Cypria: Materials for A History of Cyprus*, Cambridge, The University Press, 1908.

Constantinidou, K. A. *I Angliki Katochi tis Kyprou tou 1878*, Nicosia, 1930.

"Correspondence between President Johnson and Prime Minister Inonu", *Middle East Journal*, 20(3):386-393, Summer 1966.

Coufoudakis, Van, *Essays on the Cyprus Conflict*, New York, Pella Publishing Company, 1976.

Couloumbis, Theodore A., and Sallie M. Hicks, eds., Conference Proceedings, *U.S. Foreign Policy Toward Greece and Cyprus: The Clash of Principle and Pragmatism*, Washington, The Center for Mediterranean Studies and the American Hellenic Institute, 1975.

—, "Five Theories on Kissinger's Policy on Cyprus" (in Greek), *Kathimerini*, 11 October 1975.

Crouzet, Francois, *Le Conflit de Chypre*, Brussels, Etablissements Emile Bruylant, 1973.

Cyprus Geographical Association, *International Symposium on Political Geography*, Nicosia, 27-29 February 1976, Proceedings.

Cyprus Turkish Information Centre, *The Clearing up of Certain Misrepresentations*, Nicosia, 1969.

Cyprus Turkish Information Centre, *Double Measure of Facilities in Cyprus,* Nicosia, 1970.

Democritos, *I Akeliki Igesia kai o Enoplos Agon: Marxistiki Kritiki,* Nicosia, 1959.

Denktas, Rauf R., *A Short Discourse on Cyprus*, Nicosia, February 1972.

—, *The Problem of Cyprus: Constitutional and Political Aspects,* Nicosia, 1974.

Diamantouros, Nikiforos P., "NATO and the Political Disintegration of Cyprus: A Case Study in Linkage Politics", paper presented at the 1975 Meeting of the Midwest Political Science Association, Chicago, May 2, 1975.

Dobell, W. M. "Division over Cyprus", *International Journal*, 22:278-292, 1966/67.

Doob, Leonard W., "A Cyprus Workshop: An Exercise in Intervention Methodology", *The Journal of Social Psychology*, 91:161-78, 1974.

Drooz, Daniel, B. "The Quiet Civil War", *The Times of Israel*, April 1974.

Duncan-Jones, Anne, "The Civil War in Cyprus", in E. Luard, ed., *The International Regulation of Civil Wars*, London, Thames and Hudson, 1972.

Economidi, Chr., "I Exelixi tou Ellinikou kai Tourkikou Plithysmou tis Kyprou epi Tourkokratias", *Kypriaka Chronika*, 53:5-16, June/July 1966.

Eden, Anthony, *The Memoirs of Anthony Eden: Full Circle*, Cambridge, The Riverside Press, 1960.

Ergin, Feridun, "The History of Cyprus and the Turks on the Island", *Turkish Economic Review*, 4:14-16, 1964.

Erlich, T. *International Crises and the Rule of Law: Cyprus 1958-67*, Oxford, The University Press, 1974.

Evdokas, T. Ch., *To Aitima tis Enoseos: Psychika Empodia kai Planes*, Nicosia, Epitropi Kypriakou Agonos, 1965.

Evriviades, Marios L., "The Problem of Cyprus", *Current History*, January 1976.

Fantis, A., "Imperialist Intrigues Around Cyprus", *World Marxist Review*, 9(2):48-9, February 1966.

Foley, C., *Legacy of Strife: Cyprus from Rebellion to Civil War*, London, Penguin, 1964.

—, and W. I. Scobie, *The Struggle for Cyprus*, Stanford, Hoover Institution Press, 1975.

Gabriilides, A. Ch. *Ta Ethnarchika Dikaiomata kai to Enotikon Dimopsephesma*, Nicosia, 1950.

Garouphalias, P. "Apomnimonevmata", *Akropolis*, September-October 1974.

Georgallides, G. "Churchill's 1907 visit to Cyprus: A Political Analysis", *Epetiris Kentrou Epistimonikon Erevnon*, 3:167-220, 1969/70.

—, "The Commutation of Cyprus's Payment of the Turkish Debt Charge", *Epetiris Kentrou Epistimonikon Erevnon*, 4:379-415, 1970/1.

—, Report on the International Symposium on Cyprus, Panteios School of Political Science, Athens, 10-14 March 1975, mimeo.

—, "Turkish and British Reactions to the Emigration of the Cypriot Turks to Anatolia, 1924-7", *Institute of Balkan Studies Journal*, forthcoming.

Georghiadis, Cleanthis, *I Katagogi ton Kyprion*, Nicosia, 1936.

Gillesen, Günther, "Hundert Jahre türkischer Erbfolgkrieg", *Frankfurter Allgemeine Zeitung*, 27 July 1974.

Government of Cyprus, *Census, 1881*.

Great Britain, *Disturbances in Cyprus in October, 1931*, London, H.M.S.O., 1932.

Great Britain, *Terrorism in Cyprus: The Captured Documents*, London, H.M.S.O., n.d.

Grivas-Dhigenis, G., *Apomnimonevmata Agonos EOKA 1955-59*, Athens, 1961.

Hald, M., *A Study of the Cyprus Economy*, Nicosia, The Government Printing Office, 1968.

# Bibliography

Harbottle, M., *The Impartial Soldier*, Oxford, The University Press, 1970.

—, "Why Cyprus is doomed to become a Political Volcano", *The Times*, 17 October, 1974.

Harding, Field Marshal the Lord of Petherton, "The Cyprus Problem in Relation to the Middle East", *International Affairs*, 34(3):291-296, 1958.

Heinritz, Gunter, "Der griechisch-turkische Konflikt in Zypern", *Geographische Rundschau*, 27:93-99, March 1975.

Hill, Sir George, *A History of Cyprus*, Cambridge, The University Press, 1952.

Hitchens, Christopher, "Talking Geography over Cyprus", *New Statesman*, 5 September 1975.

—, "How Cyprus was Betrayed", *New Statesman*, 24 October 1975.

—, "Detente and Destabilization: Report from Cyprus", *New Left Review*, 94, 1975.

—, "Taking Jim's Word For It", *New Statesman*, 26 March 1976.

Hotham, David, *The Turks*, London, John Murray, 1972.

Hughes, James, "The Cypriot Labyrinth", *New Left Review*, 29, 1965.

Hutchinson, J. T. and Cobham, C. D., *Handbook of Cyprus, 1901*, Nicosia, Government Printing Office, 1901.

Ierodiakonou, Leontios, *The Cyprus Question*, Stockholm, Almqvist and Wiksell, 1971.

The International Institute for Strategic Studies, *Strategic Survey*, 1974.

Ioannou, N. "Cyprus", in Conference of the Communist Parties of the British Empire, February 26-March 2, 1947, *We Speak of Freedom*.

Jenness, Diamond, *The Economics of Cyprus: A Survey to 1914*, Montreal, McGill University Press, 1962.

Kadritzke, Nils and Wolf Wagner, *Im Fadenkreuz der NATO: Ermittlungen am Beispiel Cypern*, Berlin, Rotbuch Verlag, 1976.

—, "Limitations of Independence in the Case of Cyprus", Paper presented to the Conference on the Survival of Small Countries, Nicosia, September 1976.

Kardianou, Dionysiou, *O Attilas Plitti tin Kypro*, Athens, 1976.

Karpat, Kemal H. and contributors, *Social Change and Politics in Turkey: A Structural-Historical Analysis*, Leiden, E. J. Brill, 1976.

Katalanos, N. *Kypriakon Lefkoma: Zenon*, Nicosia, 1914.

Kedourie, Elie, *The Cyprus Problem and Its Solution: An International Seminar Report*, Rome, The Center for Mediterranean Studies, American Universities Field Staff, January 1974.

Pazarkaya, Yüksel, *et al., Zypern,* Berlin, Verein Links von der Mitte der Türkei in West-Berlin, 1974.

Kitromilides, Paschalis M. and Theodore A. Couloumbis, "Ethnic Conflict in a Strategic Area: The Case of Cyprus", *The Greek Review of Social Research,* 24, 1975.

—, "From the Dialectic of Intolerance to an Ideology of Ethnic Coexistence: Notes on the Experience of Cyprus", paper presented to the Conference on the Survival of Small Countries, Nicosia, September 1976.

Kommounistikon Komma Elladas, *Saranta Chronia tou KKE 1918-1958: Epilogi Ntokoumenton,* Athens, Politikes kai Logotechnikes Ekdoseis, 1958.

Koumoulides, John, *Cyprus and the War of Greek Independence 1821-1829,* London, Zeno, 1974.

Kyriakides, S. *Cyprus: Constitutionalism and Crisis Government,* Philadelphia, University of Pennsylvania Press, 1968.

Kyrou, A., *Elliniki Exoteriki Politiki,* Athens, 1965.

Kyrrhes, K. P., *Istoria tis Mesis Ekpaidevseos Ammochostou 1191-1955,* Nicosia, 1967.

Lanitis, N. C. "Our Destiny", *Cyprus Mail,* 3-7 March 1963.

Lewis, B., *The Emergence of Modern Turkey,* Oxford, The University Press, 1968.

Loizos, Peter, "Cyprus: Exclusion and the Ethnic Factor", *New Society,* 2 December 1971.

—, "Aspects of Pluralism in Cyprus", *New Community* (Journal of the U.K. Community Relations Commission), Summer 1972.

—, "The Progress of Greek Nationalism in Cyprus 1878-1970", in J. Davis, ed., *Essays in Honour of Lucy Mair,* London, Athlone Press, 1974.

—, *The Greek Gift: Politics in a Changing Cypriot Village,* London, Blackwell, 1975.

Luke, H., *Cyprus Under the Turks 1571-1878,* Oxford, The University Press, 1921.

MacHenry, Jr., J. A., "Prelude to Confrontation: An Historical Sketch of Cyprus between 1923 and 1945", *Dis Politika,* 4(2/3), Ankara, 1974.

Markides, K., "Social Change and the Rise and Decline of Social Movements: The Case of Cyprus", *American Ethnologist,* 1(2):309-330, May, 1974.

Mayes, S., *Cyprus and Makarios,* London, Putnam, 1960.

Melamid, Alexander, "The Geographical Distribution of Communities in Cyprus", *The Geographical Review,* 46:355-74, 1956.

—, "Partitioning Cyprus: A Class Exercise in Applied Political Geography", *The Journal of Geography,* 51:118-122, 1960.

Meyer, A. J., "Cyprus: The 'Copra-Boat' Economy", *The Middle East Journal*, 13(3):249-261, 1959.

Moskof, X., *I Ethniki kai Koinoniki Seinidisi stin Elleda 1830-1909*, Athens, 1974.

Newham, Rev., F. D., *The System of Education in Cyprus*, London, Board of Education Special Reports, No. 12, 1905.

Notel, Rudolf, "Economic Integration on Cyprus", paper presented to an Inquiry into the Resolution of the Cyprus Problem, a Seminar held at The Center for Mediterranean Studies, American Universities Field Staff, Rome, 19-24 November 1973.

North Atlantic Assembly, *Report on the Activities of the Sub-Committee on the Southern Flank*. International Secretariat, September 1975.

Oren, Stephen, "Turkey Moves Right—And East" *Contemporary Review*, July 1975.

Orr, Captain, C. W. J., *Cyprus Under British Rule*, London, Zeno, 1972.

Panagides, S. S., "Communal Conflict and Economic Considerations: The Case of Cyprus", *Journal of Peace Research*, 1968.

Papadopoulos, Th. *I Krisis tis Kypriakis Syneidiseos*, Nicosia, 1964.

—, *Social and Historical Data on Population (1570-1881)*, Nicosia, Cyprus Research Centre, 1965.

—, and M. Christodoulou, eds, *Praktika tou Protou Diethnous Kyprologikou Synedriou*, Nicosia, 1973.

Papageorgiou, Sp., *Archeion ton Paranomon Engraphon tou Kypriakou Agonos 1955-59*, Athens, 1961.

Papaioannou, E., *Dyo Chronia Agones kai ta Nea mas Kathikonta*, Nicosia, 1951.

—, "Cyprus Fights for Liberation", in The Report of the Second Conference of Communist and Workers Parties of Countries within the Sphere of British Imperialism, *Allies for Freedom*, London, The Communist Party of Great Britain, 1954.

—, "Die Einheit des Volkes Festigen", *Probleme des Friedens und des Sozialismus*, August 1974.

Pefkos, George, "Cyprus: Striving for a Solution", *Comment*, 6(15):237-8, 13 April 1968.

Papandreou, Andreas, *Democracy at Gunpoint*, London, Penguin, 1973.

Patrick, R. A., *A General System Theory Approach to Geopolitical Aspects of Conflict between Communities with particular Reference to Cyprus since 1960*, Doctoral Dissertation, London School of Economics and Political Science, University of London, 1972.

Plaza, G., *Report of the U.N. Mediator on Cyprus to the Secretary General*, 1965.

Pollis, Adamantia, "Intergroup Conflict and British Colonial Policy: The Case of Cyprus", *Comparative Politics*, 5(4):575-599, July 1973.

—, "Colonialism and Neocolonialism: Determinants of Ethnic Conflict in Cyprus", paper presented to the Conference on the Survival of Small Countries, Nicosia, September 1976.

Polyviou, Polyvios G., Cyprus: *The Tragedy and the Challenge*, London, John Swain and Son, 1975.

—, *Cyprus in Search of a Constitution: Constitutional Negotiations and Proposals 1960-1975*, Nicosia, 1976.

Psychari, S., *70 Krisimes Meres*, Athens, Papazisis, 1976.

Public Information Office of the Turkish Cypriot Administration, *A Legal Expose on Land Consolidation in Cyprus*, Nicosia, 1971.

—, *Cyprus: The Paradox of Enosis*, Nicosia, n.d.

Purcell, H. D., *Cyprus*, London, Ernest Benn, 1969.

Ramady, Mohammed A., " 'Two States' or One?" *Friends of Cyprus Report*, No. 9, March 1976.

Republic of Cyprus, Department of Statistics and Research, *Census*, 1960.

—, Public Information Office, *Brief Biographies of the President, the Vice-President and the Ministers of the Republic of Cyprus*, 1963.

—, *Cyprus: The Problem is Perspective*, April 1968.

—, *The Cyprus Question: A Brief Analysis*, June 1969.

—, *Facilities Granted to the Turkish Cypriots*, February 1971.

—, *The Attila Peacemakers, 1974.*

—, *Economic Consequences of the Turkish Invasion*, October 1974.

—, *The Cyprus Problem: Historical Review and Analysis of Latest Developments*, December 1975.

—, *Colonization of Cyprus: Facts and Figures*, May 1976.

—, *Proposals of the Greek Cypriot Side on the Various Aspects of the Cyprus Problem*, April 1976, mimeo.

—, *Proposals of the Turkish Cypriot Side on the Various Aspects of the Cyprus Problem*, April 1976, mimeo.

—, *Certain Facts About the Cyprus Problem: An Analysis of Turkish Policy*, Nicosia, June 1976.

Royal Institute of International Affairs, *Cyprus: The Dispute and the Settlement*, Oxford, The University Press, 1959.

Salih, H. Ibrahim, *Cyprus: An Analysis of Political Discord*, Brooklyn, Theo Gaus Sons, 1968.

Servas, P., "I Kypriaki Aristera", *Anti*, January/March 1975.

—, *I Kypriaki Tragodia*, Athens, 1975.

Solomides, R., *Analysis Katamerismou tou Varous tis Ektaktou Forologias Eisodimaton. Nicosia, Chamber of Commerce & Industry, 1975.*

Spain, James, W., "The United States, Turkey and the Poppy", *The Middle East Journal*, 29(3):295-309, Summer 1975.

Spyridakis, C., *A Brief History of Cyprus*, Nicosia, Greek Communal Chamber, 1964.

Stavrinides, Z., *The Cyprus Conflict*, Nicosia, 1976.

Stegenga, J. A., *The United Nations Force in Cyprus*, Ohio, The State University Press, 1968.

Stephens, Robert, *Cyprus: A Place of Arms*, London, Pall Mall Press, 1966.

Stern, Laurence, "Bitter Lessons: How We Failed in Cyprus", *Foreign Policy*, Summer 1975.

Tachau, F., "The Face of Turkish Nationalism as Reflected in the Cyprus Dispute", *The Middle East Journal*, 13:262-72, 1959.

Tenzel, J. H., "Problems in Cross-Cultural Communication: Cyprus a Case Study", paper presented at the Fifth International Congress of Psychiatry, December 1971.

—, and M. S. Gerst, "The Psychocultural Aspects of a Conflict", paper presented to the American Psychological Association Annual Meeting, Dallas, Texas, 1972.

Terlexis, P., *Diplomatia kai Politiki tou Kypriakou: Anatomia Enos Lathous*, Athens, 1971.

Thomas, Ann Van Wynen and A. J. Thomas Jr., "The Cyprus Crisis 1974-1975: Political-Juridical Aspects", Southwestern Law Journal, 29: 513-546, Summer 1975.

Tremayne, Penelope, "Ringed with a Lake of Fire: Cyprus 1976", *The Army Quarterly and Defense Journal*, 106(1):101-107, January 1976.

Tsolaki, A. L. *Politiki Istoria tis Neoteras Kyprou: Vol. A 1950-54*, Famagusta, 1972.

Turkish Information Centre, *The Cyprus Problem in the Light of Truth*, Nicosia, 1967.

U.S. Congress, *Controlling the Damage: U.S. Policy Options for Greece*, Report of a Study Mission to Greece, January 18 to 21, 1974, Washington, U.S. Government Printing Office, 1974.

U.S. Congress, *Europe, South and East: Redefining the American Interest*, Report of a Study Mission to Portugal, Greece, Yugoslavia and Hungary from January 1-12, 1975, Washington, U.S. Government Printing Office, 1975.

U.S. Intelligence Agencies and Activities: Committee Hearings, *Proceedings of the Select Committee on Intelligence*, U.S. House of Representatives 94th Congress, 1st Session. September 11, 12, 18, 25, 30, October 7, 20 and 31, 1975, Part 2, Washington, U.S. Government Printing Office, 1975.

U.S. Intelligence Agencies and Activities: Committee Hearings, *Proceedings of the Select Committee on Intelligence*, U.S. House of

Representatives 94th Congress, 1st Session. September 10, 29, October 1, November 4, 6, 13, 14 and 20, 1975, Part 4, Washington, U.S. Government Printing Office, 1975.

U.S. Senate, Committee on the Judiciary, Sub-committee to Investigate Problems Connected with Refuges and Escapees, *Crisis on Cyprus: 1975 One Year After the Invasion*, Staff Report, Washington, U.S. Government Printing Office, 1975.

U.S. Senate, Committee on the Judiciary, Sub-committee to Investigate Problems Connected with Refugees and Escapees, *Crisis on Cyprus 1976: Crucial Year for Peace*, A Staff Report, Washington, U.S. Government Printing Office, 1976.

Vanezis, P. N., *Makarios: Pragmatism Versus Idealism*, London, Abelard-Schuman, 1974.

Vatikiotis, P. J., *Greece: A Political Essay*, Washington, The Centre for Strategic and International Studies, 1974.

Weintal, E. and A. Bartlett, *Facing the Brink: An Intimate Study of Crisis Diplomacy*, New York, 1967.

Weinstein, Adalbert, "Zypern ist nicht Kuba", *Frankfurter Allgemeine Zeitung*, 16 July 1974.

—, "Zyperns Strategische Bedeutung", *Frankfurter Allgemeine Zeitung*, 19 July 1974.

—, "In Zypern behält Clausewitz recht", *Frankfurter Allgemeine Zeitung*, 23 July 1974.

—, "Das Atlantische Bündnis hat den Krieg verhindert", *Frankfurter Allegemeine Zeitung*, 26 July 1974.

Williams, P., *Athens under the Spartans*, Fabian Social Research Pamphlet No. 264, London, 1967.

Windsor, P., *NATO and the Cyprus Crisis*, Institute of Strategic Studies, Adelphi Papers No. 14, 1964.

Xydis, A. G. *et al.*, *O Makarios kai oi Symmachoi tou*, Athens, Gütenberg, n.d.

Xydis, S. G., *Greece and the Great Powers 1944-47*, Thessaloniki, 1963.

—, "Toward 'Toil and Moil' in Cyprus", *The Middle East Journal*, 20(1):1-19, Winter 1966.

—, *Cyprus: Reluctant Republic*, The Hague, Mouton, 1973.

Zoidi, G. and T. Adamou, *I Pali tis Kyprou gia tin Levteria*, Athens, Politikes kai Logotechnikes Ekdoseis, 1960.

# INDEX

Acheson, Dean 18–20, 66–7, 69, 115
AKEL 14, 106, 108–16, 119
anti-communism 11, 13, 15, 17, 58, 59, 90, 98, 117, 121, 129, 133, 136, 148–9, 154, 190–1
Ataturk, Kemal 83–4, 90
Baghdad Pact 11
Balkan Pact 11
Bases, British 13, 112, 128, 132, 158–9
Boyd, Lennox 47, 48
British colonial policy 3, 6–7, 8–9, 12, 22–5, 40–2, 46, 47, 62
CENTO 13
church 1, 22, 24–5, 26, 31, 33, 39, 40, 60, 87, 114, 117, 122
civil service 51–2
Clerides, Glavkos 16, 19, 67, 72, 73, 153, 164, 169, 170, 173
Communal Chambers 52, 78
communism in Cyprus 5, 10, 15, 31, 59, 73–4, 86
conversions 80
Deniz incident 51, 53
Denktas, Rauf 55, 100, 101, 102
detente 15–6, 138–9
Eastern Question 3–4, 11, 21, 140
Ecevit, Bulent 86, 164, 175–6, 186
Eden, Sir Anthony 6, 8
education 25–9, 42–3, 55, 124
Egypt 6, 7, 15, 17, 44, 54
emigration 44
enosist opposition 119–20, 121, 124–6, 127, 128, 133, 136, 154
EOKA 47–9, 50, 110, 117–8, 119
EOKA B 135, 136, 154–5, 162–3, 168, 169
Ethnarchy 1, 108, 109, 110, 117, 122
Evkaf 41–2, 46
Greece 3–4, 6–7, 8, 17, 19, 21, 25, 34, 58, 59–73, 92, 98, 99, 121, 123–5, 127–35, 145–9, 154–6, 172–3
Grivas, George 12, 17, 48, 49, 52, 62, 63, 69, 70, 117–8, 119–20, 126, 128, 129, 134–5, 154, 157, 163
Hatay 83
Inonu, Ismet 17
intercommunal talks 98–103, 162

Johnson letter 142
Karamanlis, Constantine 164
Kuchuk, Dr Fazil 46, 55
Lanitis, N. C. 77–8
Lausanne, Treaty of 8, 44, 90
Lisbon agreement 132–3, 153–4
London Conferences 8, 17, 55, 62, 64, 84, 85, 141
Macmillan plan 12, 54
Makarios 12, 14, 20, 52, 59, 61, 63, 67, 71, 115, 119, 120, 121–4, 127, 128, 129, 145, 151, 163–4, 165, 168, 188
Montreux, Treaty of 45
Municipal elections 109
NATO 4, 5, 9, 11, 12, 13, 15, 16–17, 35, 57, 85, 105, 119, 128, 132, 139, 144, 148, 155
non-aligned policy 14, 15, 20, 54, 119, 145, 178–9
oil 6, 138, 160–1
Ottoman empire 36–40, 87
partition 7, 8, 11–12, 17, 18, 19, 48, 53, 84, 90, 114, 115, 128, 138, 150–2, 166
passive resistance 118
Patriotic Front 119
Plaza, Gallo 81–2, 86
plebiscite, *enosis* 109
Papandreou, George 17, 20, 64–68, 71
population 88–90
publishing 43
refugees 91–2, 93, 94, 179, 187–8
riots, 1931 24, 27, 29, 44–5, 59
Social Progress Society 77–8
Soviet Union 13, 15, 16, 17, 65, 68, 69, 121, 138, 140–5, 177–9, 188
standard of living 76, 87–8, 94–7
T.M.T. 47–9, 55, 87, 90, 91, 112
trade unions 49, 112, 113
Treaty of Alliance 53
Treaty of Guarantee 53
Treaty of Establishment 13, 53
Turkey 7–8, 17, 19, 44, 83–6, 92, 93, 98, 120, 139–42, 143–4, 154, 174–7, 186–7, 188
Turkism 37

225

## Index